Advance Praise for *Solutions for Agile Governance in the Enterprise*

"This book is an essential tool in filling the knowledge gaps we have in being Agile on complicated projects. The other way to fill these gaps is through expensive and painful trial and error. From now on, I'll recommend reading this book instead."

Mike Cohn Mountain Goat Software
Author, *Agile Estimating and Planning*

"Dr. Kevin Thompson is a recognized thought leader who has researched and written extensively on all things Agile. In his newest book, he describes how Agile can be used at scale for complex products (those that include software and hardware), programs, and portfolios. I highly recommend this book to team members and executive leaders who want to apply Agile throughout their organizations and learn from one of the true masters of the field."

John Carter principal, TCGen Inc.
Author, *Innovate Products Faster*

"Dr. Thompson understands the differences and similarities between software and hardware, and is moving Agile / Scrum methods beyond their software origins. He paints the clearest picture of that world and all its moving parts that I have seen."

David G. Ullman emeritus professor of
mechanical design and ASME Life Fellow
Author, *The Mechanical Design Process*

"*Sage* presents an overarching vision of integrating Agile throughout an organization. Regardless of your familiarity with Agile, or your role within the organization, you will find valuable insights on how to turn your project, business unit, or company into an Agile powerhouse."

James Kolozs staff systems engineer, Syncroness

"This book explores in depth the issues surrounding scaling Agile development, including many recommendations based on the author's experience."

Jeff McKenna Certified Scrum Trainer

Kevin W. Thompson, PhD

Solutions for Agile Governance in the Enterprise (Sage)

Agile Project, Program, and
Portfolio Management for Development
of Hardware and Software Products

SOPHONT
PRESS

Screen images of Planview PPM Pro® by permission of Planview, Inc. Screen images of 1000minds® product by permission of 1000minds.

ISBN 978-0-578-42058-5 (paperback)
ISBN 978-0-578-42059-2 (ebook)

Produced by Page Two
www.pagetwostrategies.com

Cover design by Setareh Ashrafologhalai
Interior design by Peter Cocking
Printed and bound in the United States of America

19 20 21 22 23 5 4 3 2 1

www.cprime.com

Contents

List of Figures

List of Tables

Foreword

WHAT does "Agile" mean? And why is it so important for companies to adopt Agile practices for developing software and hardware products? I have dedicated my career to helping others answer this question—providing tools, training, and solutions for them to succeed.

The short answer is that Agile styles of product development reduce waste, decrease time to market, and improve the quality of working life for engineers, management, and executives. Today more than ever, Agile practices are essential to success. Businesses and technology has evolved so quickly in the past twenty years that it poses a real challenge for companies to keep up, let alone seize new opportunities.

I have had the pleasure of working with Kevin Thompson for over eight years. As a PhD from Princeton University, his insight into Agile processes is unparalleled. His dedication to his work is meticulous. Every theory, every customer engagement, is thoroughly analyzed, revised, and reapplied to real-life situations. Kevin goes into details and provides examples as to how one approach may work in one situation but fail in another, or how alternative approaches may lead to similar results. He is a true thought leader and has proven to be indispensable. And now, after years of theorizing, experimenting, and successfully repeating the process, Kevin has narrowed down the core components to optimizing and perfecting Agile methodologies.

As you read through this book, you may be surprised by how relatable it is and how easy it is to apply the practices and techniques to your own projects. The same tools, charts, and techniques have worked effectively across our client base, from small businesses to large corporations. This book is immensely practical, and an indispensable resource for successful product development. Read on! You will be glad you did.

Zubin Irani
Chief Executive Officer
cPrime, an Alten Group Company

Preface

MY background is in science, and my journey to the world of Agile product development has been long and complex. The tale is a classic example of how life can veer from expectations.

I received my BS in physics from Santa Clara University in 1979 and my PhD in the field from Princeton University in 1985. I also spent eight years at the NASA Ames Research Center's Space Sciences Division, performing research into bipolar flows from galactic nuclei and stars, and turbulence in the solar nebula. I enjoyed writing and publishing articles on computational fluid dynamics (CFD) in scientific journals, especially on the topic of boundary conditions for hyperbolic systems of differential equations.

However, I gradually realized that working on CFD simulations was much more interesting than working on astrophysics. I also became more concerned with making enough money to afford a house for my family. I eventually made the difficult decision to leave the practice of science for the world of commercial software development in 1992.

Writing software in Smalltalk, Object Pascal, C, and Java for a few different companies kept me occupied through 2006. The four years I spent at Macrovision, writing Java code for Web applications, made it clear that I was losing interest in writing software. Because I'd spent much of the past two years planning work rather than doing it, I decided to move into a new career in software project management.

I joined OnVantage in 2006 as a full-time software project manager. I managed work on event management products with the classic "Waterfall" process. I learned that the Waterfall process worked well—on paper. In reality, it gave the illusion of understanding and control while providing neither.

My education in the Agile world began in 2007 when our chief operating officer told us that the company needed to be more Agile in our development process. Taking him at his word, another project manager found some information on Agile development (largely Henrik Kniberg's book *Scrum and XP from the Trenches*[1]) and started a successful pilot project.

I started the second and third Agile pilot projects. I filled the roll of Scrum Master, training the Team members and the Product Owner in Scrum on the fly as we went through the work. My teams brought to market the company's first successful new product in a number of years. As the manager of the company's project management office, I then led the effort to roll out this new "Scrum process framework" across the rest of the company.

Layoffs hit the company in 2008, and I took advantage of my new leisure time to pursue Project Management Professional (PMP) certification from the Project Management Institute (PMI), and certification as a Certified ScrumMaster (CSM) and Certified Scrum Professional (CSP) from the Scrum Alliance. Later that year, I began my first consulting engagement to facilitate a successful Agile transformation for Zuora, Inc.

In December 2009, I joined cPrime, Inc., as a full-time employee. At the time, cPrime's focus had been on project management consulting for IT organizations, but the company wanted to move into the new market of Agile training and consulting. I was hired as the first employee who really knew what the words "Agile" and "Scrum" meant.

cPrime was, finally, the right place for me. I felt at home there in a way I had never experienced. I was fascinated by Agile concepts. I enjoyed the intellectual challenges of Agile training and consulting for our clients. I derived tremendous satisfaction from the very real improvements I could bring to the working lives of so many people. Finally, and critically for me, I had the space to develop new concepts, new strategies for helping clients, new Agile training classes, and new markets.

Over the years, cPrime grew from a small firm to a much larger one. In the early years, I mostly developed training material on Scrum and related topics, delivered classes to clients, and trained cPrime people on Agile content. As we grew, I spent less time training and more time organizing and facilitating Agile transformations for our clients.

Client opportunities grew in size as well. I discovered that managing an Agile transformation for a hundred people was quite different from managing one for ten. Thinking through how to do Agile software development on large scales led to six months of furious concept development and writing, culminating in my 2013 paper, "Recipes for Agile Governance in the Enterprise: The Enterprise Web."[2]

The paper had the somewhat unfortunate acronym of RAGE. That aside, it represented a huge shift in the way I thought about large-scale Agile product development. I had come to realize that program and portfolio management applied just as much to the Agile world as to the world of classic project management. These topics had to be redeveloped along Agile lines to truly address the needs of large organizations, and the RAGE paper showed how this could be done.

The RAGE paper provided a springboard for initiatives in two different directions.

The first direction was organizational scaling of Agile development. I developed training materials for Agile Program Management and Agile Portfolio Management. Events proved that the time was indeed right for an Agile style of program management, but the market was not yet ripe for the next level up.

The second direction was to bring the advantages of Agile techniques to the world of hardware product development, which really meant the integrated development of products that contain both hardware and software.

The opportunity to launch this second initiative came in late 2013, at the annual convention of the Silicon Valley chapter of PMI. I was speaking on the topic of Agile governance, as derived from my RAGE paper. Another speaker, John Carter, gave a presentation on Agile techniques for use in developing hardware products.

John was deeply knowledgeable about hardware development, with a pedigree that included development of the original noise-canceling headphones for Bose. I buttonholed him to discuss combining our areas of expertise to develop standard and reusable Agile processes for the development of integrated products. He was indeed interested, and looped in his colleague, Dr. Scott Elliott, to join the endeavor.

Eighteen months later, we'd learned what there was to be learned from the roughly twenty clients whom the three of us selected to interview. All did some form of hardware and / or large-system development. Most had done some "Agile things" at some point, but none had a systematic and reproducible approach for Agile hardware development.

While the research did not prove fruitful for its intended purpose, our collaboration was fruitful in a different way. John and Scott knew hardware development inside and out, and I was knowledgeable about the Agile space.

Together, we hammered out the details of how to create an Agile approach to hardware development.

Much to my surprise, Scrum emerged as the appropriate process framework for hardware development at the team level. This was not at all what I was expecting, but the data led in that direction. However, working out just how to use Scrum to develop hardware products was not simple.

The practical realities of hardware development are different from those of software development. While the decision-making techniques of Scrum work in both worlds, much of the day-to-day experience of product development is quite dissimilar between the two worlds. Many concepts that are taken for granted as "the right way" in the software world are inappropriate for hardware development. In fact, the realities of hardware development can seem deeply wrong to experts in Agile software development. Overcoming that mindset, and finding the right techniques for the hardware world, was challenging.

The results of our lengthy collaboration appeared in my 2015 paper, "Agile Processes for Hardware Development,"[3] which has stood the test of time remarkably well.* I was pleased to see that my concepts of Agile Program and Portfolio Management, originally developed with software product development in mind, applied without modification to the world of integrated hardware–software development.

Looking back, the history makes sense, but I could not have envisioned the road in advance. In this book, I want to share with you what I have learned along the way. I hope you will enjoy it.

---

* If I had to do it over, the only thing I would change would be to recommend a Sprint length of two weeks, or three at the most. Everyone we interviewed was firmly convinced that four weeks, or even eight, would be required in a hardware development context. I did not think so but bowed to the pressure. I now take it back. Two weeks is almost always the right length.

Introduction

AGILE processes for software product development first saw the light in the 1990s, under names such as Extreme Programming[4] (XP) and Scrum.[5] The years since then have seen an explosion of books on Agile development, and, more specifically, on the Scrum framework. Many excellent books—by highly regarded authors such as Mike Cohn, Ken Rubin, Kent Beck, and others—have provided a wealth of guidance and insight into the theory and practice of Agile development.

Why, then, write another book? What is there to say that has not been said many times already?

Two things, really.

First, many books and papers excel at "team-level" or "project-level" concepts and practices. I have seen far fewer provide useful insight for large-scale Agile development involving many collaborating teams, and none (yet) that provide adequate guidance for Agile approaches at the level of Business Strategy and Portfolio Management.

Second, and fueling the first, the explosive growth of hardware and software technologies is driving a new world of integrated hardware–software products. From aerospace to robotics to the "Internet of Things," products often contain both hardware and software elements. This means that products are now larger than the hardware or software elements, and their development must be conducted on larger scales than has been common in the past. We must learn to excel at the concurrent development and integration of software and hardware technologies in order to produce the complex products that are becoming the norm. The use of the same Agile techniques and frameworks across the entire span of complex product development simplifies both the long-term planning and day-to-day integration of work across the concurrent technology streams.

This book is not intended as an introduction to the Agile world. The excellent books listed at the end of this chapter already address the needs of the neophyte well. They emphasize, quite properly, the importance of free and open collaboration without fear, the need to focus on maximizing value produced over time instead of completing planned scope on a planned date, and other critical and cultural aspects of Agile product development. As no book can be all things to all people, I will assume an understanding of these matters and focus, instead, on the structural and process-related aspects of a large-scale Agile enterprise.

Levels of Organization

Much of this book addresses the upper layers of the Agile product development hierarchy. It provides concrete guidance for Agile Portfolio, Program, and Project Management, based on a common set of underlying principles. It defines effective techniques and practices at all levels in a way that provides enough guidance to be useful while avoiding excessive prescription.

The techniques I will describe ensure alignment of plans and work vertically (portfolio on down) and horizontally (across collaborating teams) in an organic and holistic fashion. The intent behind the Program and Portfolio Management solutions presented here is that these solutions be applied when necessary and omitted when not necessary.

At the team or project level, all of the techniques and practices of Scrum (or Kanban) should be used. As an organization grows from a single Scrum Team to many teams, informal cross-team collaboration becomes insufficient, and it becomes necessary to implement Agile Program Management. Similarly, as the organization grows to the point of having multiple products, informal approaches to business strategy and investment decisions will become inadequate to the needs at some point, and a formal Agile Portfolio Management process will be required.

One of the insights I hope to provide in this book is that similar concepts apply at all levels of the organization's product development hierarchy. (Scope-versus-time tradeoffs are a frequent example.) These concepts lead to common themes that recur at different levels. However, the expression of these recurring themes, in the form of specific practices, does not literally duplicate the same practices at all levels. Instead, the specific needs of each level drive that level's practices in ways that resemble, but are not the same as, those at other levels. Fortunately, the commonality of themes across levels simplifies the process of learning how the different levels operate.

Another insight I want to provide is that Agile techniques can be used outside the world of software product development. They can be used for the development of hardware and integrated hardware–software products as well, such as electronic and electromechanical devices. Scrum in particular is well suited for all types of product development. The degree to which the nature of the work (software versus hardware) affects the nature of the process is addressed primarily at the project (team) level, not at the program or portfolio levels. Specific examples in this book are provided from software and hardware contexts, as appropriate.

The Kanban approach to managing work is also presented in some depth here. Kanban differs from Scrum in a variety of ways, but both apply to the project or team level of the organization, as both define the practices by which a team plans, executes, and tracks its work. A key difference is that Kanban is generally not an effective basis for creating large product development organizations, as it omits the planning and synchronization opportunities required for large-scale collaborative work. For this and other reasons, Kanban is generally not appropriate for product development work and is more suited for customer support, operations, and other request-driven environments. Kanban is, however, an important Agile process framework, and is included here for that reason.

Framework versus Process

The term "framework" is common in the Agile world. Sometimes it appears in the phrase "process framework," and it may be perceived, by a casual reader, as a synonym for process. This is not the case: framework and process are not the same, although they are related.

A *framework*, or *process framework*, defines a specific set of characteristics that must be incorporated into a particular process in order for us to say that the process implements that framework. The most widely used and well-known example of an Agile process framework is the Scrum framework, which is defined by "The Scrum Guide."[6] In other words, a particular organization commonly implements a process that contains *all* elements of the Scrum framework, along with other elements that address organizational needs that are not defined or addressed in the Scrum framework. I would call this implementation a "Scrum process," as distinct from the "Scrum framework."

For a framework to be widely usable, it should focus on a minimum set of required elements. The attempt to solve all problems that could occur in places where the framework is used generates large process documents stuffed with ideas that are too numerous and prescriptive to be incorporated in toto into any particular process. The inevitable result is that one must pick and choose which elements to incorporate into a particular process, at which point the notion that we are using a framework is no longer valid.

As to what, exactly, a framework should contain, I consider the basic content to be the roles (specific responsibilities and areas of authority) assigned to certain individuals and the ceremonies (standard meetings) at which certain kinds of decisions are made. I would also say that the framework's description of the ceremonies is oriented toward what the ceremonies accomplish rather than on defining how the goals are accomplished. This approach allows for local choices of how best to achieve the goals, based on local needs.

What a framework does *not* address are the "best practices" for achieving the goals or outputs of ceremonies. Thus, while certain best practices are commonly used for Scrum processes (User Stories for specifications, Planning Poker for estimation), these are not defined to be part of the framework.

Trouble can arise when people conflate the framework definition with preferences for specific techniques used to carry out the work required by the framework. This is a common source of confusion, and an occasional bone of contention.

In this book, I attempt to lay out my frameworks for Kanban, Agile Program Management, and Agile Portfolio Management, and do so in the context of a larger organizational concept and meta-framework (see the next chapter). Aside from Scrum, which I have attempted to align to "The Scrum Guide," these frameworks are my definitions and are not intended to represent any kind of consensus across any industry.

In practice, a framework is important but not sufficient. We do need specific techniques to estimate work, write specifications, and make various decisions beyond what a framework can provide, and I will present my preferred approaches for these items. As with Scrum, though, other techniques may be employed as needed.

Finally, I use the word "process" more frequently than the word "framework" because I am commonly focusing on practical details that provide useful solutions but that should not be baked into a framework. I hope this practice does not cause confusion.

Recommended Reading

As mentioned, I recommend these authors and books for their accessible coverage of Agile fundamentals.

Kent Beck with Cynthia Andres

Extreme Programming Explained: Embrace Change. 2nd Edition (The XP Series). Boston: Addison-Wesley, 2004.

Kent Beck's work to develop *Extreme Programming* pioneered Agile software development and the associated engineering practices that make much of the Agile software world practical.

Mike Cohn

User Stories Applied: For Agile Software Development. Boston: Addison-Wesley, 2004.

Agile Estimating and Planning. Upper Saddle River, NJ: Prentice Hall, 2005.

Mike Cohn's books say most of what there is to say on how to write specifications and estimate work. These pioneering books are so insightful that their relevance remains high more than a decade later.

Kenneth Rubin

Essential Scrum: A Practical Guide to the Most Popular Agile Process. Boston: Addison-Wesley, 2012.

Kenneth Rubin provides an excellent introduction to the basics of Scrum. Highly recommended.

James Schiel

Enterprise-Scale Agile Software Development. 1st Edition (Applied Software Engineering Series). Boca Raton, FL: CRC Press, 2017.

James Schiel's focus is not on the conduct of Agile product development (although he provides a good summary of the concepts) but on how to plan and execute the transformation of potentially very large companies to Agile development principles.

Jeff Sutherland

Scrum: The Art of Doing Twice the Work in Half the Time. New York: Currency, 2014.

Jeff Sutherland invented Scrum. This book not only provides a superb introduction to Scrum but also fascinating historical information about just how he came to identify the key elements of the Scrum framework.

1

Agile Is about Making Decisions Quickly

"AGILE" is an umbrella term that refers to styles of managing work that deal well with unexpected developments. The term encompasses more than "Scrum," but there is much to be learned more generally by examining Scrum for a moment.

The in-depth details of the Scrum framework are presented in Chapter 3 and will not be discussed here. However, it is important to note that the Scrum framework does not contain any concepts or language that are specific to software development. This critical point is often mentioned, usually in a context referring to other areas where Scrum could be applied (e.g., in marketing departments). In essence, the definition of the Scrum framework separates *process* (which it addresses) from the *practices* required to do a specific type of work (such as software development, which it does not address).

It may seem counterintuitive to focus on the characteristics of a process in a way that is divorced from the specifics of the work, but this way of thinking provides important benefits:

- It enables use of the process in different contexts, for different kinds of work.

- It restricts the problem domain to an extent that enables effective general solutions.

- It focuses on concepts that have lasting value by avoiding entanglement with techniques and technologies that may change rapidly over time.

It is obvious that a company that uses Scrum to organize a team's product development work produces a product of some kind. The team's output consists of the deliverables of the planned work, which collectively define the product. It is therefore easy to conclude that the output of the team's Scrum process is that set of product-related deliverables, which are ultimately provided to customers for their use.

Yet I have also said that Scrum does not describe the mechanics of producing any particular kind of product. The work of the team does indeed produce a product, but the practices of Scrum itself do not. What, therefore, does Scrum produce, if not a product? What are the "outputs" of the various Scrum practices? The answer is simple, if not obvious:

The outputs of Scrum practices are decisions.

Now we can view Scrum in a new light. The purpose of Scrum is to generate the *decisions* about what things need to be done and who will do them. We can assume that the individuals on the Scrum Team know how to do their jobs, that is, they are competent in their particular areas of expertise. What they lack as individuals, and what Scrum provides, is an approach to making the decisions about what work each of them should do and how they should work together to get the work done.

The remainder of this book focuses on the types of decisions that need to be made, and the supporting practices for making those decisions, from the portfolio level on down. The journey begins with a closer look at how decisions are made in an Agile way.

1.1 Governance

The term "governance" is widely used but seldom defined. In writing "Recipes for Agile Governance: The Enterprise Web" (hereafter the RAGE paper),[7] I developed a definition that focuses on the central role of decision-making identified in the preceding section:

Governance is the formalization and exercise of repeatable decision-making practices.

As organizations grow, so does the need for governance. Small organizations can often function with informal governance but are unlikely to grow to a large size successfully without some degree of formality and uniformity. A key challenge that arises when scaling up to a large enterprise is that of managing the tension between the need for uniform and well-defined practices that can be applied widely and the need for flexibility to handle specific local issues in appropriate ways.

This challenge is best met by providing just enough of the right kind of governance to enable successful collaboration, while avoiding the peril of excessive governance that becomes an impediment to success.

The introduction of Agile frameworks and principles has introduced a new wrinkle in the concept of governance.

Agile principles emphasize rapid adaptation to unexpected change over the execution of an existing plan. Agile processes have arisen partly in reaction against governance over-reach and yet, paradoxically, are highly disciplined. Agile frameworks have essentially reformulated governance in a fashion that combines a light touch with rigorous enforcement. Agile governance, like Agile frameworks in general, focuses much more on collaboration than on documentation, and is effective precisely because it involves the spirit of collaboration, not just the form.

To put it another way, governance is organic to Agile processes because it is conducted automatically in the normal course of planning and executing work by the people who do the work. This style of governance stands in stark contrast to the more common perception of governance as heavy-handed oversight that imposes an intrusive regime of inspections and enforcement.

In this book, I will use the term "Agile governance" to refer to an Agile style of governance, not specifically to the governance of projects that use Agile processes. This style of governance emphasizes rapid decision-making based on lightweight artifacts that are developed with minimum effort and that are part of the natural flow of work. Thus, Agile governance can be exercised for projects that are inherently non-Agile or that contain a hybrid mixture of Agile and other processes.

1.2 The Three Levels of Governance

Conceptually speaking, organizations can be divided into levels in many ways. For my purposes, the levels that matter are the levels of decision-making in the context of product development, and three will suffice for most purposes. A large organization may have more than three levels, but the levels that they do have will draw on the three patterns I describe below.

The classic world of project management provides a starting point for thinking about levels of governance, namely Portfolio, Program, and Project. With minor modifications, these terms are applicable to the governance of an Agile world as well,[8] and so it is worth reviewing the following terminology from the Project Management Institute.

A Project is a temporary endeavor undertaken to create a unique product, service, or result.[9]

A Program is comprised of multiple related projects that are initiated during the program's life cycle and are managed in a coordinated fashion. The program manager coordinates efforts between projects but does not directly manage the individual projects.[10]

A Portfolio is a collection of projects or programs and other work that are grouped together to facilitate effective management of that work in order to meet strategic business objectives. The projects or programs of the portfolio may not necessarily be interdependent or directly related.[11]

Given these definitions, the management of these entities can be defined as follows:

Project Management is the application of knowledge, skills, tools, and techniques to project activities to meet the project requirements.[12]

Program Management is the centralized coordinated management of a program to achieve the program's strategic objectives and benefits. It involves aligning multiple projects to achieve the program goals and allows for optimized or integrated cost, schedule, and effort.[13]

Portfolio Management is the coordinated management of portfolio components to achieve specific organizational objectives.[14]

Less formally, we might say that Project, Program, and Portfolio Management operate at tactical, strategic, and business levels, respectively. Project Management is about doing work correctly, while Portfolio Management is about selecting the correct work for the business to do. Program Management is the layer in between, which addresses the integration of tactical work (projects) into strategic (program-level) deliverables.

It should be noted that changes in the business environment may result in the cancellation of projects or programs that no longer represent appropriate investments for the business. A well-functioning portfolio management process can be expected to terminate programs or projects that are successful by their own objectives but that have ceased to represent the best investment of the company's resources.

The strict interpretation of the above definitions for "project" and "program" do not apply readily to an Agile world. In the latter, we are less focused on the concept of a project or a program as an entity in its own right and more focused on how Team members and teams can collaborate to produce business value over time. The classical concept of projects commonly assumes that a project team is drawn from some resource pool, that the project is funded as a line item in some larger budget, and that the project team is disbanded back into the resource pool on completion of the project. I consider the Agile perspective to be team-centric, meaning that we organize people into persistent teams, which may do the work of many "projects" over time. (I am anticipating the concept of Initiatives, from Chapter 6, here.)

Nevertheless, the concept of a hierarchical organization of work remains relevant, and I find it useful to think of this hierarchy in terms of three levels. The levels are not project-oriented but framework- or process-oriented. Each level conducts its work via a particular framework, which I expect to vary from one level to the next.

- The *Project level* (or *Team level*) refers to how a single team conducts its work. Possible frameworks include Scrum, Kanban, or variations on classic project management or Waterfall approaches.*

- The *Program level* refers to the collaboration between teams.

- The *Portfolio level* refers to the development and management of business initiatives that lead to Program- and Project-level work.

A key point to note is that the various teams may use any of a variety of approaches to manage their own work (although I expect that Scrum will be the most common solution at this level). We only require that the interfaces between levels are standardized and managed properly. These interfaces are defined by the Agile Program Management practices addressed in Chapter 3.

Figure 1.1 provides a high-level overview of the interaction of the three levels, for the specific case of a team-oriented organizational structure. At the top level, a Portfolio Management Team makes strategic investment decisions in the form of Initiatives that reflect business priorities and that

---

* I use "Project level" and "Team level" interchangeably partly because classic Project Management techniques may be in use for some teams at this level, as opposed to more Agile approaches, and partly because the three-tier hierarchy predates the Agile world and is well-defined in the context of classical Project, Program, and Portfolio Management. I have opted to preserve the familiar terminology for this hierarchy rather than attempt to rename any levels. That said, you should feel free to use whatever terminology you wish for the lowest level.

ultimately must feed work to the Project / Team level. The Program level then makes the decisions about how the work is partitioned across teams and maintains vertical alignment up and down through the organization. Each level has a specific set of decisions to make and uses a specific set of techniques to make those decisions.

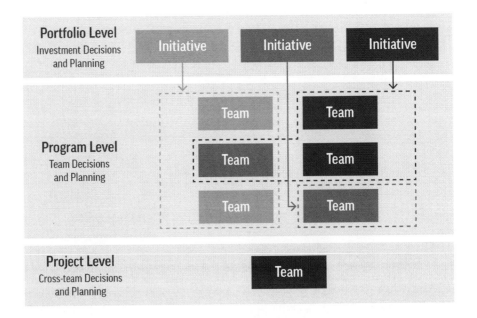

Figure 1.1: Flow of Decision-Making from Portfolio Level on Down

The teams are persistent structures, while Initiatives come and go. Thus, the work of each Initiative must be mapped to the appropriate set of teams; that is, the teams that do the kind of work required by the Initiative. This mapping is dynamic and may vary from one Initiative to the next.*

Governance is important at all levels. I will address governance for Agile methodologies, but not for plan-driven (e.g., Waterfall) methodologies, at

---

* Note that the Program and Project levels always have work to do that does not derive directly from any Initiative, such as setting up test environments. If, for accounting purposes, the organization requires that all work be traceable to some Initiative, then it is a good idea to create Initiatives that represent such work and for which the work is actually defined at the lower levels rather than at the top.

the Project level. At the Program level, where the distinction between Agile and plan-driven processes starts to blur, I will address governance for Agile and hybrid processes. Finally, Portfolio planning and monitoring strongly resembles the Agile perspective by default, and governance at that level can easily be described in Agile terms.

1.3 The Principles of Agile Governance

One of the most common ways to discover useful patterns is by observing examples in action and isolating the important commonalities into abstractions. Unfortunately, attempts to apply this approach to the three levels of Agile governance suffer from an absence of real-world examples.

An alternative approach, used in the RAGE paper, is to employ one of Albert Einstein's favorite techniques, which he called a *Gedankenexperiment* (a "thought experiment"). A Gedankenexperiment is an imaginary scenario developed to provide insight into situations, phenomena, or theories. It is a useful technique for generating insight and formulating hypotheses, especially when it is not possible to find relevant real-world data.

The RAGE paper performed a Gedankenexperiment in the conduct of large-scale organizational behavior that is intended to be Agile but not intended to be perfect. The paper describes a fictitious company, TelCorp, which develops medical products. The company's different Business Units develop hardware, embedded software, and Web applications. While the different Business Units do much of their work with Scrum or Kanban, they do so imperfectly and thus experience various real-world issues and variations in practices from one Business Unit to another. The result is a laboratory for investigating effective and ineffective ways of conducting Agile Portfolio, Program, and Project Management.

In writing the RAGE paper, I discovered that the same set of standard elements applies across Agile processes at the different levels. Every such process could be defined in terms of five basic elements:

1. **Roles:** A role defines areas of responsibility and authority associated with different aspects of governance. People who fulfill these roles collaborate with others in the process of making decisions but have specific areas of authority that are theirs alone and not shared with any other people or roles. This authority is constrained by checks and balances (often in the form of other roles with other types of authority) so that no one person can rule in an autocratic fashion. This conception of roles provides:

a. clarity, in terms of which people are the sole sources for certain types of information or decisions, and

b. decisiveness, by avoiding "rule by committee," which can otherwise produce endless debate and little action.

2. **Ceremonies:** Ceremonies are recurring meetings, with specific and standardized agendas, attendance, and practices. Each ceremony has a particular purpose.

3. **Artifacts:** Different artifacts serve different purposes, but most decisions make use of artifacts to some degree.

4. **Tracking and Metrics:** Tracking performance of work against plans is important. Without tracking, the actual deliverables and delivery dates may have little in common with the needs we are attempting to address. Tracking always involves the collection of status information, the creation of useful metrics that depend on this information, and comparison of the metrics to the planned or desired values. Effective tracking enables swift detection of problems and speeds their resolution, while ineffective tracking does the opposite. In some cases, the information provided by tracking may provide information that leads to large changes in direction, or even cancellation of planned work.

5. **Governance Points:** A governance point is a moment at which someone who fulfills a role makes a decision in the domain of that role's authority, based on standard practices, metrics, and artifacts. Many governance points are ceremonies, but some occur informally, as needed.

1.4 Common Role Types

Removing considerations specific to the type of work to be done simplifies the definition of roles by allowing us to focus on roles associated with making key decisions. Each role has a set of responsibilities that can be defined clearly, and certain patterns of responsibility occur at all levels of decision-making. These responsibilities are:

1. Defining specifications of deliverables to be produced

2. Prioritizing deliverables into a sequence to be implemented over time

3. Implementing the deliverables

4. Ensuring that the process is followed, and that work is being done in an effective and productive fashion

In Scrum, for example, the Product Owner owns the first two responsibilities, the Team members own the third, and the Scrum Master owns the fourth.

Other roles must always exist in an organization of any size. For example, there are people responsible for Architecture, User Experience, Release Management, Manufacturing, Human Resources, and so forth, and there is no intention here of slighting those people. The reason those responsibilities are not mentioned here is because they are domain-specific, and the focus here is on domain-independent responsibilities that are associated with the decision-making required for product development.

1.5 Decision Cycles

It is, of course, possible to define roles and the other elements mentioned above for processes that are anything but Agile. A slow-moving, ineffective, and wasteful process can be well defined in the sense described above, so there must be more that separates an Agile process from other kinds than just the five elements I've described.

For a process to be consistent with Agile principles, it must adapt swiftly to unexpected developments in a way that optimizes the value of the deliverables that the teams produce over time. Swift adaptation requires both quick discovery and quick action. In other words, it requires a short *decision cycle.*

A decision cycle is a sequence of steps that not only yields a decision but also feeds the results of the decision back into the same cycle to yield a new decision on a recurring basis.

Many examples of decision cycles exist, such as W. Edwards Deming's Plan-Do-Check-Act (PDCA) Cycle[15] in quality control and Colonel John Boyd's Observe-Orient-Decide-Act Cycle (OODA Loop).[16]

A key point in the theory of decision cycles is that the competitor with the shortest decision cycle has an advantage over other competitors. This point is often phrased as "getting inside the adversary's decision loop." If you can learn and change direction more quickly than the adversary, then you can push the adversary into a mode of increasingly ineffective attempts to catch up. For Boyd, this meant that you could win an aerial dogfight. In business, this means that you can deliver better value to customers more quickly than the competition and thus win market share.

For our purposes, a simple example of a decision cycle will suffice:

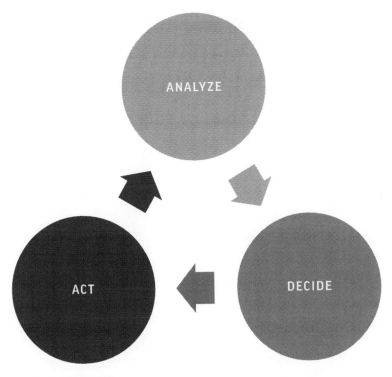

Figure 1.2: Simple Decision Cycle

The decision cycle of Figure 1.2 represents the following steps:

1. Analysis of results guides decisions.

2. Decisions drive actions.

3. Actions produce new results.

The effectiveness of our decisions depends partly on how good the decisions are and partly on how fast we make them. It is generally better to make adequate decisions quickly than to make perfect decisions slowly.

The benefits of rapid decision-making are core to what makes a process Agile. The elements described in the preceding section, while appropriate, will be ineffective unless they are implemented in a way that yields fast decision cycles.

What we need in Agile governance is to devise our process to enable rapid decisions based on lightweight artifacts that are developed with minimum effort.

1.6 Planning Horizons

Agile approaches both enable and require planning for some time horizon, which can be as long or short as desired. Figure 1.3 shows a common set of standard Agile planning horizons.[17]

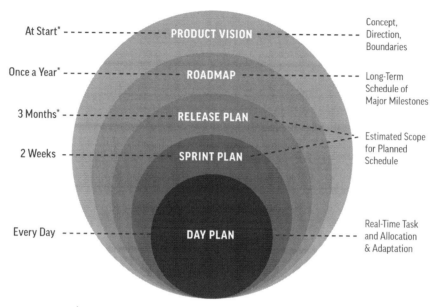

*Revise as often as needed (per Release, per Sprint,…)

Figure 1.3: Five Time Horizons of Agile Product Development

The language of Figure 1.3 is drawn from the world of Agile product development, but the concepts are widely applicable.

Classic project management often views work as a linear sequence of activities whose completion delivers the desired scope. The Agile perspective is better characterized as a set of nested cycles, or time horizons. Each cycle has some concept of a plan of work over time, and each larger cycle contains an integral number of smaller cycles.

The above cycles may be defined as follows:

- **Product Vision:** Not a plan of work against a calendar but a concise description of what the product is, and is not, which guides development work across multiple versions over time. Product Visions can be changed but tend to evolve slowly over years.

- **Roadmap:** A long-term schedule of major milestones, commonly over a span of six months to two years. A Roadmap spans multiple Release Cycles.

- **Release Plan:** The estimated scope (the *Release Backlog*, or deliverables to be developed) for a Release Cycle. A Release Cycle spans multiple Sprints.

- **Sprint Plan:** The estimated scope (the *Sprint Backlog*, or deliverables to be developed) for a Sprint.

- **Day Plan:** The work of the day, carried out in the form of real-time task allocation and adaptation to circumstances.

In the simplest case, a Scrum Team plans and executes Sprints (i.e., iterations, or short development cycles) of uniform length (usually two weeks) on a just-in-time basis. More complex scenarios may have a set of such teams collaborating over a longer Release Cycle to produce a larger product.

In principle, the decision of how far into the future one should plan and how many teams need to collaborate are separate issues. We might have one team who needs some forecast of work over the course of the next year or four teams who work closely together and only need to plan the next two-week Sprint.

In practice, the need for longer-term planning is driven in large part by the number of teams who must collaborate. As we grow an organization to more teams, we also grow the number of cross-team dependencies. As the latter increase, the potential for disrupting other teams' work due to broken dependencies also increases. The increasing cost of broken dependencies drives the need for longer-term planning so that we can identify dependencies and plan our work to satisfy them.

In short, Release Planning becomes a necessity as the number of teams grows. I usually recommend Release Planning for any organization that has three or more teams.

The linkage between organization size (number of teams) and Release Planning suggests that they be considered together. For this reason, I will present Release Planning as part of the content on Agile Program Management.

1.7 Where to Go from Here

We now have the basic pieces needed to develop Agile processes. The elements of an effective Agile process will draw from the set described in

Section 1.3. Each process will be designed to enable rapid decisions based on lightweight artifacts that are developed with minimum effort. The next few chapters will present solutions for the Project, Program, and Portfolio levels, focusing on the decisions to be made and the techniques for making them. Subsequent chapters will address other key topics in Agile product development.

This book provides specific Agile solutions for common situations that arise in organizations that develop products. It is not intended to address all possible aspects of product development but a core set that addresses common needs.

The obvious acronym for this book is SAGE. I like the implication of wisdom, but do not like the capitalization of the acronym. It is my wish that this collection of frameworks be called "Sage," with only the "S" capitalized, and I will use this convention throughout.

I anticipate that more solutions may appear over time and "nucleate" around the content presented here. My philosophy is that solutions intended to be widely useful should have the property that they are usable in more than a single domain. They should not incorporate or rely upon the specific content or technologies in those domains, other than as examples. In other words, they should address the *patterns* of decision-flow and decision-making, not the *content* of the decisions.

Roles, therefore, must relate to governance (decision-making) separately from domain knowledge. Thus, while we might have a "Program Manager" in such a solution, we will not have an "Architect" or an "Engineer." Domain-specific concepts must be addressed for the organization to function but should be addressed outside of the Agile-process definition.

Why focus in this fashion? Because to do otherwise is to expand the problem domain to incorporate the entire company, and in a way that is tightly coupled not only to the specific product development technologies but also to their rapid evolution over time. The combination of unbounded solution space and rapid change over time makes such a definition too large, too cumbersome, too prescriptive, and too fragile to be widely useful over time.

With all of the above said, welcome, and read on.

2

Overview of Approaches to Project Management

OUR journey begins with a brief review of the classic styles of project management, as defined in *A Guide to the Project Management Body of Knowledge* (hereafter PMBOK4). In this classic model, someone (commonly referred to as a "sponsor") approves some conception of project scope, which leads to the budgeting and staffing of a project team to implement the project scope. The project team works to refine and finalize the scope, plans the work to implement and test the scope, executes the plan, and delivers the planned scope as appropriate at the project's termination.

The above style of project management is sometimes referred to as a "plan-driven" approach, meaning that one first develops the plan and then drives the work according to the plan. A common example of this plan-driven style of work in software development is the Waterfall process. In this chapter, I will review the Waterfall process, identify its limitations, and use this understanding as a springboard for developing a broader understanding of why certain approaches to managing work do or do not work well in different situations. The organizational scope for this chapter will be a single team of modest size, from three to nine people. Later chapters will address scenarios of larger organizational scope.

2.1 Defining "Plan"

The word "plan" can be used in several ways. I might say, "I plan to stop at the store on the way home," or "We are planning to serve fish" or "This plan shows how five deliverables are completed over a two-month period."

Even though the word "plan" was used in all three examples, the meaning varied. The first example expressed an intention, the second some concept of "scope" (fish) without any reference to time, and the third described how a specific concept of scope (five items to be produced) will be sequenced and scheduled over a period of time.

In classic project management, a "project plan" consists of a set of documents that define what is to be done, when the work is to be scheduled, and anything else that is useful to know about how the work is to be done. A "project schedule" is a subset of this plan and shows the intended dates for various milestones, tasks, and deliverables. The famous (or infamous) Gantt chart is one example of such a schedule.

In other contexts, the word "plan" may refer to something quite different than Gantt charts and related artifacts. For this book, I will take the word "plan" to mean some conception of work to be done over some kind of time frame. The plan may not be detailed, but it must involve some attempt to align the work with our understanding of what is achievable in the time frame of interest.

The word "plan" does not imply anything about reliability. In some cases, the plan may be a very reliable guide to the future. In others, it may turn out to be wholly unrealistic. In general, we plan our work not to ensure that it can be done as planned but to prepare ourselves to achieve the best results that can be achieved in the time frame. In this sense, "planning" is very much part of "preparation."

The word "forecast" is sometimes a useful alternative to the word "plan" for people who have negative reactions to the latter based on their history. People understand that a weather forecast has some reliability in the very near term but decreasing reliability as the time scale grows. The concept of "decreasing reliability with increasing time scale" is relevant to virtually any concept of planning, so the word "forecast" does a good job of capturing this behavior in an intuitive fashion.

The drawback to "forecasting" is that it lacks the intentionality of "planning." We do not have any control over the weather we forecast, while we do have substantial control over what we plan. Thus, the use of "forecast" risks a different conceptual error than does "plan."

I will use "plan" rather than "forecast" because I want to focus on decision-making, which is very intentional. That said, our plans do become less reliable as time scales grow, just as forecasts do.

Much of this book focuses on various ways to plan work over time. The time scales and techniques vary from one case to another, but all address the basic need to generate some insight about the future and what we may be able to accomplish.

2.2 The Waterfall Process

The Waterfall process, as described most famously by Winston Royce in 1970,[18] was the dominant process for software development until roughly through the year 2000. Although Royce did not coin the term "Waterfall," he did describe a process whose characteristic stair-step structure and flow inspired the term.

The "Waterfall" term has achieved such wide usage that it has largely become synonymous with any kind of "non-Agile process" or "plan-driven project management," although Royce's original intent related only to software development. (Many hardware developers have told me, "We use a Waterfall process here," although their actual process does not much resemble the Waterfall diagram in Figure 2.1.) While I personally do *not* use the "Waterfall" term outside of its original context, it has become impossible to avoid it elsewhere. Regardless, the lessons of Waterfall development *do* apply far beyond the bounds of strictly -Waterfall environments.

The basic concept of a Waterfall process is that the project scope (in this case, the feature set of a software product) is first defined and then moves through a sequence of stages until the complete product is delivered at the end. Royce diagrammed the process in this manner:

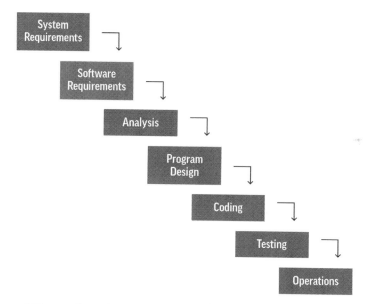

Figure 2.1: Winston Royce's Original Waterfall Diagram

Royce's own commentary on this diagram foreshadowed the difficulties to come:

I believe in this concept, but the implementation described above is risky and invites failure. The problem is illustrated in [Figure 2.1 above]. The testing phase which occurs at the end of the development cycle is the first event for which timing, storage, input / output transfers, etc., are experienced as distinguished from analyzed. These phenomena are not precisely analyzable. They are not the solutions to the standard partial differential equations of mathematical physics for instance. Yet if these phenomena fail to satisfy the various external constraints, then invariably a major redesign is required. A simple octal patch or redo of some isolated code will not fix these kinds of difficulties. The required design changes are likely to be so disruptive that the software requirements upon which the design is based and which provides the rationale for everything are violated. Either the requirements must be modified, or a substantial change in the design is required. In effect the development process has returned to the origin and one can expect up to a 100-percent overrun in schedule and / or costs.[19]

Software product development processes commonly adopted the "Waterfall" term and concepts. Hardware development processes have often adopted the term and concepts as well, even though the logical sequence of development steps does not follow those of Royce's diagram. In fact, the concept of a "Waterfall" process has become essentially synonymous with any concept of "plan-driven" work, independent of the nature of the work or the steps involved.

Royce correctly identified the key problem with a Waterfall approach to product development: it is not possible to get the requirements, design, and implementation of a product done exactly the right way in a single pass. Every aspect of product development is subject to such high uncertainty that one cannot simply lay out a plan and follow it because reality diverges swiftly from the plan.

Attempts to reduce uncertainty to the point where one can create a Waterfall-style plan that works are doomed to failure because the uncertainty cannot be reduced to low levels. In other words, it is not possible to "plan out" the unknown unknowns, and there are always many unknown unknowns in the development of a new product.

The impact of uncertainty applies in very much the same ways to any kind of product development work, whether the product is software, hardware, or a mix of the two.

The solution to this problem lay almost thirty years in the future from Royce's paper, with the development of Agile processes. A core component of this solution is the practice of defining and implementing scope in small pieces, sequentially, and providing frequent opportunities to correct errors and change direction as understanding of the true needs emerges over time.

2.3 Guidance for Selecting a Process: The Adaptive Spectrum

It would be easy to infer from the Waterfall example that plan-driven approaches to planning and implementing work are always inappropriate, but this is not the case. The real problem is that the characteristics of a plan-driven approach are not well suited for the characteristics of the work to which it has often been applied.

Many approaches to the practicalities of planning and executing work have been developed. When attempting to decide which approach to use, the single most important characteristic to consider is the amount of uncertainty that we encounter in the day-to-day experience of doing the work.

For my purposes, uncertainty comes in two varieties:

- *Scope Uncertainty* is about the reliability of our understanding of the scope of the product or project. If the requirements for the work are comprehensive, detailed, clear, and stable, then uncertainty is low. Otherwise, scope uncertainty is higher.

- *Effort (or Cost) Uncertainty* is about the reliability of our forecast of the effort (or cost) required to deliver the completed scope. Uncertainty is low only if the forecast is truly reliable.

Figure 2.2 shows the connection between the total amount of uncertainty (across scope and effort) and the type of process best suited for the work. I refer to Figure 2.2 as the Adaptive Spectrum because it lays out the spectrum of uncertainty to which an effective process must adapt.

	UNCERTAINTY →	
	The Agile Zone	
Predictive	**Adaptive**	**Reactive**
Plan-Driven	Scrum	Kanban
Waterfall		
• Emphasize efficiency (minimum cost, duration) • Perform well when work is well understood • Perform poorly when uncertainty is high	• Emphasize adaptability to rapid change • Enable detailed short-term planning • Evolve longer-term specs, plan over time • Overhead of enabling change is costly for predictable work	• Emphasize continuous re-prioritization, efficient allocation of work to people • Do not require work to be planned against calendar • Handle unpredictable work well

Figure 2.2: The Adaptive Spectrum for Process Selection

As total uncertainty encountered in doing work increases from very low to very high values, the process that is best suited for the work changes. Figure 2.2 divides the space of possible process into three columns (Predictive, Adaptive, and Reactive), which I'll examine below. As we'll see, processes that occupy the middle and right columns are Agile because they deal effectively with unpredictable events.

2.3.1 Predictive Processes

Predictive processes work well for low-uncertainty work. When uncertainty is low, it is possible to develop a plan for work over time that can be executed very much as the plan predicts. This is commonly the case for routine and repeatable styles of work, such as carpet installation, painting, and so forth. One can develop and reuse the same project plan, with adaptations for the size of the job.

Predictive processes are well-suited for repetitive work but not for work that has high uncertainty. When applied to high-uncertainty situations, the plan "breaks" and must be revised frequently. Frequent revisions are costly to develop, leading to frustration and low morale over time.

The Waterfall process is predictive but was intended for software development, whose work is characterized by such high uncertainty that the process is generally unsatisfactory in the software domain.

2.3.2 Adaptive Processes

Adaptive processes work well for high-uncertainty work, where some conception of scope and work estimates are available but are highly uncertain. Product development fits in this category, as it is not possible to foresee all of the details of work to be done at the start of product development. This statement holds for products of any kind: software, hardware (electronic, mechanical, or electro-mechanical), or any mix of software and hardware. In other words, product development inevitably encounters numerous "unknown unknowns" that cannot be planned out in advance.

The concept of known versus unknown aspects in project planning is an old one. Table 2.1 provides some examples relevant to product development.

	Known	Unknown
Known	• Basic product capabilities • Intended market	• Technology readiness levels • Vendor qualifications
Unknown	• Internal capabilities not yet known to be relevant to the product	All disruptions that cannot be foreseen • Vendor goes out of business • Part specs are incorrect • Physics is impossible

Table 2.1: Known-Unknown Matrix Examples for Product Development

The "known knowns" are items that are well understood, for which reliable estimates and plans can be developed.

The "known unknowns" are items whose definition or impact is not yet known but that can be identified as areas that require research or risk mitigation.

The "unknown knowns" are areas that have not been identified but that we do have the ability to address once identified.

The "unknown unknowns" are the most disruptive items because they cannot be identified or mitigated in advance or managed without significant impact when they occur. Any attempt to do non-routine work of any size (which is the norm for product development) will encounter numerous unknown unknowns.

An effective approach to planning this type of work is to plan at a detailed level for the near term (say, two weeks), and at a high level for longer periods of time, while also adapting to unforeseen changes and disruptions that may occur frequently.

Scrum is the most widely used and standardized approach for this style of work. Scrum focuses on maximizing value delivered over time by sequencing work to ensure that the most valuable items are done as soon as possible.

Scrum does *not* eliminate the disruption and cost of unforeseen events but *does* reduce both to a practical minimum. The techniques used in Scrum to adapt to these unexpected events entail a certain amount of overhead, whose value is justified when changes are frequent. However, if the work is highly predictable, then this overhead does not serve a useful purpose, and a predictive approach is likely to be more efficient.

2.3.3 Reactive Processes

A reactive process is most appropriate when work cannot be planned over any reasonable time frame. This is a common situation for reactive environments, where the people who do the work must react to a stream of requests whose timing and urgency (or value) varies unpredictably from one to the next. Examples of reactive environments include firefighting, triage in hospital emergency rooms, and customer-support departments. In these environments, scope uncertainty is large, as scope cannot be defined with any kind of reliability far enough in advance to enable the creation of meaningful plans.

Kanban[20] is widely used for reactive environments. Kanban focuses on rapid prioritization, workflow definition, and optimization of throughput by constraining Work in Process and reducing the Cycle Time from start to completion of work.

Kanban is not well-suited for product development work, as the latter typically requires some concept of a schedule of work over time, which Kanban does not provide.

2.4 Velocity

The classic plan-driven style of project management builds a project schedule out of a set of tasks. The tasks have estimates, and their sequence is determined by constraints such as dependencies and resource limitations. The forecasted duration of the project is then given by the resulting end date of the project schedule.

Scrum uses a different set of scheduling concepts. We start by defining a set of teams, each of which will develop and validate deliverables for some portion of the product. Each team must have the set of skills needed to do the work in its area, and work on the complete product is allocated to one team or another based on the teams' areas of specialization.

Instead of summing task estimates to derive project durations, we try to quantify how fast each team can work or, equivalently, how much work each team can do in a specific period of time, such as a two-week Sprint.

This approach introduces *Velocity* as a central concept in the exercise of planning work against the calendar and is used heavily for this purpose in Scrum.

One of the oddities in Scrum is that the term "Velocity" has no standard definition, even though the term itself is widely used. For my purposes, I will define "Velocity" as the amount of work a team completes in a Sprint. The units for Velocity are the same as the units used to estimate the work required to implement and test a team's deliverables. (See Sections 3.4.2 and 3.4.3 for details on units and estimation for Velocity.)

3

Agile Project Management with Scrum

THIS chapter presents the fundamental concepts of Scrum, in the standard context of how a single cohesive team plans and executes work.*

Scrum is not only well suited for product development work but also provides the effective building blocks (in the form of Scrum Teams) needed to construct the larger organizational structures that are required when building large products. The techniques presented here apply to the development of software, electronic, mechanical, or electro-mechanical products by a single cohesive team of people.

The decisions that must be addressed for a Scrum Team to function effectively include:

- What things to do sooner versus later
- What deliverables are to be implemented in the next Sprint
- What tasks need to be done to implement and validate the intended deliverables
- Who should do the tasks for the deliverables
- How to know when work for a deliverable is done
- How to adjust when obstacles appear

---

* Some readers might object to the title of this chapter, as Scrum is more commonly employed to build products whose scope is uncertain, rather than to manage fixed-scope projects. The criticism is valid, but alternative choices of nomenclature also have drawbacks. In this case, alignment with the project-program-portfolio hierarchy is the driver behind the name, as I am focusing on the bottom level of that hierarchy.

At the most basic level, people who work according to a Scrum process do so by defining and implementing small deliverables over time. We divide time into short periods, officially termed "Sprints" in Scrum. A Scrum Team plans a Sprint with the specific intent to start and complete a set of deliverables in the time frame of that Sprint. The concept of completion is critical: while it will happen, on occasion, that a team starts a deliverable in a Sprint that it cannot complete by the end of the Sprint, this situation is an exception, and teams do everything they can to avoid it.

When a Scrum Team is developing a product, the product is built through the aggregation of these small deliverables over time. For software products, these deliverables are most commonly portions of the product (e.g., features, infrastructure capabilities, and so forth). The software product accretes functioning capabilities over time, until the accumulation of capabilities reaches the set desired for release to customers.

For hardware products, the development work focuses on creating the detailed design of a product that will then be handed over to a manufacturing process for production. Hardware product development does not typically yield accretion of features over time. Instead, it more commonly accretes design elements for components that address a target level of functionality. The product does not really function in any meaningful sense until the accumulation of components is complete, or nearly so.

The common case of hardware products that have embedded or associated software proceeds as one might expect: both modes of accretion occur, and the software and hardware aspects require synchronization in order to yield a workable plan.

A key aspect of Scrum is that each deliverable must be tested to confirm acceptability at the time of implementation. This means that we must define acceptance criteria for each deliverable, test the deliverable immediately, and fix any defects that are uncovered by testing. Working in this fashion results in building products out of pieces that are known to be of good quality at all times and avoids the classic Waterfall problem of massive testing and defect-fixing exercises late in the development cycle.

The need to conduct integration testing of components or subsystems of a product must always be addressed. The Waterfall approach emphasizes large-scale integration testing of previously "siloed" components after completion of the components, which yields late discovery of numerous integration problems. With the Scrum approach, we fold as much integration work as possible into the Acceptance Criteria for each deliverable, doing integration testing incrementally. This approach minimizes the amount of integration testing done late in the development cycle and reduces the number of late integration errors that occur.

A Scrum process has no inherent concept of architecture or design phases. Rather, Scrum provides a mechanism for planning and tracking work, leaving the nature of the work up to the team. Thus, a team's effort in a Sprint may deliver a mix of architecture- or design-related deliverables, research efforts, and infrastructure capabilities, along with development of features or components of the product. It falls to the Scrum Team to choose the optimum pacing and scheduling of these types of deliverables over time.

The following sections describe the elements of Scrum in more detail.

3.1 Overview of Roles and Process

Scrum Teams work in *Sprints* (iterations) typically of two weeks in length. Each Scrum Team consists of a set of people fulfilling one of three roles: *Team member* (usually three to nine members in a team), *Product Owner*, and *Scrum Master*. The term "Scrum Team" refers to all three roles. The term "team" refers to the set of three to nine people who do the hands-on work of developing and testing deliverables and excludes the Product Owner and the Scrum Master.

Sprints are most commonly two weeks long, and this length should be chosen unless there is a particular need for a different length. For example, a one-week Sprint might better suit organizations that need to go to production weekly, while three weeks might work better in cases where two weeks is found to be just a bit too short. Longer Sprints risk a return to Waterfall-style work, can cause degradation of tracking and discipline, and lead to late discovery that the team is behind schedule.

The Product Owner is responsible for ensuring that the team has a large-enough set of specifications for deliverables to enable planning of the next Sprint. The Product Owner is also responsible for identifying the proper ranking (sequencing) of the deliverables. All such specifications that have been defined but not yet scheduled for implementation reside in a set called the *Product Backlog*. Each item in the Product Backlog is officially called a *Product Backlog Item* (PBI).

In practice, specifications come in more than one form, and PBIs are usually written as short narrative descriptions (*Stories*) or as *Defect* reports. Prior to the Sprint Planning Meeting, the Product Owner selects and ranks a subset of the Product Backlog for use by the team in planning. The whole Scrum Team prepares the Product Backlog Items and themselves for the *Sprint Planning Meeting* through two or more Backlog Refinement Meetings in preceding Sprints.

The Scrum Master facilitates the Sprint Planning Meeting, in which the Team members collaborate with the Product Owner to clarify and estimate the work of each PBI and select the top subset of PBIs that can be implemented in the Sprint. Team members then decompose the work of implementing and validating PBIs into tasks (with estimates), finalize the scope of the Sprint (the *Sprint Backlog*), and begin work by self-organizing to assign themselves to the top PBIs to be implemented.

Team members continue implementing and testing PBIs in rank order, throughout the duration of the Sprint. They are mentored, guided, and assisted by the Scrum Master, as needed, and collaborate with the Product Owner daily to ensure the deliverables are as desired. Planning and execution of work is guided by the principle that Team members never start a PBI in a Sprint unless they believe at that time that they can complete it in the Sprint.

The three Scrum roles meet in the *Daily Stand-Up* meeting to maintain a coherent understanding of Sprint status. After completing as much work as possible in the Sprint, the team demonstrates all completed deliverables to the Product Owner in the Sprint Review meeting, and all three roles participate in a Retrospective meeting to identify how to improve their process and environment over time.

Governance is built into Scrum through the definition of roles, *ceremonies* (recurring meetings with standard agendas), artifacts (PBIs, Epics, and the *Definition of Done*), tracking, and metrics.

3.2 Roles

A "role" is a set of responsibilities, and accompanying authority, assigned to and carried out by a person or set of people. The Scrum roles of Product Owner, Scrum Master, and Team members are clearly defined, as shown below.

Product Owner: The sole authority over a team's deliverables (definition and sequencing), for up to three teams. Responsibilities include:

- Developing specifications of the user-oriented deliverables, in collaboration with customers, stakeholders, and Team members
- Collaborating with Team members to ensure necessary technical deliverables are defined
- Providing near real-time guidance to the Scrum Team during implementation and testing of deliverables
- Reviewing and approving deliverables

Scrum Master: The sole authority over the process, for up to three teams. A Scrum Master does whatever is needed to make the Scrum Team as productive as possible. Scrum Master responsibilities include:

- Enforcing the process
- Facilitating meetings
- Maintaining situational awareness of the work
- Knowing Team member strengths and weaknesses
- Mentoring the team
- Protecting the team from interference
- Monitoring progress
- Removing obstacles, ensuring issues are addressed

Team member: The Team members have sole authority over estimates, task definitions, and task assignments. A team includes three to nine members who do the hands-on work of implementing each deliverable and testing it to ensure that it performs as intended.

Team responsibilities include:

- Implementing and validating (testing, fixing) deliverables
- Completing work to standard *Definition of Done* (Section 3.5.5)
- Estimating work for deliverables
- Allocating tasks within team (self-organizing) based on skills and availability

Note also the following guidelines around selecting people to fill the Scrum roles.

3.2.1 Things to Never Do

- No person should serve as Scrum Master and Product Owner for the same team. This person becomes vested with too much authority and can easily destroy the team's effectiveness and morale in the absence of the usual checks and balances that are present when the roles are fulfilled by different people.

3.2.2 Things That Are Allowed but Should Be Avoided

- One person can be a part-time Scrum Master and part-time member of the same team. This situation should be avoided, if possible, because the distraction of being a Team member (who must focus for long periods in a very narrow area) can lead to failing as a Scrum Master (who must maintain constant situational awareness of team activities, status, issues, and limitations).

- It is commonly advised that a Scrum Master for a team should not be the functional manager of anyone on that team. The concern with this situation is that the presence of management authority can distort the team's behavior, even without conscious intent. Subordinates may feel motivated to decrease estimates or behave in ways that are counterproductive for the team's effectiveness, in an effort to please their manager.

  - The point is valid, but the likelihood of this problem depends very much on the relationship between the Team members and their manager. In practice, one should assess the situation and the options before making a decision on this point.

  - It is also worth noting that a functional manager's organizational responsibilities often relate to deciding what work should be done, and thus align with the role of the Product Owner. If so, the functional manager may best work with the team as the Product Owner, while another person takes on the role of the Scrum Master. In this case, the manager must take care not to infringe on the authority of the Scrum Master.

It is best by far to dedicate people full-time to their teams and to avoid sharing of people across teams if possible. Context switching between areas of responsibility takes a large toll on productivity. In *Quality Software Management*,[21] Gerald Weinberg quantified this toll as follows:

Number of Simultaneous Projects	% Time Available per Project	% Loss to Context Switching
1	100	0
2	40	20
3	20	40
4	10	60
5	5	75

Table 3.1: The Impact of Context Switching on Productivity

There are times when context switching cannot be avoided. A common example is the case when one person with a deep specialty (such as Database Analyst or Antenna Engineer) is needed by several teams, but no one team has enough of that kind of work to employ the person full-time. In such cases, it may be necessary to share the person across teams. If so, then estimates for that person's ability to contribute should reflect the cost of context switching, and it is often necessary to make some ad hoc adaptions to avoid consuming that person's time with multiple sets of Scrum Team meetings.

It is rarely the case that all people who contribute to the work of product development are members of Scrum Teams. Membership on a Scrum Team does not make sense when a person's skills are needed only occasionally. In these cases, it makes sense to consider the person to be an *external resource* who collaborates on a more contractual or as-needed basis. As no company consists entirely of Scrum Teams, external resources (as individuals or groups) are commonly encountered.

3.2.3 Things That Are Acceptable

One person can be a part-time Product Owner and part-time member of the same team. The challenge is that Product Owners are "on call" for frequent consultations with Team members, who need insight and approval of work, which distracts from developmental work.

In feature-oriented software development, Product Owners commonly hail from a marketing or business analyst background, and do not have the skills required to serve as Team members. This pattern does not apply so much for highly technical back-end software development or for hardware product development. In these cases, Product Owners very often do have the technical expertise to serve as Team members and may do so on a part-time basis. Taking on the part-time role of Team member does, of course, mean that the Product Owner has less bandwidth to be available for other purposes (such as being a Product Owner for a second Scrum Team).

Other combinations of Scrum roles, including management roles with Scrum roles, are possible and allowed, with the only criterion for acceptability being the ability of the person to fulfill all relevant responsibilities (e.g., an Engineering Manager might be an acceptable Product Owner, as long as he or she abides by the Scrum rules and carries out other responsibilities required by his or her position).

3.3 Ceremonies and Time Boxes

Ceremonies are recurring meetings with standard agendas.* A *Time Box* is a period of time with a specified start and end (or duration), devoted to a

---

* The terminology for meetings has drifted over time. I first encountered "meetings," then "ceremonies" became common, followed by the term "event." I do not consider "event" to be a good name for a meeting, however, and do not use it.

specific purpose. Many Time Boxes are meetings (or ceremonies), but Time Boxes may also be longer periods of time (such as Sprints).

Each ceremony has a particular purpose, as summarized in Table 3.2.

Ceremony	Time Box	Input	Output	Value
Backlog Refinement	1 hr, weekly	Draft User Stories, Epics from Product Owner	Finalized User Stories Technical Stories Ranking for top PBIS	Product Backlog & Team are ready for Sprint Planning
Sprint Planning	2–4 hrs	Ranked Product Backlog with Acceptance Criteria	Sprint Backlog: • Selected PBIS + estimates • Tasks + estimates	Team has a plan to implement Sprint Backlog
Daily Stand-up (Daily Scrum)	<15 min, daily	In-progress tasks	Tasks updated Impediments raised	Team members on same page re: Sprint progress and impediments
Sprint Review	1 hr	Demo prepared for completed PBIS	New PBIS, based on review by Product Owner Ranking may be revised	Deliverables reviewed; feedback from stakeholders, other teams
Retrospective	1–1.5 hr	Sprint performance data, e.g., Burndown chart	Short list of improvements for next Sprint, with owners	Learn from experience, enable continuous improvement

Table 3.2: Scrum Ceremonies

The durations of the Time Boxes in the table are suggestions and should be modified based on experience. They should always be kept to as short a time as will suffice, to minimize overhead. (The exception is for the Daily Stand-Up, which should always be capped at fifteen minutes.)

The practice of Backlog Refinement drives effective decisions about the definition, sequencing, and scheduling of deliverables to be implemented by a Scrum Team. Sprint Planning produces the Sprint plan, or Sprint Backlog (selection of deliverables to be developed and associated tasks and estimates), which defines the scope of the Sprint for the team. The Sprint Review meeting gives the Product Owner a final opportunity to approve deliverables (or to specify what changes will be required), while the Retrospective meeting drives rapid improvement in the team's ability to deliver. The Daily Stand-Up meeting maintains a coherent picture of work across all the Team members, identifying issues and potential impacts quickly so they may be resolved quickly.

Figure 3.1 shows a typical schedule for a two-week Sprint. Note that the meetings take up ten of the eighty hours of working time in the Sprint. While Figure 3.1 shows the Sprint beginning on a Monday, this is not a requirement. A team may choose any weekday that is convenient for them to start the Sprint. Wednesdays and Thursdays are also common as starting days for Sprints.

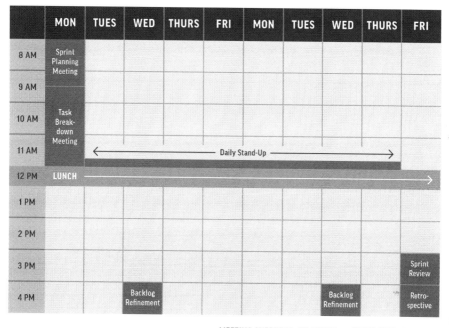

MEETING OVERHEAD: 70 HOURS   WORK TIME: 10 HOURS

Figure 3.1: Typical Sprint Schedule

3.3.1 Backlog Refinement Meeting

The purpose of Backlog Refinement is to prepare the team and a subset of the Product Backlog for future Sprint Planning meetings. Backlog Refinement meetings are held at least twice per Sprint, or weekly for Sprints of two weeks or longer.

In order for a Sprint Planning meeting for a set of PBIs to be effective, these prerequisites must be satisfied:

- The PBIs must be clear and complete.

- The set of PBIs must have no "holes"; that is, none of the PBIs can depend on some other deliverable that has not been defined or developed.

- The PBIs must be ranked (sequenced) appropriately, based on their value and dependencies.

- The Team members must understand the PBIs and the relationships between them.

The Product Owner facilitates the meeting, which all Team members and the Scrum Master attend. In the meeting, Team members provide feedback on draft Stories selected in advance by the Product Owner, identifying any issues or omissions that need to be corrected. The Team members and Product Owner collaborate to identify what changes are needed (and who will make them). They also develop a ranking of the PBIs that is driven by the Product Owner's assessment of value, which also ensures that dependencies between items are satisfied.

After the meeting, the authors of the Stories revise or draft new Stories based on feedback.

Some Scrum Teams prefer to estimate the PBIs in Backlog Refinement meetings as well. Whether to perform estimation in these meetings, or in Sprint Planning meetings, is up to the Scrum Team, and the choice is often driven by logistical issues.

There is no assumption that refinement is restricted solely to meetings. Some refinement of specifications should be ongoing, as routine work. The Backlog Refinement meetings provide an opportunity for full-team collaboration that is intended to enhance, not replace, informal collaboration on Backlog refinement.

The goal of Backlog Refinement is to ensure that Stories and the team are prepared for Sprint Planning and the Stories' implementation. Thus, the Team members should be in agreement that each PBI is ready for implementation before allowing the PBI to enter a Sprint Planning meeting. Some teams ensure readiness by defining a "Definition of Ready" for Stories, which lists the explicit criteria the team uses to ensure readiness. Others find informal consensus to be sufficient.

3.3.2 Sprint Planning Meeting

The purpose of the Sprint Planning meeting is to create the plan for the Sprint. The plan consists of the scope (the *Sprint Backlog*) in the form of the ranked Product Backlog Items selected for implementation in the Sprint, the PBI estimates, the list of tasks associated with each PBI, and the task estimates in hours.

The Sprint Planning meeting is held no later than the start of the Sprint but may precede the start of the Sprint by a day or two if necessary. (A common reason for holding Sprint Planning meetings prior to the start of a Sprint is that the Scrum Master, Product Owner, or some Team members may need to participate in more than one such meeting, for different teams, which means that the meetings cannot be held in parallel.)

A Sprint Planning meeting has two parts. In the first part, the Scrum Team develops a preliminary plan, based on PBI size, ranking, and Sprint Velocity (see Section 3.4.3). In the second part, the team decomposes the work of all PBIs into tasks and revises the Sprint scope as needed based on task-level work estimates.

3.3.2.1 Sprint Planning, Part 1

The Scrum Master, Product Owner, and all Team members attend. The Scrum Master facilitates the development of the Sprint plan, which consists of the Sprint schedule (already known) and the Sprint Backlog (the scope of the Sprint, in the form of a set of ranked PBIs).

The participants work through a set of ranked PBIs provided by the Product Owner for planning. If the PBIs have not been estimated, the Scrum Master facilitates estimation of the PBIs by the team, working through the supplied set in rank order.

In the simplest model, the Scrum Master adds each PBI to the Sprint Backlog until the latter is filled to the level of this Sprint's estimated Velocity (which must be estimated by the Scrum Master prior to this meeting, using the techniques described below).

Planning is often not quite this simple, though. There is usually some specialization of skills across Team members, and some care must commonly be taken to ensure that no one person is overloaded or underloaded. The impact of specialization on loading of people is particularly intense for hardware-oriented teams. For these cases, I suggest making tentative assignments of Story work across team members as the planning continues and modifying the ranking and scope decisions to avoid inappropriate loading of anyone in the Sprint. (Note that the Velocity-forecasting technique of Section 3.4.3.4 provides capacity information for each team member.)

The Product Owner answers questions about the content and priority of the PBIs and may make quick revisions to them on the fly. The Product

Owner may also modify the ranking to optimize the value that the team can complete in the Sprint, given their estimated Velocity.

3.3.2.2 Sprint Planning, Part 2

The Product Owner does not normally attend this part of the meeting as the focus is on task decomposition, not clarification of deliverables. The Scrum Master's presence is optional and depends on whether the team needs him or her to facilitate the work (usually the case for inexperienced teams) and the extent to which the Scrum Master wants to be familiar with the finer details of this Sprint's plan.

Team members create a Task Breakdown for each PBI in the form of a list of specific tasks they will perform in order to implement, test, and do whatever else is necessary to produce a tested and working deliverable that meets the PBI's specifications. (In other language, each completed deliverable must satisfy the Definition of Done, as in Section 3.5.5.) The Team members also estimate each task, in units of hours. The team should have a standard for minimum and maximum allowed task sizes, such as 2 and 16 hours, in order to avoid pathologies that tend to arise when tasks are very small or very large.

- The lower limit avoids creating numerous small tasks, which are typically not worth tracking. However, it is perfectly fine for a team to create and track small tasks for the purpose of ensuring that those tasks are not forgotten.

- The upper limit reduces the risk of discovering that work is behind schedule at a time that is too late to attempt corrective measures.

There are two common strategies for creating Task Breakdowns.

1. The first strategy has the whole team talk through each PBI, agree on the tasks needed for it, and then estimate the tasks. This is more time-consuming than the second strategy, but I recommend it for new teams, who need to develop a common understanding of how to do this work.

2. The second strategy has Team members divide PBIs among the team, after which individuals or pairs draft Task Breakdowns. The whole team then reassembles to review and revise the Task Breakdowns and develop consensus estimates for the tasks. This is faster than the first strategy but should only be chosen after the team has developed a common understanding of how to develop Task Breakdowns.

On completion of the Task Breakdowns, Team members and the Scrum Master review the initial scope decision for the Sprint to see if it is still valid in light of the task estimates and availability of skill sets across Team members.

If the conception of PBI size has changed due to the task estimates, it may be necessary to remove PBIs from, or add PBIs to, the Sprint Backlog, in order to ensure that the plan has an achievable scope and delivers the maximum value in the Sprint. All scope-change decisions must be discussed with and approved by the Product Owner to finalize the plan.

Here again we may need to consider how specialization of skills leads to inappropriate loading of Team members. When specialization is a major issue, I suggest making tentative assignments of tasks to Team members in the meeting and adjusting Sprint scope and ranking as needed to ensure that no one has too much or too little to do in the Sprint. (Note again that the Velocity-forecasting technique of Section 3.4.3.4 provides capacity information for each team member.) Actual assignment of tasks to people is done throughout the Sprint and need not match the tentative assignments made in the planning session.

There is generally no need to replace the original PBI-level estimates with new estimates generated by aggregating the PBI's task estimates. Most tracking systems have separate fields for these two quantities. While nothing bad is likely to happen if a team does revise the PBI-level estimate, revision of the original Story-level estimate has negligible practical impact on the planning or execution of the work.

3.3.2.3   How Work Assignment Is Done

Centralized and up-front assignment of work to Scrum Team members at the start of a Sprint is generally regarded as undesirable. The preference is to use a technique known as *swarming* in order to maximize the rate of completion of each deliverable. Swarming is desirable in principle, but the extent to which it can be employed varies. I will address what swarming is, why it is desirable, and when it does or does not work below.

3.3.2.3.1 Swarming

Swarming is a technique for work assignment intended to minimize the risk of delivering less than the greatest possible value in a Sprint. It addresses the very real possibility that the work a team intends to accomplish in a Sprint may not, in fact, be possible to complete in that time. If this situation arises, we want to finish as many of the top-ranked items as possible, and to avoid working on items that cannot be finished by the end of the Sprint.

Suppose, for example, that a team with six Team members has six PBIs ranked and planned for its next Sprint. For the sake of simplicity, assume that the all PBIs require about the same amount of effort.

Consider what happens if the Team members can complete only 50 percent of the planned work. If each Team member works on one PBI, then no

PBIs are completed by the end of the Sprint. However, if two people share the work of each of the top PBIs, then the first three PBIs can be completed, and the others will be deferred for a future Sprint.

The second scenario produces more value from the Sprint than does the first. This approach is an example of swarming, which I define as allocating as many people as practical to each PBI, in order to work through as many of the top-ranked items as possible in the Sprint. If no surprises occur, all PBIs the team selected will be finished in the Sprint. If surprises do occur, then the team will finish as many of the higher-ranked items as possible, instead of being partway through several at the end of the Sprint.

Ideally, swarming begins at the end of the Sprint Planning meeting. The three roles on the Scrum Team identify how best to allocate Team members to the top-ranked PBIs in order to complete each as swiftly as possible. Rather than pre-assign all work to all Team members, we end the assignment as soon as everyone has something to do. The remaining allocations occur on the spot during the rest of the Sprint, as each Team member ends work on one PBI and seeks out the next one where his or her presence will yield the greatest value. (This decision often involves guidance from the Scrum Master, who has more situational awareness than Team members do.)

The swarming technique requires that a Team member remain with a PBI as long as there is a task that he or she can perform, even if it doesn't match the member's particular specialty. Only if there is literally no work that the member can do does the member move on to another PBI, in which case the member moves to the nearest PBI in the ranking after this one, where his or her presence will get the PBI done sooner than would otherwise be the case. The departed swarm member may even return to the previous PBI at some point, if returning expedites that PBI's completion.

3.3.2.3.2 The Relationship between Swarming and Generalizing Specialists

The swarming technique makes an implicit assumption that each Team member could work on several PBIs in a Sprint and not be limited by specialization of skills to just one or two. This assumption holds reasonably well if the Team members are *generalizing specialists*.

A generalizing specialist is a person with deep knowledge in one particular area but who is also capable of doing work outside that area if the skill level required is not high. For example, an engineer whose specialty is writing software in Java may also be able to do database work, as long as the latter does not require advanced skills. If most Team members are generalizing specialists, then swarm sizes of two or three are common, and the benefits of swarming for risk reduction are very real.

When Team members have different skills and little overlap in what they can do, the swarming concept has much less utility. This situation is common on teams that develop physical products, where one Scrum Team might have a mix of mechanical engineers, electrical engineers, and firmware engineers. People with these skills generally cannot function as generalizing specialists. Sprint Planning must then consider the allocation of work (at both the PBI and task levels) to Team members based on the skills and availability of each Team member. In this case, we may well need to spend time in the Sprint Planning meeting to make at least tentative assignments of people to all the tasks planned into the Sprint.

3.3.3 Daily Stand-Up Meeting

The purpose of a Daily Stand-Up (also called *Daily Scrum*) meeting is to maintain a coherent perspective on the part of all Team members as to what is happening in the Sprint. Team members lose track of what other Team members are doing, and how their work can impact each other, because they are focusing on their current tasks. This meeting provides an opportunity for everyone on the Scrum Team to update their common picture of the Sprint.

All three roles attend this meeting. The Scrum Master is responsible for ensuring that the meeting does not exceed its fifteen-minute Time Box. Since all roles are present, and the meeting occurs daily, it is critical to keep the meeting short. If allowed to expand, this daily meeting can consume an unfortunate amount of the team's working time.

Team members do most of the talking, while the Scrum Master facilitates, and the Product Owner observes and contributes as needed.

I recommend the following agenda, which is common:

First, the Scrum Master displays the current Burndown chart for the Sprint, providing relevant commentary on the overall status of work (e.g., potential need to pick up the pace, remove scope, add scope, etc.) and other information of general interest to the team. For example, if the Burndown chart at mid-Sprint shows that the planned Sprint scope is not going to be completed, the Scrum Master might say as much, asking the Product Owner and Team members to remain after the Stand-Up meeting to decide which planned items to drop. The focus of the follow-on meeting would be on how to de-scope the Sprint in a way that maximizes the value that can be completed in the remaining time.

Next, each Team member describes:

1. What I've been doing since our last meeting

2. What I plan to do before the next meeting

3. What issues are slowing me down, which I may need help to resolve

A small amount of informal discussion about the items raised is appropriate. However, if the resolution of an issue takes more than a minute of discussion, we do not resolve it in this meeting but identify who will meet afterwards in a "Sidebar meeting" to address the issue. The Product Owner is often one of the people who will be involved in such resolutions, which is a large part of why his or her attendance is important (the other part being that the Product Owner also needs to understand how the Sprint is going).

It is common to have a need for the whole team to discuss topics of interest to all. A good time for this kind of discussion is directly after the Daily Stand-Up meeting. However, to avoid confusion of what is happening and who must be present, the Scrum Master should announce the end of the Daily Stand-Up meeting first, describe the topics to be discussed, and state that anyone who does not need to be present can leave. After that, discussion may continue as needed.

The Daily Stand-Up meeting is often the first opportunity to inform the Product Owner of the discovery that the planned scope cannot be completed in the Sprint. Approaches to handling this discovery are addressed in Section 3.7.

3.3.4 Sprint Review

The Sprint Review meeting serves multiple purposes:

- To give the Product Owner a final opportunity for a go / no-go decision about product capabilities developed in the Sprint

- To motivate Team members to ensure that PBIs are demonstrable, which means the PBIs are truly finished

- To give Team members an enjoyable opportunity to "show off" their work to an audience that can appreciate it

The Product Owner, Scrum Master, and Team members attend this meeting. Some Scrum Teams use the Sprint Review as an opportunity to show the new deliverables to a wider audience. This is acceptable, provided that the Team members do not find the presence of the additional observers to be disruptive and that observers observe but refrain from speaking during the meeting. (Observers who wish to give feedback should do so after the meeting, to the Product Owner.) However, it is most commonly the case that the content of the Sprint Review is too detailed, too narrow in scope, or simply irrelevant to the interests of stakeholders outside the team for this meeting to serve the needs of these stakeholders. For these reasons, I typically suggest that the Product Owner conduct separate demonstration meetings for stakeholders, focusing on aspects of the product that are more relevant to that audience.

The Sprint Review is held after all of the development and testing work in a Sprint is completed; that is, after all of the PBIs that will be completed in the Sprint have been completed. It commonly occurs just before the Retrospective meeting. However, the timing of this meeting can be changed if logistical constraints require. The meeting can even occur after the beginning of the next Sprint, if no other options exist, but in that case any follow-up actions identified as necessary in the meeting may have to wait for a couple of weeks to be started.

The Scrum Master's facilitation of the meeting is minimal, and mostly concerned with keeping the pace fast enough to avoid overrunning the time box. Team members demonstrate every completed deliverable from the Sprint, meaning every PBI and Defect that was completed. Deliverables that appear in the product's user interface are demonstrated through the user interface. Other deliverables are demonstrated in whatever fashion works best: "Before and After" screenshots for refactored code, measured times for performance improvements, schematic diagrams, mechanical and electrical mock-ups, video recordings of a new motion for a robotic arm, and so forth.

Any deficiencies the Product Owner discovers and decides to rectify are addressed by new PBIs, which describe the necessary changes and which will be scheduled for a future Sprint (possibly the very next one). We do not "reopen" PBIs that have been completed through their Definition of Done (Section 3.5.5), as this practice is confusing and distorts the tracking metrics.

If, however, a PBI that was declared to have been completed is found not to have been completed after all, then the PBI is declared to be unfinished, and its estimate does not contribute to the recorded Velocity of this Sprint. This should be a rare occurrence.

3.3.5 Retrospective

The purpose of the Retrospective meeting is to improve the team's process over time by identifying what does and doesn't work well and working to improve the latter.

The Product Owner, Scrum Master, and Team members attend the Retrospective (generally, with no additional observers allowed, although this is always a team decision). This meeting is usually held immediately after the Sprint Review, in the same room, although there is no requirement that the timing be done exactly in this fashion. The only requirement is that this meeting occurs once for each Sprint and after the work of that Sprint has been completed.

The Scrum Master facilitates, and all three roles (including the Scrum Master) participate and supply information. I recommend this agenda:

1. Review the status of action items from the previous Retrospective to understand what has been done, what is in progress, what issues are blocking progress, and so forth.

2. Each participant provides information about
   a. What went well in the Sprint, that should be continued.
   b. What did not go well, that we'd like to do better.

3. Decide what changes to make.

Any meeting where we seek information from a group of people has the potential to become lengthy and ineffective. For this reason, I advise against the "round-robin" technique of soliciting information from one person at a time. Methods that allow all of the people to work in parallel are faster and more effective.

Any technique that proves effective is fine, but I favor the following approach, which is designed to be swift:

Each participant writes the "went well" and "want to do better" items on sticky notes (one item per note) and sticks them on a wall or whiteboard under "went well" and "want to do better" headings. This usually takes about ten minutes.

The "want to do better" notes are often repetitive, so the Scrum Master may group them into a smaller number of distinct topics as people post their notes.

Next, the Scrum Master reads the "went well" items so that everyone knows what they are. The group may discuss these items briefly, as needed.

Attention then turns to the items under the "want to do better" heading.

The Scrum Master describes the first topic, and the participants hold a quick discussion about what to do about it. Often the result is simply a policy change, which might lead to a revision of the Definition of Done. Examples include:

- A decision that Team members will confirm that the application builds after each check-in.

- A decision that measurement equipment must always be calibrated before measurements are conducted.

After the above discussion, those topics requiring follow-up effort are prioritized to identify the optimum subset that the team can address given their finite bandwidth. Some of these follow-up actions may be to write Technical Stories that will enter the Product Backlog and be scheduled for a future Sprint. (For example, if the desire is to unpack and set up a new piece of test equipment that has already been purchased, the action item would be to write a Technical Story about this work.) Some items may require working with people outside the team, and these may simply be taken on without representing the work as Stories in the Product Backlog.

The participants select owners to drive the selected follow-up actions, and then adjourn.

Finally, I suggest the Scrum Master record the decisions, action items, and owners for future use.

3.3.6 Attendance at Ceremonies

Many opinions exist regarding who should or should not be allowed to attend the various Scrum ceremonies. The discussions usually involve the following considerations:

- How well the meeting achieves its purpose
- How long the meeting takes
- Concerns Team members have about safety and confidentiality
- Concerns about the possibility of micromanagement

Meetings should always be kept as short as possible, to preserve the attendees' time for other things. They should also accomplish their intended purpose. These two goals are most easily ensured when attendance is limited to the Scrum Team membership (Team members, Scrum Master, and Product Owner).

The presence of additional attendees has the potential to impair the speed and effectiveness of the meetings. Questions and comments from "external attendees" can lengthen the meeting and distract from its purpose. Attendance by detail-oriented managers might lead to micromanagement of Team members' work and second-guessing of their decisions. Finally, the presence of anyone considered to be critical or judgmental may cause fear on the Team members' part, preventing the meeting from achieving its goal (a particular concern for Retrospective meetings).

The decision about who can be present at Scrum ceremonies is therefore surprisingly complex. My thoughts on the subject follow.

First, my personal policy is that all three Scrum roles (i.e., the complete Scrum Team membership) attend all Scrum ceremonies. This policy stands in opposition to some writers' recommendations that Product Owners not attend the Retrospective meeting out of concern that Team members may feel intimidated or afraid to speak up if the Product Owner is present. My position is that this fear is unlikely to be common, in the first place, and if it is present, we need to solve the problem of fear, not allow it to cripple the team. I also consider exclusion of the Product Owner from this critical meeting to be demeaning and divisive, not beneficial.

Second, my basic policy regarding meeting attendance by people outside the Scrum Team is that the Scrum Team membership decides what is appropriate. I have seen some Scrum Teams simply assume that their managers are free to drop into any meeting, and no one has any concerns or problems. However, other Scrum Teams might feel quite differently.

In general, if the Scrum Team has no objections to observers, then I set the expectation that observers should avoid speaking in the meetings so as not to divert or lengthen the meetings. They are there to learn, not participate. Their comments and questions should be reserved for after the conclusion of the meeting.

The Review and Retrospective meetings merit additional discussion.

The Review meeting is sometimes considered to be a good opportunity to show newly developed functionality to interested stakeholders. In reality, it is usually not a good choice for this purpose. It is held more often than most stakeholders wish to attend, much of the content is incomprehensible or irrelevant to the stakeholders, and the review does not convey a holistic or usage-oriented perspective of the product. For these reasons, I suggest that the Product Owner demonstrate the product features in a more useful fashion to these stakeholders at regular opportunities of mutual convenience.

The Retrospective meeting is usually considered to be the most sensitive, and many writers state that only the Scrum Team membership attend. I don't go quite that far but do agree that the Retrospective meeting is the one in which Scrum Team members are likely to have the most concern with respect to external attendees. Having said that, my policy is again to go with the Scrum Team's wishes.

The findings of the Retrospective meeting are often of particular value to managers as they relate very much to how well the department or organization is functioning. Thus, managers are likely to be eager consumers of the Retrospective findings and are often engaged in addressing findings from the Retrospective that require the manager's attention.

The responsibility for providing relevant Retrospective findings to managers normally falls to the Scrum Master. Scrum Masters may provide whatever information managers are likely to find useful while taking into account possible sensitivity of some of the findings. That said, I have never observed a Retrospective meeting that produced very sensitive information, and I believe such scenarios are rare.

3.4 Estimation

Three types of estimations are required in the course of Sprint Planning. We need estimates for the Sprint Velocity, the Product Backlog Items considered in Sprint Planning, and the tasks associated with each Product Backlog Item. I will address these categories in the following sections.

The concept of work estimation is very old, and many techniques exist. For our purposes, we need estimates of Product Backlog Items to plan Sprints. The standard in Scrum (and the Agile world in general) is that all estimates to be used for "official" planning must be produced by the people who will do the work. The obvious reason for this policy is that the people who do the work will generally have the most insight into the amount of work to be done. An important side benefit is that this policy avoids the situation of having one group of people estimate and commit work for another group, which leads to a variety of unfortunate consequences.

A second policy in the Agile world is that the entire (Scrum) Team estimates all work to be done, as a whole team. The reasoning behind group-based estimation is that the team as a whole knows more than any one person, and tapping their group expertise is likely to yield better results than any one person can supply. An additional, but very important, benefit of group estimation is that it educates the entire team on the details of the work to be done and prepares them to do the work more effectively.

3.4.1 Challenges with Group Estimation

A common argument against whole-team estimation is that specialization of skills makes this approach impossible. In practice, whole-team estimation may devolve into, say, the mechanical engineers providing estimates for one PBI while the members with other skills abstain.

Here again we encounter the concept of generalizing specialists. If all team members are generalizing specialists, then whole-team estimation is clearly the best approach. It provides the greatest possible pooling of knowledge and insight, yielding the best possible work estimates.

If the Team members are not generalizing specialists, then we are faced with a dilemma. It is tempting to divide PBIs into skill categories and have the specialists in each category estimate those items. The downside is that even non-specialists can ask insightful questions, and excluding them from the discussions can lead to integration errors that could have been avoided through whole-team discussion.

For example, imagine that a particular Story involves adding components to a circuit board. It may well be that only the two electrical engineers on the team can provide insight into the work estimates. However, a whole-team discussion of the Story might lead to one of the mechanical engineers asking, "You mentioned that one of the capacitors has greater height than the other components. How much vertical space does it take up?" The resulting discussion might lead to the discovery that the "tall capacitor" will conflict with the chassis that is also under development.

I do suggest a way to deal with these two opposing drivers: estimate *quickly* in the planning meetings, and let whole-team discussions happen. If the estimates are developed quickly, then no one is spending a great deal of time idle.

Unfortunately, rapid estimation is more easily described than done. The labor of estimating a PBI can explode if the PBI is not well understood and if the engineers involved dive too deeply into the technical details in the middle of the estimation discussion. These issues can be addressed but require discipline. The PBIs should be clarified in the Backlog Refinement meetings so they are well understood before the planning meeting. In the planning meeting, the Scrum Master will have to be diligent about identifying discussions that will impact estimates and discussions that make the engineers feel more comfortable but have little impact on estimates. The latter should be avoided.

A final challenge with group estimation methods is the problem of *anchoring*, which is the tendency of a group to adopt one person's perspective instead of contributing insights from everyone. The Planning Poker technique described below addresses this issue effectively.

3.4.2 Units for Estimation

The purpose of estimation is to enable planning of work over time, on some kind of calendar. Any units that serve this purpose will suffice. The categories of units in common use may be described as *relative sizing* and *time-based sizing*. Other units are possible but seldom encountered.

3.4.2.1 Relative Sizing

In *relative sizing*, the units are called *Story Points*. Story Points do not relate directly to time or any measurable attribute of the PBI. Instead, Story Points are defined by association with a set of reference PBIs.

Prior to its first Sprint, a new team reviews a set of PBIs, identifies a small one, and arbitrarily assigns it a small size, such as "two Story Points." The team then identifies smaller and larger ones, assigning them sizes of "one Story Point" and "three Story Points," respectively.

The team next conducts a *triangulation* assessment for the validity of the scale, by asking three questions:

1. Is the 2 SP PBI twice the size of the 1 SP PBI?
2. Is the 3 SP PBI three times the size of the 1 SP PBI?
3. Is the 3 SP PBI one and a half times the size of the 2 SP PBI?

If all three questions have a "Yes" answer, the PBIs size scales consistently with the numbers. If any question has a "No" answer, the team goes through the process again until they do identify a consistent set. They then continue in this fashion to identify reference PBIs to associate with other allowed numbers (e.g., the Fibonacci sequence, with 5, 8, 13,... for the larger numbers).

Having established this reference scale, future PBIs are estimated by comparison with the reference items. For example, a Team member might say, "This item has a size of five Story Points because I think it is closer in size to our reference item of that size than it is to any of the other reference items."

While Story Points are not defined in terms of time, the practical reality is that a Scrum Team should be completing at least five PBIs per Sprint, and often ten or fifteen. This reality does constrain the meaning of a Story Point, with the result that a one-Story-Point PBI usually does not take more than a day or two to complete, in the absence of interruptions.

3.4.2.2 Time-Based Sizing

In *time-based sizing*, the units define an amount of *effort*, which is the aggregated time spent by all people who work on a PBI. The unit is commonly called a *person-day* (sometimes referred to as a *man-day*). A person-day is defined to be eight hours of time expended on some particular piece of work. Thus, a PBI that requires eight hours of work by one person has a size of one person-day, as does a PBI that requires four hours from each of two people.

The effort required to complete a PBI does not map directly to the *duration* of the work. A PBI with a size of one person-day will often require two or three calendar days to complete because the eight hours of work will not be done in a single eight-hour span of time. It is important to understand the distinction between effort and duration, as the most common failure mode for time-based sizing is to estimate duration in calendar days. For estimation purposes, it is effort that matters.

The distinction between relative and time-based sizing can blur in practice. Teams that choose time-based sizing can define reference Stories for different sizes and use the style of thinking employed in relative sizing while still yielding time-based estimates. Similarly, teams that use relative sizing often base their numbers on an informal concept of time.

3.4.2.3 Comparison of Time-Based and Relative Sizing

The purpose of work estimation, in any units, is to support development of a useful plan of some kind. In the context of Scrum and Sprint planning, the purpose of estimation is to give us the insight we need in order to decide which PBIs we should attempt to complete in the Sprint.

The most important observation regarding units of estimation is that both Relative and Time-Based strategies are in use and have been found effective for Sprint planning in the context of *software* development. That said, many proponents of Relative sizing are adamant that it is the only effective approach and that time-based estimation is risky and ineffective. I will investigate those arguments here.

Proponents of relative sizing often state that people understand "larger versus smaller" more readily than they do individual numbers, and therefore relative sizing is more effective than a time-based approach. However, while the former may be true, it says nothing about what meaning we should ascribe to the units of estimation. At most, the argument relates to *techniques* for estimation, not the meaning of the numbers. After all, five units are always bigger than three units, no matter what the units are.

The other most common motivations I have heard for advocating for Story Points, specifically, are that:

- Use of units that are not based on time shields the team from management criticism for "not meeting their hours" when work takes longer than expected.

- Estimation in Story Points can show a team's progress toward maturity, as the observed Velocity values increase over time and plateaus at an optimum value after some number of Sprints.

- Team members are less likely to be distracted by debates about how much time will be required to implement a Story as these debates will be shorter if the units of estimation are decoupled from units of time.

The first point is about fear, not effectiveness of estimation. I consider fear a problem that must be solved, not a justification for avoiding the problem. If management acts in a way that creates fear in the teams, then the management behavior is the real problem and must be addressed. Effective approaches include clarifying for management that estimation is a planning technique, not a guarantee. In other words, all estimates are wrong—the only meaningful question is "How wrong are they?" and this can only be determined after the fact. No amount of practice at estimation will ever yield perfection. Clarifying this point for management and Team members is important.

The second point is about team maturity. As the purpose of estimation is to enable effective planning, any benefit beyond that should be considered serendipitous, not a key driver for choosing a particular approach. Teams will improve to a plateau whether we are measuring that improvement in this manner or not, and other metrics (e.g., ratio of Stories completed to ratio of Stories planned) can provide similar insight into team maturity.

The third point is the only one that relates specifically to the merits of relative sizing with Story Points. The extent to which it is valid can only be assessed by observation.

I have conducted a simple experiment over my career as an Agile consultant. I explain both systems of units to teams, let them pick which they wish to use, and watch what happens. Overwhelmingly (more than 95 percent of the time), teams select time-based units and find that this approach is intuitive and effective. Moreover, I have also found that teams that have used Story Points in the past often prefer to switch to time-based sizing when they have the opportunity. For these reasons, I do not advocate relative sizing, although I do not oppose it as a team-based estimation practice.

Time-based units of estimation move more toward a necessity than an option in two cases:

1. Story Points require creating a team-based norm that all Team members understand and that makes no explicit reference to time. While this is a possibility for many software teams, the greater specialization of skills found in hardware development teams can make this team-based norm impossible because the size of many Stories cannot be understood by all Team members. In this case, only time-based units are applicable.

2. Large organizations usually have multiple Scrum Teams who must collaborate to produce a product. It is important to have metrics (such as Burn-Up charts) that show aggregate progress across all teams. Aggregation of status information across teams requires that all teams provide numbers than can be added together in a meaningful way. This requirement, in turn, means that all teams either use the same units, or can convert to common units. Time-based units are, by definition, the same across teams, and thus provide the simplest approach to meeting this need.

Selection of units for estimation is both necessary and often a matter of some sensitivity. Discussions about motivations for preferring a particular system can yield useful insights and may identify organizational dysfunctions that should be addressed. In the end, the decision must be made, and it is not always possible to satisfy all participants in the process. It is therefore important to handle the decision in a considerate and diplomatic fashion.

3.4.3   How to Estimate Team Velocity for Use in Sprint Planning

I define the Velocity of a Scrum Team to be the amount of work the team completes in a Sprint (as per Section 2.4). The Velocity for a completed Sprint is computed as the sum of the PBI estimates for the PBIs completed in that Sprint. (By convention, PBIs that were started but not completed in the Sprint do not contribute to that Sprint's Velocity. They will contribute to the Velocity of any subsequent Sprint in which they are completed.) Over time, a team develops a history of Velocity values that may be used to forecast the Velocity of future Sprints.

The process of Sprint planning requires some forecast of the Velocity expected for the Sprint, which is used to bound the scope of work for the Sprint. Thus, the Scrum Master must provide a forecast of the team's Velocity prior to the Sprint Planning meeting.

Many techniques for estimating Velocity exist, and none is mandated. Possibilities includes estimating Velocity as:

1. The observed Velocity for the last Sprint

2. A running average of the last three Sprints' observed Velocities

3. (Team size) × (# days in Sprint) × (focus factor), where "focus factor" is the fraction of time a team spends developing and testing PBIs in a Sprint (e.g., 60 percent)

4. The sum of the times Team members are available to work on PBIs in the Sprint, based on meeting schedules and individual availability for Sprint work (resource model forecast).

The first two methods may be used in the context of relative sizing. While all four techniques could be used in the context of time-based sizing, the third and fourth are most commonly used for that case.

3.4.3.1   Yesterday's Weather

This technique is the simplest. We look at the Sprint that was just completed, calculate the Velocity that the Scrum Team achieved in that Sprint based on the Stories and Defects that were implemented to completion, and forecast the next Sprint to have that same Velocity.

3.4.3.2 The Last Few Days' Weather

This technique is similar to the previous one, but instead of forecasting the next Sprint's Velocity to be that of the previous one, we define the forecast as the average of the last three Sprints' Velocities. This approach provides a smoother forecast over time by averaging out potential saw-tooth variations that can occur from Sprint to Sprint.

3.4.3.3 Focus Factor Method

This approach assumes that time-based units will be used. We know the team size and the number of working days in the Sprint, and forecast the Velocity via the formula:

Velocity = (Team size) × (Working days in Sprint) × (Focus factor).

For example, suppose we have five Team members and a two-week Sprint that contains ten working days. A forecast of (5 people) × (10 days) yields 50 person-days, but this is too large, as the Team members will not be able to spend 8 hours per day working on the Scrum Team's deliverables. The various Scrum meetings and other distractions will take time away from the development and testing work. We attempt to capture the impact of these distractions by incorporating a "focus factor" that describes how much of the available working time can actually be devoted toward the Sprint's deliverables.

Suppose we chose a focus factor of 60 percent, or 0.6. This choice would yield a forecasted Velocity of 30 person-days, which is a reasonable value in most cases.

3.4.3.4 Resource Model

This approach also assumes time-based units. It is the most complex but provides the most realistic and flexible strategy for Velocity forecasting.

What we want to know is how much time each person can contribute to working on the Scrum Team's deliverables in the course of the Sprint. In the course of a two-week Sprint, each Team member has up to ten days' time available, but each will lose some of that time due to Scrum meetings, other meetings, email and other communications, holidays, vacation time, sick time, and other things. The amount of time these activities consumes may vary substantially from person to person in the Scrum Team. Ideally, therefore, a Scrum Master could perform the forecast by asking each Team member how many hours of actual working time he or she can contribute to the Sprint. Adding up these numbers, and converting the total to person-days, would yield the Velocity forecast.

In practice, Team members would not generally be able to answer the above question, so it falls to the Scrum Master to do this on their behalf, in a reasonably effective manner.

We can start by assessing how much time people spend in the Scrum meetings. The table shows a reasonable scenario.

Sprint Start Date	22-Mar-17
Sprint End Date	4-Apr-17
Workdays in Sprint	10
Work Hours in Sprint	80
Daily Scrum hours	2
Backlog Refinement hours	4
Sprint Planning hours	2
Task Breakdown hours	4
Sprint Review hours	1
Retrospective hours	1
Net Work Hours in Sprint	**66**

Table 3.3: Net Hours of Working Time in a Sprint

Of the eighty "calendar hours" in a two-week work schedule, only sixty-six are available for work outside of the Scrum meetings.

Next, we ask how much time the Team members are planning to take off in the Sprint. For example, one person might be taking three days of vacation time, and a half-day for a doctor's appointment. Subtract off from that person's time "in office" time the known time away, and the time consumed by Scrum meetings, to yield the time that the Team member is present and not in Scrum meetings. Do this for all Team members.

Finally, multiply each person's potential hours available by an "Availability" fraction that reflects other distractions, to get the final hour total for that Team member's working time. Summing these numbers up for all Team members and dividing by eight to convert hours to person-days yields the Velocity forecast.

Assuming that the net work-hours in the Sprint is sixty-six, we can compute Velocity as follows:

Team Member	Role / Skill	% Avail	Hrs Off	Hours
Henry	Hardware, Algorithms	75%	8	43.50
Babita	Firmware	75%	8	43.50
Tim	Software	75%	8	43.50
Pat	Firmware	75%	56	7.50
Chris	Software	75%	56	7.50
Velocity: 18.2	Net Team Resources: 1.82		Team Hours:	145.50

Table 3.4: Team Member Availability and Velocity Forecast

This calculation yields the hours each Team member has available for work on Stories and Defects in the last column. Summing these yields a total of 145.50 hours, and division of this total by 8 forecasts a Velocity of 18.2 person-days.

Of interest, if not actually used in planning, is the field named "Net Team Resources." The number in this field represents the number of imaginary full-time employees, who work on Stories and Defects for eight hours in each workday, whose contribution equals that of the real people. This number tends to be around half of the actual Team members and shows in an aggregate sense how much of these peoples' time is spent on the planned development work.

The formulas used for this calculation are:

1. Hours = Availability * (Net work hours in Sprint – Hours off)
2. Net Team Resources = Team Hours / (Work hours in Sprint)
3. Velocity = Team Hours / 8

I suggest an Availability value of 75 percent, or 0.75, for Team members who have no responsibilities outside the Scrum Team. Choose lower values for people who spend significant time on distractions such as outside responsibilities, supporting Team members with technical expertise, or in other ways.

One benefit of this approach is that it enables a realistic assessment of what is admittedly an undesirable situation: the case where one person works for two Scrum Teams concurrently. While I strongly recommend against this situation, there are times that it will happen, and we can at least plan more realistically if we can provide a meaningful insight into how much time that person can spend on our team's work. We might, for example, make such a shared member available at 35 percent instead of 75 percent.

3.4.3.5 Which Velocity-Forecasting Model Is the Best Choice?

The short answer to "Which is the best choice?" is that the simplest method that works well enough is the best choice. Beyond that, I can add:

- Only the first two approaches will work if we are using units of Story Points. In this case, I would suggest simply observing how much work (in Story Points) a team does accomplish in the first Sprint, using the first approach for the second Sprint, and migrating to the second approach as we develop a longer history.

- If we are using time-based units, the first two approaches can be used but in most cases prove less appealing than the third and fourth. The third is effective in an environment with high stability, but it is not clear how to employ it if we have substantial and varying time-off schedules or changes in team size. If such variation does exist, the fourth approach is likely to be more satisfactory.

3.4.4 How to Estimate Product Backlog Items with Planning Poker

The estimate of work for a Product Backlog Item is a single number that encompasses all work required to create and validate the desired deliverable. More precisely, it encompasses all work required to achieve the *Definition of Done* for that item (Section 3.5.5). This effort includes development work, testing work, and any other kind of work involved.

A Scrum Team may use any estimation technique for Sprint Planning that works for them, but I recommend Planning Poker[22] specifically. With the Planning Poker technique, each Team member is given a deck of cards, printed with numbers such as 0, ½, 1, 2, 3, 5, 8, 13, and so forth.

Most card decks used for Planning Poker are based at least approximately on the Fibonacci sequence, where each number is the sum of the previous two. The logic behind this selection is that we want values that are spaced far enough apart to be clearly distinct. For example, the difference between 1 and 2 is large (a factor of 2), while the difference between 10 and 11 is small (10 percent). A deck that contains closely spaced numbers will lead to time-wasting discussions between numbers that are closer to each other than either is likely to be to the actual value to be estimated. Hence, we use a relatively coarse scale, such as the Fibonacci sequence, for which numbers increase by around 50 percent from one to the next.

A second but critical reason for this selection of numbers has to do with the way humans think. People have an instinctive feel for numbers in the single-digit to low double-digit range, as opposed to much larger or smaller numbers. Thus, any estimation technique that relies on human judgment should involve numbers in this range. As a corollary, the units of estimation should always be chosen to yield numbers in this range.

At the time of the estimation session, it is assumed that Team members are already familiar with the PBI based on previous discussions. The Scrum Master normally facilitates the estimation process, during which the Team members commonly estimate a number of PBIs.

The Product Owner reads the current PBI to the team. All participants then ask questions and discuss the item, briefly, to clarify any remaining issues. The Scrum Master then asks that each Team member pick a card with his or her estimate and hide the card. When all Team members have selected cards, the Scrum Master asks them to show their cards, and then asks the low and high voters to explain the reasoning behind their numbers. The group then has a brief discussion to clarify and resolve issues and questions resulting from the vote, and re-votes. A third vote is often useful for achieving consensus, but additional rounds of voting are not usually productive.

If Team members stabilize at a small range of values by the third vote, they should discuss the values and agree on a consensus number. This is a common scenario and happens about half of the time in my experience.*

Rarely, the numbers are far apart and do not converge. In this case, it is likely that the PBI is poorly written and poorly understood, and its estimation should be deferred until it has been rewritten.

The participants continue in this fashion until they have estimated enough PBIs for their current purpose (most commonly, enough to fill a Sprint).

The Planning Poker technique offers two key benefits of comparable importance:

- It minimizes anchoring; that is, the tendency for a team to adopt a consensus belief driven by the influence of a single person, who is often perceived as the expert.

- It produces a dramatic improvement in the team's consensus understanding of what the deliverable is and what must be done to create it and confirm that it is acceptable.

Planning Poker prevents anchoring for the first round of voting but cannot prevent anchoring in latter rounds. Fortunately, preventing anchoring in the first round is sufficient, as it gets different perspectives out in the open for discussion.

---

* Technically, "consensus number" means that the Team members agree this is the best single number they can produce. It does not necessarily mean that everyone agrees this is the right number.

3.4.5 How to Estimate Tasks

During Sprint Planning, Team members decompose the work of each PBI into a set of tasks, which are the actions required to implement and validate the deliverable of the PBI. Team members also estimate the work of each task. These estimates are usually provided in units of hours, which denote the effort required to execute them.

Tasks are smaller and more numerous than PBIs. Because they are numerous, their estimation via Planning Poker would take an impractical amount of time. Fortunately, I find that Team members can produce an adequate estimate of task hours through quick and informal discussion. This approach works for tasks, if not for PBIs, because tasks are so much simpler than PBIs that implicit assumptions and anchoring are seldom problems.

Since Planning Poker is not used, there is no restriction on the possible numbers, which need not correspond to the values in a Planning Poker card deck. Values such as ½, 7, or any integer in the allowed range are acceptable.

However, I suggest setting floor and ceiling values for allowed task times. My preference is a floor of two hours and a ceiling of sixteen. Setting a floor value too small generates a large number of small tasks, for which the overhead of defining and tracking is large. Setting a ceiling value too high risks late discovery that a PBI will not be completed within the current Sprint.

3.5 Artifacts

The following artifacts are widely used in Scrum.

3.5.1 Product Backlog Items

Decades of experience in product development work has shown that it is not possible to write a comprehensive and detailed product specification that is complete, correct, and stable over time. Such documents always contain numerous errors: some details prove undesirable, some prove impossible, parts of the document are inconsistent with other parts, and some things that prove necessary are omitted. Too much is unknown at the time of writing to get all of these details right prior to the onset of development work.

I am not advocating that no overall product definition be performed. In fact, I do believe that a solid definition is important, as long as it does not attempt to provide the finer details that are best deferred to a later time. Scrum Teams, however, require a level of detail in the specifications for their deliverables that is much finer-grained than the basic product and design concepts.

The solution adopted in Scrum embodies the concept of *Progressive Elaboration*, meaning continuous refinement over time of scope and work to be done to achieve the scope. Instead of writing a large and detailed requirements document that is going to be wrong in many respects, we write many small documents about small pieces of scope, each of which is written at a high-enough level that it is reliable at that level. We then implement a process of stepwise refinement to work out the fine details before and even during implementation. These high-level summary specifications are then known as *Product Backlog Items*.

A Product Backlog Item (PBI) is a specification for a deliverable that one team can implement in a modest fraction of a Sprint. (I recommend that no one PBI exceed one-third of a team's Sprint Velocity. Most teams I have observed complete from five to fifteen PBIs in one Sprint.)

The Scrum world does not have a standardized conception or format for PBIs. There is general agreement that User Stories should be used, less agreement about the fine details of how to write a User Story, and no general agreement on other Backlog artifacts.

I will define three types of Product Backlog Items, called *User Stories, Technical Stories*, and *Defects*.

- A *User Story* describes a user's experiences of some aspect or capability of a product.
- A *Technical Story* describes a deliverable that no user of a product experiences directly.
- A *Defect* is a report of a failure of some aspect of the product to perform as intended.

3.5.1.1 User Stories

A *User Story* is a short narrative description of some aspect of a product that a user experiences. A User Story describes the user's interaction with the product, in a brief format that conveys a basic understanding, without attempting to spell out all of the details. User Stories are most often written by Product Owners, who act as proxies for the actual users.

The term "User" refers to a category of person who experiences the deliverable in some fashion. Many types of user experience are possible, such as:

- A doctor uses a cardiac monitor to view an electrocardiogram.
- A firefighter selects a communication channel on a portable radio.
- A customer buys products from a store.
- An operator powers up a machine.

In other words, the User is the consumer of functionality that he or she perceives directly. By definition, Users are not members of the Scrum Team who is developing the product but may be members of another Scrum Team.

The format presented here is a reasonably common one, with the content of the User Story represented by a *Title*, a *Narrative*, and *Acceptance Criteria*:

- The *Title* is a one-sentence summary of the PBI.

- The *Narrative* contains one to a few paragraphs that describe the user experience:

  - The first sentence is of the form "As a <Role>, I want to <perform an action>, so that <this benefit occurs>." Any following text expands on the user experience.

  - The Narrative section often contains non-narrative information as well, such as links to user interface designs, and other external documents of interest that relate to the user experience.

- The *Acceptance Criteria* summarize things that must be true, and are confirmed by testing, about the completed deliverable:

  - Many acceptance criteria provide a starting point for test-case definition during development work.

  - This is a good place to provide other useful information that does not fit naturally into narrative form.

Figure 3.2 shows a sample User Story that reflects the above description, in the context of a software product.

Title	Buyer views statistics for transactions with Vendors		Rank	3
ID	22	Estimate	8	Total task Est.	96

Narrative
As a Buyer, I can view my statistics about my transactions with Vendors so that I can understand how my history looks to Vendors.
When I click on a buyer-statistics link, I see my statistics. (This link is on the home page, under account information.)
Prototype / UI References: Landing Page: Attached (landingPage.html)
External Documents: Company Style Guide for UI: http://wiki/UI/UIStyleGuide.doc Statistics to be computed: http://wiki/apps/buyerstats.doc

Acceptance Criteria
• When the user clicks on the link, the application should display the statistics. • User can create fictitious buyers and suppliers for use in testing. • When the user submits or responds to RFPs, report shows updated statistics that reflect the user's activities.

Figure 3.2: Sample User Story about Viewing Statistics

Figure 3.3 shows a User Story appropriate for a hardware product that requires electrical power to function.

Title	Operator confirms power status before using device			Rank	3
ID	22		**Estimate**	8	**Total task Est.** 96
Narrative					
As an Operator, I want to confirm that the device is powered up so that I know whether it can be used. I move the power switch to the "On" position and observe the power light come on if the device has power or see that it is not lit if the device does not have power. See http://wiki.abc.com/scr/FrontPanel.html for a mock-up of the control panel, to see the positioning of the power light.					
Acceptance Criteria					
• Use the same light-emitting diode as we use for all panel displays (3 mm super-bright red LED, part number 800-1000MCD). • Use the standard 3mm mounting bezel to secure the LED to the front panel (part number 55-530)					

Figure 3.3: Sample User Story about Power-On Indicator

3.5.1.2 Technical Stories

Not all deliverables that a Scrum Team creates represent a user's experience of a product. Attempts to represent such deliverables in User Story form tend to produce User Stories that have peculiar wording and require non-user roles. I prefer to represent deliverables other than user-facing product elements as *Technical Stories*, instead of User Stories. As they do not represent any kind of user experience, and tend to have a technical orientation, Technical Stories are most commonly written by Team members.

A Technical Story has the same format as a User Story, except that it omits the user role from the Narrative. Thus, a Technical Story for a software product might look like Figure 3.4 below.

Title	Messaging API Refactoring			Rank	7
ID	32		**Estimate**	3	**Total task Est.** 14
Narrative					
We need to refactor the Messaging API to make it easier to use. The current API grew in an ad hoc fashion and requires several calls and some awkward logic to use. We want an API that is easier to use, requires fewer calls, and is much less confusing than the current interface.					
Acceptance Criteria					
• At least two Team members agree that the new API is appropriate. • All existing Unit Tests that rely on the Messaging API continue to work.					

Figure 3.4: Sample Technical Story for Software Development

In the case of hardware–software system development, there are many physical requirements, such as voltage levels and signal types among the various modules, that are necessary to make the system functional. Internal signals are not seen by the user of the product but must be implemented for the product to work. Technical Stories such as the following are therefore appropriate.

Title	16-bit Digital-to-Analog Converter Motherboard Integration			**Rank**	9
ID	25	**Estimate**	8	**Total task Est.**	60
Narrative					
Design into the motherboard a Digital-to-Analog converter (DAC) in order to provide the high-level analog voltage required to drive the analog display. Assume that the digital drive presented at the input of the DAC module is of sufficient amplitude to activate the unit properly, but not so large as to damage the input gates. Since no DAC has been chosen for this purpose yet, select an appropriate one for incorporation into the motherboard design.					
Acceptance Criteria					
• 16-bit output with +/- 0.5 bit nonlinearity • Single supply operation: 2.7 to 5.5V • The maximum current to drive the unit is 500mA. • The maximum clock rate is 3.4 MBit/sec. • The output will be a time-varying analog signal varying from 0V to 5V at steps of 7.5 µV, with a maximum output impedance of 1 Ohm. • Device meets the other requirements of the I2S serial bus					

Figure 3.5: Sample Technical Story for Hardware Development

Hardware products tend to have a much higher ratio of Technical Stories to User Stories than do software products. This implies that most of the Stories for hardware products are written by the Team members who will then develop the products, and not by the Product Owner. Product Owners still have the responsibility to define the product, but much of their effort is devoted to ensuring that the right Stories are being written rather than writing most of them personally.

Common reasons for writing Technical Stories include the following:

- **Infrastructure:** An infrastructure capability. This is done to support specific functional or non-functional requirements, such as product components that have no meaningful user interactions.

- **Research:** A Time-Boxed research project to gain knowledge required to support future decisions, designs, or work. This is done when the solution to a problem is required but not known.

- **Spike:** A throwaway implementation used to demonstrate the solution to a particular technical problem. This is done to clarify the nature of a solution and enable estimation of future work. ("Spike" is essentially synonymous with "Research Story," but the term "Spike" is a common one.)

- **Tracer Bullet:** A first attempt to integrate previously separate components or technologies that must interface and work together in order for the product to function as required. The emphasis is on making the integration work rather than on developing sophisticated capabilities at the time. This is done to minimize technical risk or integration effort.

- **Chore:** Any non-product work that requires scheduled time from the team. This is often done to implement improvements selected in Retrospectives.

3.5.1.3 Defects

A *Defect* is a report of a specific failure of the product to function as intended. No standard format is required for Defects in the context of Scrum.

Defects reported by users of the product most commonly enter the Product Backlog via reports from customer-support personnel, which migrate to the Product Owner for action. The Product Owner ranks Defects alongside other PBIs, with the ranking based on the value of correcting the Defect sooner rather than later.

Team members usually do not enter Defects into the Product Backlog for problems found in Stories that are currently in process, when there is no need to retain a record of such problems beyond the lifespan of the Story. (Defects that *do* require such tracking should be captured.) Defects found in other parts of the product, in the course of normal work, may of course be reported and entered into the Product Backlog.

Defects are a common, if unfortunate, artifact in the world of software development. They are not so common, and are often not used at all, in the world of hardware development. The reason for this difference is that software products go through many production releases, which provide opportunities to fix Defects in shipping products. However, hardware products have no comparable opportunity, and so a Defect artifact loses much of its intended utility. I have heard hardware developers object to the concept of a Defect on the grounds that everything a user experiences is simply an attribute of the product. Rather than quibble on the terminology, I simply suggest that teams use Defects as PBI types if it is useful to do so and omit them otherwise.

3.5.2 Epics

Larger specifications, called *Epics*, must be decomposed into Stories prior to implementation. Epics of modest size may be decomposed directly into a few Stories, while the decomposition of larger Epics may yield a tree structure whose interior nodes are child Epics and whose leaf nodes are Stories. The implementation of an Epic is completed, by definition, when the Stories comprising it have been completed. (To the greatest extent possible, the integration testing of the pieces of an Epic should be completed incrementally, as each Story in the Epic is completed, rather than deferred to a later integration stage.)

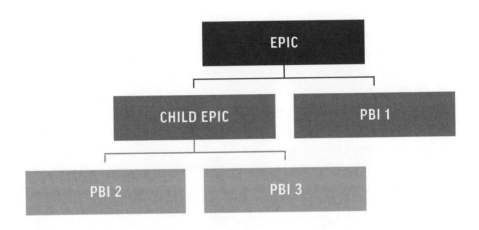

Figure 3.6: Decomposition of an Epic into PBIS

Epics are commonly used as a convenient organizing principle for deliverables or features that are too large to be completed in a few days' time or that require the work of more than one team. (They also arise by accident, when what the author thought was a PBI turns out to be larger than expected.)

The written format for Epics is identical to that of Stories, meaning that an Epic contains a Title, Narrative, and Acceptance Criteria. Only the size of the implementation and testing work of Epics, not the format, differs from that of PBIS.

It is acceptable, but not usually necessary, to refer to "User Epics" and "Technical Epics." In these cases, "User" and "Technical" refer to the focus of the Epic, but there is no assumption that a User Epic cannot contain a Technical Story and vice versa. In fact, each type of Epic very often will contain the other type of Story.

Many Epics that are primarily about user-facing behavior involve multiple roles and cannot be written in a fashion that involves a single role performing an Action. In this case, the Narrative still describes a user experience, but that experience may involve multiple roles, explicitly or implicitly.

3.5.3 Product Backlog

The *Product Backlog* is the set of specifications for deliverables to be developed by a specific team, which have not yet been assigned to a particular Sprint for implementation. The Product Backlog contains Stories and Defects. The Product Backlog is often thought of as having two parts, the top (which is ranked, or sequenced, for near-term planning purposes) and the bottom (which has not been ranked).

Technically, Epics are not part of a Product Backlog, as Epics are not implemented directly, and many Agile project management tools do manage them separately from Product Backlogs. However, in casual conversation, Epics are often spoken of as if they were elements in a Product Backlog, especially when they are treated as placeholders for Stories that have not yet been written (i.e., the Epic has not yet been decomposed into Stories).

3.5.4 Sprint Backlog

The Sprint Backlog is the ranked sequence of Product Backlog Items (Stories and Defects) assigned to a particular Sprint for implementation by a particular team. During Sprint Planning, items are moved from the Product Backlog into the Sprint Backlog. After a Sprint has been completed, the Sprint Backlog for that Sprint is the set of all Product Backlog Items that were completed, which may not be the same as what was planned.

3.5.5 Definition of Done

The *Definition of Done* clarifies and standardizes the team's understanding of what must be accomplished in the course of creating each deliverable (as described in its PBI), testing the deliverable, and fixing defects found in it. It contains a set of policy statements regarding how quality is assured and how organizational standards are met. Figure 3.7 shows a typical set of such policies for a software-development team.

Policies about Quality Assurance

- All defects found when testing a PBI must be fixed immediately
- Acceptance tests must be satisfied
  - Validation is performed in QA environment
- Unit tests must be satisfied
  - Stub out messaging calls, but use live subsystems in QA environment for other unit tests
- Regression tests must be satisfied
  - Execute regression suite daily, and fix regression bugs first thing each day

Policies about Organizational Standards

- Code is checked in to repository
- Build from repository is successful
- Deployment process is successful, with no errors
- Code has been reviewed by peer, team lead
- DB design has been reviewed by DB architect
- Unit tests have been developed
- Acceptance tests are automated
- Continuous-integration server builds app and runs tests

Figure 3.7: Example Definition of Done for a Software Team's PBIs

A team that is developing a hardware product might have a Definition of Done that resembles the following.

Policies about Quality Assurance

- Defects found when testing a Story must be addressed immediately
  - Software defects must be fixed immediately
  - Defects in diagrams must be fixed immediately
  - CAD models cannot be checked into the database with errors
  - Defects in Printed Circuit Boards and hardware assemblies must be fixed to the extent possible. If they can't be fixed immediately, then we will identify and plan corrective action (e.g., write a Story to define the corrective action to be performed).
- Calibrate test equipment prior to performing tests.
- Confirm that schematic diagrams satisfy the standard validation checklist.
- Design documents and software must be peer reviewed.
- Confirm software builds successfully after check-ins.

Policies about Organizational Standards

- Design files must be put into the document control system.

Figure 3.8: Example Definition of Done for a Hardware Team's PBIs

3.6 Tracking and Metrics

The key tracking tools for a Sprint are the Scrum Taskboard and the Burndown chart.

Figure 3.9 displays a typical Taskboard, which shows the current status in the middle of a Sprint.

The Taskboard shows the tasks associated with different PBIs in the Sprint Backlog and the state of each task. The PBIs are listed in rank order from top to bottom. Team members move a task into the "In Progress" state when starting the task and into the "Complete" state when finishing a task. It is extremely important that everyone be diligent about keeping this Taskboard current because the Taskboard is the core mechanism for understanding the status of work in the Sprint. All other metrics (such as the Burndown chart) are derived from the raw data provided by the Taskboard over time.

BACKLOG ITEM	NOT STARTED	IN PROGRESS	COMPLETE	
As a... I want to... So that... YY POINTS			TASK 1 XX HRS / TASK 2 XX HRS	TASK 3 XX HRS / TASK 4 XX HRS
As a... I want to... So that... YY POINTS		TASK 3 XX HRS / TASK 4 XX HRS	TASK 1 XX HRS / TASK 2 XX HRS	
As a... I want to... So that... YY POINTS	TASK 1 XX HRS / TASK 2 XX HRS / TASK 3 XX HRS / TASK 4 XX HRS			

Figure 3.9: Scrum Taskboard

The Burndown chart shows the hours remaining across all tasks planned for the Sprint but not yet completed, along with a diagonal line that shows the planned values. The diagonal *baseline* is a straight line that connects the known initial state with the planned final state. Work is ahead of schedule if the bars for the daily values are below the baseline, and behind if they are above it.

The initial state for the Burndown chart is the total effort planned for the Sprint, computed as the sum of the hour estimates for all tasks associated with all PBIs planned for the Sprint. This initial state occurs on "Day 0" of the Sprint on the chart (i.e., before the start of work on Day 1 of the Sprint).

The planned final state is defined by zero hours of work remaining at the end of the last working day of the Sprint (e.g., Day 10 for a two-week Sprint). Only weekdays are plotted (not weekends).

Each day's value is given by the sum of task estimates for tasks that have not been completed by the end of that day.

If the Scrum Team has decided to track partial task completion, by providing "Hours Remaining" estimates for tasks that are in-process at the end of the day, then the sum is over the "Hours Remaining" per task, which will normally be somewhat smaller than the sum of the tasks' original work estimates. (Note that the concept of "percent done" per task does not appear and is not used, as it is not a reliable measure of progress and is not forward-looking. The "Hours Remaining" concept is more reliable, better reflecting the need for forward-looking information.)

The example in Figure 3.10 displays the history up through the end of Day 5, out of the ten working days in this two-week Sprint. Progress is good, suggesting that the team is likely to finish the planned work on time. If the bars had been, say, 30 percent higher than the baseline at Day 5, it is unlikely that the planned work could be completed, and scope reduction should be considered.

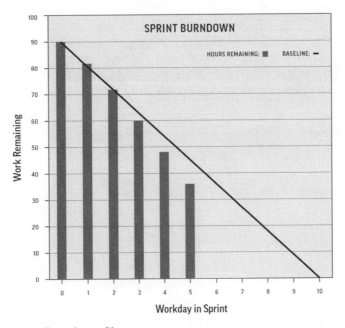

Figure 3.10: Burndown Chart

The Taskboard and Burndown chart enable a clear understanding of how well the work of the Sprint is going. The Burndown chart shows aggregate progress, revealing whether work is being accomplished at the intended rate. The Taskboard shows complete information about the current state of work. Together, they provide great insight into how the Sprint is progressing.

3.7 Scope Changes in the Sprint

The policy in Scrum is to not allow scope change requests in the current Sprint. The reason for this policy is that accepting such changes requires replanning the remainder of the Sprint, and the cost of doing so reduces productivity to an unacceptable degree.

However, the rate of progress the team is achieving in the Sprint may force a scope change if the planned scope cannot be completed. The Burndown chart is highly valuable because it provides insight about the future, which enables us to address such problems days before the Sprint ends. This means that we can identify the best fallback options while some time remains in the Sprint.

In the absence of such a forward-looking metric, we might not discover that the planned scope cannot be finished until the last day of the Sprint, at which point there is no time to develop fallback options. It is quite possible that the Sprint might end with one or more PBIs started but not completed, which is highly undesirable.

The Scrum Master should be monitoring Sprint status daily, and so it is often the Scrum Master who first becomes aware that the planned scope cannot be completed. The mechanism for this identification is simple: one puts a best-fit straight line through the last three, say, days' data on the Burndown chart to extrapolate where the team's amount of uncompleted work will be at the end of the Sprint. Typically, this trend is clear by the halfway point in the Sprint, and it is easy to see if the remaining work can be accomplished in the remaining time.*

When it is clear that the planned scope cannot be achieved, the Team members and Scrum Master should discuss fallback scenarios with the Product Owner, who will then select the best course to take. Common scenarios include:

- Remove a specific Story (e.g., the seventh, out of ten planned) to allow the team to complete all of the others. Or remove multiple PBIs, if needed.

---

* This can be determined by holding a ruler or other straight-edged item up to the chart and using it to make an educated guess about the likely end-state of the Sprint's planned work.

- De-scope a planned Story to reduce the work required by implementing a subset of the original scope. The smaller Story can be completed, along with other planned Stories, and the remainder of the original Story may be written as a new Story for implementation in a later Sprint. For this approach to work, it must be possible to define and plan the reduced scope quickly.

Similarly, we may discover that work is proceeding more rapidly than planned, and the team will finish all planned work a day or two in advance of the end of the Sprint. In this case, the response is typically one of the following:

- Add a new PBI to the end of the Sprint Backlog. For this to work, the new Story must be well understood, and it must be possible to estimate it and create its Task Breakdown quickly.

- If no appropriate PBIs are available, then the team may devote unstructured time to any useful activities they agree are an appropriate use of the remaining time.

Scope changes impact the metrics we use to track work against the plan—in this case, the Burndown chart. When we choose to reduce scope, I suggest that the team follow the approach as described above but do not change the scope of the Sprint from a tracking perspective. Leave the scope as-is in the tracking system, and only remove the deleted Story or Stories from the Sprint scope after the Sprint is over. This allows the Burndown chart to finish in a way that shows that the team's accomplishment was less than what was planned.

When adding scope to a Sprint, I suggest adding the scope to our tracking numbers at the time we begin work on the new PBI.

3.8 Testing and Integration and "Potentially Shippable Increments"

One often hears the statement that, "Every Sprint should produce a potentially shippable increment of product functionality." This statement is often misinterpreted as saying that every Sprint should produce new and useful functionality. In reality, the latter is not usually possible in a software context, and even less so for hardware development.

In the context of software development, I would interpret the statement as saying that the quality of the deliverables produced in the Sprint must be high enough that if the new business value was high enough, we could ship the product at that moment, and customers would find the product of acceptable quality.

I say this because it is often not possible to ensure that every Sprint delivers a new and usable software feature. This is even truer for hardware development, where the first approximation to a usable product is a late occurrence, not the result of accumulating features over time. Either way, we want to ensure high quality of everything the team develops by engineering quality in at all times.

The need to keep quality high leads to the core and very much iron-clad rule of Scrum that every deliverable must be tested and confirmed to be built and working as intended before the work of the Story can be considered done. The Story's Acceptance Criteria are expanded into Test Cases during the work of the Story, and the Story's deliverable must satisfy all Test Cases.

This simple description is very powerful. Not only does it drive quality to high and sustained levels on a per-Story basis, but it also provides the foundation for how we want to conduct *integration testing* in an Agile world.

Suppose Story A produces a deliverable that provides some capability, and a subsequent Story B likewise produces a deliverable that provides some capability. Suppose now that the combination of A and B produces more functionality than what the two do in isolation from each other. We now face the need to do integration testing to ensure that the integration of the two deliverables produces the larger set of desired functionality.

The best way to handle this scenario is by including in the scope of Story B's work all of the work required to do the integration testing of the two Stories' combined deliverables. In other words, whenever we add a deliverable to a system that makes new integration testing possible, we do that testing as part of the work of the new Story.

This practice turns integration testing from a later phase into the ongoing "business as usual" of building our deliverables. This style of integration testing provides immense value in finding and fixing integration problems as soon as possible, reducing one of the largest burdens of product development: the late discovery of integration problems.

Conducting integration testing on a per-Story basis can be difficult, if it requires substantial infrastructure to enable such rapid testing. Integration testing also tends to be more costly and time-consuming for hardware components than for software components. The necessary infrastructure may take substantial time to build and may be seen as impractical or "not how we do things here" in companies with long-established Waterfall processes. However, those companies will also have long-established problems with integration issues and resulting schedule overruns that should provide powerful incentives to do better!

I do not mean to say that there is no place for later-stage integration testing for software or hardware products. Such testing may well be required. The change here is from a common pattern of "build pieces now, and test all of them together later" to one of "do as much integration testing as early as possible, to discover and correct integration problems as early as possible."

With this approach, late-stage integration testing becomes work that truly could not be done earlier, and begins with higher product quality, and thus fewer integration problems to be found.

3.9 How Specifications Are Developed

The development of product specifications is an ongoing process, which takes serious and sustained effort over time, much as implementation does. Product Owners commonly work with marketing and other personnel to gather basic product requirements at a summary level and then develop a coherent concept of the product based on these requirements.

At some point, the higher-level conception of product requirements must inform the more detailed specifications provided to a Scrum Team for use in planning and executing a Sprint. The Product Owner has the responsibility of ensuring that teams receive implementable specifications for consideration in the Sprint Planning meetings. These specifications are always specifications for *deliverables*; that is, each one must provide a clear description of something that a team should make, which does not yet exist.

In the simplest case, a Product Owner may spend thirty minutes writing a User Story, which the team will implement a week or two later. At the other end of the spectrum, a Product Owner may spend months collaborating with usability experts, architects, subject matter experts, technology experts, marketing experts, and others to hammer out an increasingly detailed vision that is ultimately incorporated into Epics and PBIs that are written by the Product Owner and the Team members.

Thus, the day-to-day experience of a Product Owner can range from "one-man band" to conductor of an orchestra, depending on how many people's efforts must be guided and synchronized to produce the implementable specifications that a team must have. In all cases, the Product Owner makes the decisions about what to build based on business value, feasibility, and cost, and is the funnel through which *all* requests for a team's work must go (including requests that come from the team).

Detailed guidance about the mechanics of how and when to write specifications is beyond the scope of this chapter. However, these guidelines should be helpful:

- A PBI cannot enter a Sprint Planning meeting unless it contains the information required for teams to implement its deliverables. It is acceptable and expected for the team to have a number of questions for the Product Owner, about various details, throughout the Sprint. It is not acceptable for the team to be stalled for days, routinely, while others have debates about what the PBI should contain.

- User Experience, architectural, and technology guidance needed for a PBI's implementation must be made available, and incorporated as appropriate into the PBI itself, before the PBI can be considered ready for implementation. This guidance may take the form of wireframe or high-fidelity mock-ups, block diagrams, design patterns, or anything else that is required, and may be attached to the PBI, or referenced in the PBI's text by a link to a separate artifact.

- It is unwise to create large, detailed user experience or architecture specification in one big effort, and then hand the whole batch off to a team at once. It is better to develop rough conceptions of long-term needs and solutions but design and build the detailed pieces on a "just in time" basis. The former slows value delivery, usually leading to building too much of the wrong things and not enough of the right things.

4

Agile Project Management with Kanban

THIS chapter presents the fundamental concepts of Kanban, in the context of how a single team organizes and tracks work.

A Kanban process is appropriate for environments where forecasting the delivery of results on a schedule is either impossible or not needed. The focus is primarily on prioritizing incoming requests to do various kinds of work and organizing the workflow to optimize throughput. It is well suited for customer support, IT operations, and other environments with similar characteristics. It is generally not employed for product development, as some concept of scheduling is generally important when developing products but could be employed in this area if scheduling were not needed.

In a Kanban process, requests for work to be done enter a pool of pending work items. The Kanban Team members work on these items to complete them in a way that maximizes throughput and that involves moving the items through standard workflow states.

The decisions that must be addressed for a Kanban Team to function effectively include:

- What deliverable to implement next
- Who should perform the work that has been selected
- How we know when our work on a deliverable is done
- How we adjust when obstacles appear

As of this writing, the standard descriptions of Kanban as a business process most commonly focus on workflow definition, prioritization of work, and techniques for optimizing throughput (see, for example, David Anderson[23]). While these are important topics, they are not sufficient to define a process in the sense that I have discussed in Section 1.3. Thus, the presentation below differs significantly from the common descriptions of Kanban by adding elements that are important for a practical process. Addition of these elements yields a version of Kanban that provides all of the elements of Agile governance.

The following sections describe the elements of Kanban in more detail.

4.1 Kanban Queues, Workflow, and Parameters

The concepts behind Kanban were first explicitly developed by Taiichi Ohno at the Toyota Motor Corporation, in the context of automobile manufacturing. The goal for Toyota was to maintain a high level of production of high-quality automobiles, and the resulting process was christened the Toyota Production System (TPS). TPS embodies a particular instance of Kanban. It pioneered concepts of just-in-time manufacturing and continuous improvement (*kaizen*) based on respect for and participation of the people who do the work.

It is not surprising, therefore, that the language of Kanban often resembles the language of manufacturing. However, Kanban has evolved into a process for organizing work in general, outside of manufacturing, and our focus here will be on the latter, wider world.

Kanban is primarily about the flow of work in a context where the nature of that flow is uniform, standardized, and routine. I will also consider cases that are less routine, and the practicalities of using Kanban in such cases, but the baseline understanding of Kanban is the context of a routine and standardized workflow.

4.1.1 Workflow

Figure 4.1 illustrates some basic concepts of a Kanban process:

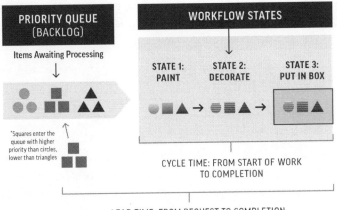

Figure 4.1: Simple Kanban System for Decorating Items

The front end of the process is a queue of work items, where *queue* means an ordered set. In Figure 4.1, the items are sets of ornaments to be custom-decorated and shipped to customers.

The queue is neither the classic FIFO (First-In, First-Out) nor LIFO (Last-In, First-Out) queue but a *priority queue*. In a priority queue, items are ordered by priority. The item at the head of the queue is the one that will be selected next for work, and the items after it are sequenced in the order desired, based on some conception of priority. The key behavior of a priority queue is that the priority of a work item, and therefore its relative position in the queue, may change over time. Figure 4.1 shows an example of such a change, as the squares to be decorated enter the queue with a higher priority than the circles and therefore push the circles back by one position in the queue.

(The similarity to a Product Backlog in Scrum is obvious, and indeed, a Product Backlog is a priority queue. The difference in language reflects the different origins of Scrum and Kanban, as the latter tends to draw more of its language and concepts explicitly from the domain of queueing theory. Nomenclature aside, however, the concepts are the same, and I will generally refer to the priority queue in Kanban as the *Backlog*.)

Work items exit the queue when work on them begins. In the example, each item (a set of ornaments to be decorated) goes through three standard workflow states: painting, decoration, and packing into boxes for shipment. While the fine details of what happens in each state vary somewhat from one item to the next, all items go through all three states.

Not shown in Figure 4.1 is what happens after the packaging state. As far as the sample process is concerned, the packaged item exits this Kanban workflow and enters a "Done" state. Whatever happens to the items after that point is not addressed by this particular workflow.

The relationship between Team members and Workflow States is not specified by the selection of Kanban alone but is a local decision. One group might decide to have one person per workflow state, passing an item along from one person to the next as work is done. Another group might have one or two people work on an item from start to finish, moving with it while it moves through workflow states. The only rule is that the organization of people and workflow states should be chosen so as to be effective in accomplishing the work, with minimum overhead. A key optimization in many cases is to minimize the number of handoffs that must be made between people or workstations, as handoffs are a key source of delay and errors.

The cardinal rule of a Kanban process is that items may not move to a state until that state is ready to begin work on them. For this reason, Kanban is often referred to as a *pull system* because an item is "pulled" into a state when capacity exists to work on it. This concept of a pull system contrasts with that of a *push system*, where items are pushed into the next state based on timing or other considerations.

Push systems may be effective for a wholly automated manufacturing process but do not work as well when the timing of work done in the various workflow states is not known reliably. Consequently, pull systems should generally be adopted when people rather than machines are doing work.

The term *Kanban* is itself a Japanese word that means "signboard." In its original context of auto manufacturing, someone who had finished work on a car at a particular workstation would signal that he has the capacity to start work on a new car, and request that a car be sent to him, by holding up a physical sign (signboard). The person or people in the adjacent upstream workstation would see the sign and send their partially built car along as soon as it was ready to go.

The concept of a worker seeking work when he or she has the capacity to do so carries on to the use of Kanban in business-process contexts as well. A Team member is expected to go find the next thing to work on, either from the previous workflow state or from the top of the queue, when he or she has the capacity to start work on a new item.

4.1.2 Parameters

The elapsed time from start of work to completion of work for an item is called the *Cycle Time*. The elapsed time from request (when an item enters the queue) to completion of work is called the *Lead Time* and cannot be less than the Cycle Time.

Each item will experience a particular Cycle Time and Lead Time, which may vary from one to the next. In a context where priorities change frequently, the Lead Times may vary widely across items, even though the Cycle Times may be quite similar for most of them.

Another parameter of interest is the *Work in Process* (WIP). The WIP is simply the number of items in workflow states at any one time, which is three (one in each state) for the example.

4.1.3 Throughput and Little's Law

The process as a whole will have the average values of Lead Time, Cycle Time, and WIP. It will also have an average throughput, defined as the rate of production of completed items per some period of time (e.g., per day). These numbers are not wholly independent but are related by a formula called Little's Law:

Throughput = WIP / Cyclé Time

Note that Little's Law refers to average values of the parameters, as averaged over many Cycle Times. It does not apply to any specific item.

The desire to increase throughput can only be achieved in two ways: increasing WIP or decreasing Cycle Time. Adding more production lines can increase throughput by increasing WIP, which may be an appropriate strategy. However, increases in WIP commonly cause increases in cost as well and are generally less desirable than decreasing Cycle Time.

The same tradeoffs also apply to pure business-process contexts as opposed to manufacturing contexts. Increasing WIP by hiring more people increases costs. Increasing WIP by requiring people to multitask on multiple concurrent items imposes a cost in the form of delays due to context switching and actually decreases throughput.

4.2 Overview of Roles and Process

In this process, *Kanban Teams* work steadily on work items over time, according to a standard workflow of predefined states. Each Kanban Team consists of a set of people fulfilling one of three roles: *Team* (or *Team member*, of which there are three to nine in a team), *Backlog Owner*, and *Monitor*. I define "Kanban Team" to refer to all three roles, while the term "Team" refers to the set of three to nine people who do the hands-on work and excludes the Backlog Owner and Monitor.

The Backlog Owner provides ranked work items, meaning that the specifications for work must be listed in the desired order of implementation. All items not yet in process reside in a set called the *Backlog*, and each item in the Backlog is officially called a *Backlog Item* (BI). (In practice, specifications come in more than one form, as the following sections will describe in detail.) The Backlog Owner is responsible for ranking work items based on value, urgency, and so forth. Periodically, the Backlog Owner selects and ranks a subset of the Backlog for review and revision by the team in Backlog Refinement Meetings.

The Monitor oversees the process as a whole, facilitating meetings, enforcing the process, removing roadblocks, and so forth.

When Team members have the capacity to start work on a new item, they select it from the top of the Backlog. They collaborate as appropriate to complete the necessary work and move the item through the workflow states until work is completed for the item.

The Team members are mentored, guided, and assisted by the Monitor, and collaborate with the Backlog Owner daily to ensure the deliverables are as desired.

The three Kanban roles meet in the Daily Stand-Up meeting to maintain a coherent understanding of work status, including the impacts of current and anticipated actions to each other. Finally, all three roles participate in a Retrospective meeting every two weeks to identify how to improve their process and environment over time.

4.3 Roles

A "role" is a set of responsibilities, and accompanying authority, assigned to and carried out by a person or set of people. The Kanban roles of Backlog Owner, Monitor, and Team members are clearly defined, as are the responsibilities and areas of authority associated with each:

Backlog Owner: The sole authority over work-item specifications and prioritization. Depending on the environment, this person may or may not develop the specifications but is always responsible for ensuring that they have the necessary quality and completeness to be executable. Responsibilities include:

- Prioritizing (ranking, i.e., sequencing) work items
- Ensuring quality of specifications for work items
- Providing near real-time guidance to team during execution of work items
- Reviewing and approving deliverables

Monitor: The sole authority over process. This role is analogous to Scrum Master in that it focuses on defining and enforcing the process and doing whatever is needed to make the team as productive as possible. Responsibilities include:

- Defining workflow states and Work-In-Process constraints to optimize throughput
- Enforcing the process
- Facilitating meetings
- Maintaining situational awareness of the work
- Knowing Team member strengths and weaknesses
- Mentoring the team
- Protecting the team from interference
- Monitoring progress
- Removing obstacles, ensuring issues are addressed

Team: The people who execute the work items. They may have specialized skills that are aligned with workflow stages. Team responsibilities include:

- Implementing and validating (testing, fixing) deliverables and executing tasks

- Completing work to standard "Definition of Done" per state or for deliverables

- Selecting appropriate work to do, based on skills, availability, and type of work waiting to be done

4.4 Ceremonies

Ceremonies are recurring meetings, with specific and standardized agendas and practices. As of this writing, there is no widely recognized standard for Kanban ceremonies, but there are actions that must be performed that are well-addressed by having a set of ceremonies. These actions include:

- Receive or define work items
- Make priority decisions
- Move items between workflow stages

Table 4.1 lists a set of ceremonies that I have found useful for a practical Kanban process:

Ceremony	Time Box	Input	Output	Value
Backlog Refinement	<1 hr	Draft Work Items at the top of the prioritized Backlog	Finalized Work Items and ranking	Backlog & Team are ready for subsequent execution of Work Items
Daily Stand-up	<15 min	In-progress Work Items	Team updated Impediments raised	Team members on same page re: progress and impediments
Retrospective	1–1.5 hrs	Recent performance data, e.g., Cumulative Flow chart	Short list of improvements for near future, with owners	Learn from experience, enable continuous improvement

Table 4.1: Kanban Ceremonies

The durations of the Time Boxes are suggestions and should be modified based on experience. They should always be kept to as short a time as will suffice, to minimize overhead.

The practice of Backlog Refinement drives effective decisions about the definition and sequencing of work to be done. The Retrospective meeting drives rapid improvement in the team's ability to deliver. The Daily Stand-Up meeting maintains a coherent picture of work across all the Team members, identifying issues and potential impacts quickly so they may be resolved quickly.

4.4.1 Backlog Refinement Meeting

Backlog Refinement meetings may be held at any useful frequency, and commonly once per week. The purpose of Backlog Refinement is to prepare the team and a subset of the Backlog Items for implementation. Before work can be started on Backlog Items, these prerequisites must be satisfied:

- The written description of each item must be clear and complete.
- The set of items must have no "holes," meaning that none depend on some other item that has not been defined.
- The items must be ranked (sequenced) appropriately, based on their value and dependencies.
- The Team members must understand the items and the relationships between them.

The Backlog Owner facilitates the meeting, which all Team members and the Monitor attend. In the meeting, Team members provide feedback on draft Backlog Items provided in advance by the Backlog Owner and identify any issues or omissions that need to be corrected. The Team members and Backlog Owner collaborate to identify what changes are needed (and who will make them). They also develop a ranking of the Backlog Items that is driven by the Backlog Owner's assessment of value, which also ensures that dependencies between items are satisfied.

After the meeting, the Backlog Owner revises and drafts Backlog Items based on feedback, while Team members write other Backlog Items that are required to address infrastructural or other needs that are outside the Backlog Owner's area of expertise.

There is no assumption that refinement is restricted solely to meetings. Some refinement of requirements should be ongoing as routine work. The Backlog Refinement meetings provide an opportunity for full-team collaboration that is intended to enhance, not replace, informal collaboration on Backlog refinement.

The goal of Backlog Refinement is to ensure that Backlog Items and the team are prepared for the items' implementation. Thus, the Team members should be in agreement that each Backlog Item is ready for implementation before the start of work on it. One useful technique for ensuring this readiness is to define a "Definition of Ready" for Backlog Items, which lists the explicit criteria the team uses to ensure readiness.

4.4.2 Daily Stand-Up

The purpose of a Daily Stand-Up meeting is to maintain a coherent perspective on the part of all Team members as to what is happening. Team members lose track of what other Team members are doing, and how their work can impact each other, because they are focusing on their current work. This meeting provides an opportunity for everyone on the Kanban Team to update their common picture of work status.

All three roles attend this meeting. The Monitor's primary responsibility is to ensure the meeting does not exceed its fifteen-minute Time Box. Since all roles are present, and the meeting occurs daily, it is critical to keep the meeting short. If allowed to expand, this daily meeting can consume an unfortunate amount of the team's working time.

Team members do most of the talking, the Monitor facilitates, and the Product Owner observes and contributes as needed.

First, the Monitor displays the current tracking information (such as the Cumulative Flow Chart) and provides relevant commentary on the overall status of work (e.g., potential need to pick up the pace, address a bottleneck, etc.) and other information of general interest to the team.

Next, each Team member describes:

1. What I've been doing since our last meeting
2. What I plan to do before the next meeting
3. What issues are slowing me down, which I may need help to resolve

A small amount of informal discussion about the items raised is appropriate. However, if the resolution of an issue takes more than a minute of discussion, we do not resolve it in this meeting but identify who will meet afterwards in a "Sidebar meeting" to address the issue. The Backlog Owner is often one of the people who will be involved in such resolutions, which is a large part of why his or her attendance is important (the other part being that the Backlog Owner also needs to understand how the work is going).

It is common to have a need for the whole team to discuss topics of interest to all. A good time for this kind of discussion is directly after the Daily Stand-Up meeting. However, to avoid confusion of what is happening and who must be present, the Monitor should announce the end of the Daily Stand-Up meeting first, describe the topics to be discussed, and state that anyone who does not need to be present can leave. After that, discussion may continue as needed.

4.4.3 Retrospective

The purpose of the Retrospective meeting is to improve the team's process over time by identifying what does and doesn't work well and working to improve the latter. This meeting should be held every two weeks or so.

The Backlog Owner, Monitor, and Team members attend the Retrospective meeting (generally, with no additional observers allowed, although this is always a team decision).

The Monitor facilitates, and all three roles (including the Monitor) participate and supply information. I recommend this agenda:

1. Review the status of action items from the previous Retrospective, to understand what has been done, what is in progress, what issues are blocking progress, and so forth.

2. Each participant provides information about how work has gone since the last Retrospective.
   a. What went well that should be continued.
   b. What did not go well that we'd like to do better.

3. Decide what changes to make.

Many techniques exist for gathering this information, some of which draw on visual metaphors or more game-like behaviors. One common and fast-paced approach to collecting and responding to the information is as follows.

Each participant writes the "went well" and "want to do better" items on sticky notes (one item per note) and sticks them on a wall or whiteboard under "went well" and "want to do better" headings. This usually takes about ten minutes.

The "want to do better" notes are often repetitive, so the Monitor may group them into a smaller number of distinct topics as people post their notes.

Next, the Monitor reads the "went well" items so that everyone knows what they are. The group may discuss these items briefly, as needed.

Attention then turns to the items under the "want to do better" heading.

The Monitor describes the first topic, and the participants hold a quick discussion about what to do about it. Often the result is simply a policy change (e.g., a decision to revise a Definition of Done). These policy decisions are made on the spot. Items that require follow-up actions are noted as such and set aside for the moment. This process repeats until all topics have been discussed.

After the above discussion, those topics requiring follow-up effort are prioritized to identify the optimum subset that the team can address, given their finite bandwidth. Some of these follow-up actions may be to write up new work items that will enter the Backlog and be prioritized for completion like any other work item. Some items may require working with people outside the team, and these may simply be taken on without representing the work as new work items in the Backlog.

The participants select owners to drive the selected follow-up actions, and then adjourn.

4.5 Artifacts, Tracking, and the Four Flavors of Kanban

The system used to track work is tied closely to the nature of the Backlog Items. In other words, a Kanban process is largely defined by the nature of the work to be done and, therefore, the nature of the Backlog Items to be processed.

In this section I will look at the four varieties of Kanban. I will characterize each variety by the type of work to be done, how this work is described in written artifacts, the workflow used to accomplish the work, and the details of tracking systems.

I will start by clarifying just what a "work item" or "Backlog Item" is. I believe that there are only two fundamental possibilities, and so a Backlog Item is a written description of one of these two things:

1. A task to be performed
2. A deliverable to be created

A *task* is an action performed by one or more people, while a *deliverable* is a thing that is produced by one or more people, based on some kind of specification.

One might conclude that these two categories imply two varieties of Kanban tracking systems, but the reality is more complex. While Kanban as derived from manufacturing assumes similar deliverables, reality in other areas is not always this tidy. Sometimes deliverables can vary markedly from one to the next.

In addition, it is entirely possible to encounter a situation of such massive confusion that the first order of business is to get some visibility into a chaotic mess that has no clear workflow and not have the time or luxury to make fine distinctions between tracking deliverables and tracking tasks. In these situations, it is still possible to set up a Kanban board to bring visibility into the status of work, at the cost of blurring the distinction between different types of work.

I have found that four varieties of the Kanban tracking system cover all practical scenarios. The selection of the appropriate system is driven by what we need to track, namely:

1. Flow of tasks
2. Flow of similar deliverables
3. Flow of dissimilar deliverables
4. Flow of a mix of tasks and deliverables

Exactly which system to choose is not always obvious, but Table 4.2 presents some examples of how different types of work might best be addressed with a Kanban tracking system.

Summary	Item Type	States	Examples	How Tracked
Simple case of uniform tasks	Task	NIC	Paint motorcycles	NIC Board
Same kind of task, but different sizes	Task	NIC	Paint motor vehicles	
Different task types, of similar size	Task	NIC	Respond to requests submitted to IT help desk	
Task type and size both vary	Task	NIC	Provide janitorial services	
Simple case of uniform Deliverables	Deliverable	Per-process	Sandwiches from a deli	Board with custom states
Same kind of Deliverable, of different sizes	Deliverable	Per-process	User-interface designs	
Different Deliverable types, of similar size	Deliverable	NIC	Meals in a restaurant	Scrum-style Taskboard
Deliverable type and size both vary	Deliverable	NIC	Bug fixes for software products	
Mix of tasks and Deliverables	Task or Deliverable	NIC	Variety of work done in IT operations	NIC Board

Table 4.2: Examples of Kanban Tracking Systems for Different Types of Work

The "NIC" task board has only Not Started, In Progress, and Complete states. All four varieties of tracking systems are discussed in detail below.

4.5.1 Flow of Tasks

A "task" is an action performed by one or more people. Common tasks in everyday life include "walk the dog," "take out the trash," and so forth. One characteristic that serves to distinguish a task from a deliverable is that task descriptions typically start with a verb.

Confusion between tasks and deliverables is common. A statement such as "Make a sandwich" is worded as a task but is really a request for someone to create a deliverable (a sandwich). One might argue that everything is really a task, since every request for something to be done can be worded in the action-oriented language of tasks, but this quibbling serves more to obscure differences and complicate tracking than it does to provide any practical benefits. While the distinction between tasks and deliverables can indeed be blurry in some cases, it is nevertheless a useful distinction in practice, and understanding the distinction leads to more effective tracking.

A good rule of thumb for distinguishing between tasks and deliverables is to try to describe the work item as a specification of a thing to be created. If the language flows naturally, then the thing is probably a deliverable. Otherwise, it is probably more reasonably described as a task.

4.5.1.1 Requirements-Definition Artifact

Definitions in terms of a Title, a Description, and Acceptance Criteria are effective.

- The Title is a one-sentence "action statement" starting with a verb.

- The Description contains one to a few sentences, in clear and simple language, that describes the action to be performed. Attachments or references to additional documents should be included as necessary.

- The Acceptance Criteria summarize things that must be true, and should be validated, about the completed task.

  - This is a good place to provide other useful information that does not fit in the description section.

Figure 4.2 shows a sample task that reflects the above definition. This task is a request for a particular person (Bert) to be given login access to the specified product, subject to certain restrictions.

Title	Create a uTracker login for Bert Winger
Description	
Please provide Bert access to our uTracker instance. His email address is bwinger@telcorp.com.	
Acceptance Criteria	
1. Bert should be able to write and edit Backlog Items and see the usual metrics (Taskboard, Cumulative Flow chart, etc.). 2. Bert is on the Vascubot Controller project and should only see information relevant to the Teams working on Vascubot.	

Figure 4.2: Sample Task

4.5.1.2 Tracking

The Kanban board used for tracking tasks is a basic "NIC Taskboard," for which the task states are defined as *Not Started*, *In Progress*, and *Complete (NIC)*. Figure 4.3 shows an example of a Kanban Taskboard, for which five items are currently displayed.

Figure 4.3 shows the three standard task states and the tasks that are in those states.

- Task 1 has been completed. Completed tasks are removed from the Taskboard periodically to avoid clutter.
- Tasks 2 and 3 are in the In-Progress state, meaning that work is progressing on them at this time.
- Tasks 4 and 5 are waiting in the queue and are not yet started.

4.5.1.3 Constraining Work in Process through WIP Limits

The Taskboard in Figure 4.3 illustrates a new concept: The *Work-in-Process Limit (WIP Limit)*. The sole meaningful workflow state (In Progress) has a WIP Limit of 2, meaning that no more than two items (Tasks) can be in that state at the same time.

NOT STARTED	IN PROGRESS (2)	COMPLETE
		TASK 1
	TASK 3 TASK 2	
TASK 4		
TASK 5		

Figure 4.3: Kanban Taskboard for Tracking Tasks

The purpose of WIP Limits is to improve the overall effectiveness of the process. In its original context of manufacturing, a WIP Limit is driven largely by logistical constraints: physical space, number of workstations, and number of workers put a practical ceiling on how many items can be in process in any given state at a time. Allowing the Work in Process to exceed these ceilings results in items piling up in workflow states, consuming more space, and increasing inventory costs relative to the optimum scenario. Thus, each state's WIP Limit is defined to prevent these space and cost problems, and we do not allow the number of items in a particular state to exceed the state's WIP Limit.

In a business-process context, physical constraints exist but tend to be relatively less important than the time and availability of people to do work. We are less concerned about the cost of too many items being in any one state because material costs are usually not an issue. There are still drawbacks, however, in that having WIP be too large causes confusion as items accumulate, increases the risk that items may be forgotten, and can promote multitasking and context switching to a degree that reduces both productivity and morale.

4.5.2 Flow of Similar Deliverables

A deliverable is a thing that is produced by one or more people, based on some kind of specification. The form of the specification varies widely, depending on the nature of the deliverable. In the simplest cases, the specification may be a selection from a menu that lists the possible choices. In the most complex case, the specification may be custom written, with significant effort required to clarify all of the details.

4.5.2.1 Requirements-Definition Artifacts

In the simplest case, the deliverables are standardized, and one can choose from a menu of options, as in Figure 4.4. The example menu lists sandwich and topping types for lunch orders. While the number of possible combinations is large, the modest number of options per category makes the compact menu format possible. The customer specifies the desired sandwich by circling the appropriate options, after which assembling the sandwich is straightforward.

Bread	Spreads	Fillings				Toppings
		Type	Slices			
Sourdough	BBQ	Roast Beef	1	2	3	Lettuce
Whole Wheat	Mayonnaise	Ham	1	2	3	Onions
White	Dill Spread	Turkey	1	2	3	Pickles
Rye	Yellow Mustard	Mushroom	1	2	3	Jalapeños
Wheat Wrap	Dijon Mustard	Pepper Jack	1	2	3	Salt
	Ketchup					Pepper
						Pepper Jack
						Cheddar

Figure 4.4: Deliverables as Menu Selections

One can have a menu for much more complex deliverables as well. For example, someone shopping for a custom personal computer may navigate through an extensive set of options in different categories, such as processor type, storage space, graphics-processing capabilities, monitor types, and so forth. Each page of the order typically displays a set of options that is partly defined by constraints arising from selections made earlier in the process. The number of possible combinations is enormous, and two different shoppers may see very different options, but all possible custom computers are nevertheless drawn from the same finite sets of components. Once all selections have been made, the vendor will then assemble the customer's computer as specified.

Menu-style specifications are useful, but not all deliverables can be defined in terms of menu selections. For example, a company may purchase ghostwriting services to generate articles for the company's website. It is not possible to specify all fine details for an article to be written without actually writing the article, which is not desirable. It makes more sense to write a description of the desired articles that clarifies the basic concept without going into so much detail that the description becomes the deliverable.

(Note that this section assumes that deliverables may be complex enough to make menu-style specifications inappropriate but are otherwise similar enough that all can go through the same set of workflow states.)

Complex deliverables require a more free-form style of specification, in a manner deliberately analogous to the User Story format of Section 3.5.1.1. However, this complex specification format for Kanban is most commonly not a description of a user experience in a software product, so the specific language used for the latter may not be appropriate. Thus, the format described here more closely resembles that of a Technical Story, as in Section 3.5.1.2.

Figure 4.5 presents an example of the complex-deliverable format for an article about test automation.

Title	Article on test automation
Description	
I want a 2,000-word article on test automation for software products. The focus is on the big picture, covering all aspects of test automation at a high level and describing how automation can reduce time to market while maintaining high quality. I'd like some nice illustrations in it too.	
Acceptance Criteria	

1. Approximately 2,000 words
2. At least three illustrations
3. Address unit testing, integration testing, user-interface testing
4. Mention at least two tools for automating each type of testing
5. Include a quantitative example showing reduction in time-to-market, e.g., for an application requiring 3,000 regression tests

Figure 4.5: Example Specification for an Article on Test Automation

This format includes a Title, a Description, and Acceptance Criteria for the deliverable.

- The Title is intended to be the shortest-possible description of the deliverable that is meaningful to the people who will be reading it.

- The Description contains one to a few sentences, in clear and simple language, that describes the deliverable to be produced. Attachments or references to additional documents should be included as necessary.

- The Acceptance Criteria summarize things that must be true, and should be validated, about the completed deliverable.

  - This is a good place to provide other useful information that does not fit in the description section.

Just as for Stories in Scrum, the Complex deliverable specification does not (and cannot) capture all significant details. We must rely on Progressive Elaboration of the specification via discussion over time, in Backlog Refinement meetings and informal conversation, in order to work out the details.

4.5.2.2 Tracking

The Kanban board used for tracking similar deliverables is the variety most commonly described in other texts about Kanban and originated in the world of manufacturing. The board contains a set of workflow states that are common to all deliverables that flow through the process.

A particular organization that uses Kanban may have multiple workflows, each with its own Kanban board and each intended to produce a particular category of deliverable.

The example below shows the organization of a Kanban board for a company that writes articles on various topics for its customers. Requests are entered into the queue (i.e., the Backlog) and flow through a variety states until work is completed. The workflow states between the Backlog and Complete state are:

1. Call with customer to clarify details (3)
2. First draft of text (3)
3. First draft of illustrations (3)
4. Call with customer for feedback on first draft (3)
5. Second draft of text (3)
6. Second draft of illustrations (3)
7. Call with customer for feedback on second draft (3)
8. Third draft of text (3)
9. Third draft of illustrations (3)

The WIP Limit for each state is indicated by the numbers in parentheses. The most common reason for such WIP Limits is the number of people available to do work. In this example, we might have three writers, each of whom does all of the work for each article as it moves through the workflow states.

4.5.2.3 Definition of Done for Workflow States

A significant risk in this workflow scenario is the problem of failed handoffs. This problem is unlikely to arise if one person shepherds the work on an item through all states but is a definite risk if a person working on an item in one state hands it off to the next person in the next state.

For deliverables and workflows of any complexity, there will usually be some ambiguity about which of the finer details should be done in one step versus another. It is often less important when the work is done than that the work be done reliably. In other words, a person who is about to start work on an item that was handed off by a previous person must be able to trust that all of the necessary prerequisite work was indeed accomplished. A failure to make clear where the details are accomplished leads to mistaken assumptions, confusion, rework, and poor morale.

A good way to address the potential for failed handoffs is to define a *Definition of Done* for each workflow state. The Definition of Done for a state clarifies what will be accomplished on an item before its handoff to the next state. It is essentially a contract, or definition of exit criteria, which ensures that an item is not passed to the next state until the specified prerequisite work has been done.

Parts acquisition state:
- All parts placed on cart
- All parts checked off on order's parts list

Computer assembly state:
- Assembled devices are on cart
- Devices turn on when powered up
- Assembler signs and completes assembly checklist

Figure 4.6: Some Definitions of Done for Computer Assembly Workflow States

Figure 4.6 gives examples for Definitions of Done for two of the states that might occur in the production of a custom-computer order. For example, the person who performs the assembly can be confident that all of the necessary parts have been provided.

4.5.3 Flow of Dissimilar Deliverables

Kanban's roots in manufacturing mean that it is well-suited as a means for organizing routine work on items that are of similar size and are performed with a standard set of workflow states. By the same token, it is less appropriate when those assumptions do not hold.

Suppose, for example, that the same group of people needs to do the following:

- Assembly of an outdoor playground set (slide, swing-set, etc.)
- Preparation of a two-course lunch for forty people
- Painting a room in a house

The above deliverables do not resemble each other and do not have a common set of workflow states.

Kanban may well not be the best approach to managing such highly diverse types of work. Scrum (for example) might be a better choice, as it is designed to handle widely varying types of work in a graceful fashion. Nevertheless, the planning-related machinery of Scrum may not be needed if the more reactive and priority-driven approach of Kanban is preferable.

I will describe a variant of Kanban that works for dissimilar deliverables, but it would be a mistake to expect smooth throughput in this case. Throughput may be highly variable, and therefore not very predictable, due to the variability of the deliverables.

From a Kanban tracking perspective, we face the challenge that the work to be done for various deliverables cannot be described by a set of standard workflow states that:

- Show all types of work that can be done
- Are relevant to all items
- Are sequential
- Have similar duration per deliverable
- Allow for meaningful WIP Limits

The solution will be to borrow some concepts from Scrum, including the practice of defining a Task Breakdown for each deliverable.

4.5.3.1 Requirements-Definition Artifact

The Complex-Deliverable format of Figure 4.5 is very flexible and applies equally well to this more complex situation. No modifications are required.

4.5.3.2 Tracking

The Kanban board used in Figure 4.7 is a derivative of the Scrum Task-board of Figure 3.9. Since the work on highly dissimilar items does not flow through a common set of workflow states, we decompose each deliverable's work into a set of tasks that are appropriate for that item and then track the task states.

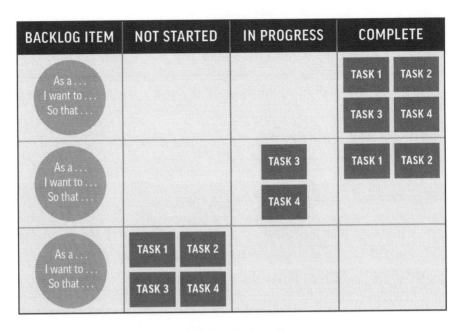

Figure 4.7: Kanban Board for Dissimilar Deliverables

The Backlog Items in Figure 4.7 are the descriptions of the deliverables, each of which has an associated set of tasks. The list of tasks will vary from one item to the next, depending on the nature of the work to be done. The only commonality across the items is that each item's tasks go through the same set of task states: Not Started, In Progress, and Complete. By definition, a deliverable is complete when all of its tasks are complete.

The concept of decomposition of work into Task Breakdowns is the same in Kanban as it is in Scrum. The details are provided in Section 3.3.2.2 and will not be repeated here. The only difference between the Scrum and Kanban scenarios is that tasks are not estimated in Kanban.

4.5.3.3 Constraining Work in Process by Swarming

A major goal of any Kanban system should be to minimize Cycle Time. A major contributor to this goal is a well-chosen strategy for constraining Work in Process to levels that optimize the process and minimize Cycle Time.

The standard perspective for constraining Work in Process in Kanban is to set explicit WIP Limits for each state. This approach makes good sense in a manufacturing context, where logistical constraints and material cost are extremely important. The argument for numeric WIP Limits is weaker in a business-process context, where the concerns have more to do with inefficiencies arising from excessive context-switching when people try to work on too many things at the same time.

Numeric WIP Limits work much less well when the process must handle dissimilar deliverables. Fortunately, setting numeric WIP Limits is not the only strategy available for constraining WIP. The swarming technique of Section 3.3.2.3.1 is more flexible and is a better strategy for constraining WIP when deliverables have high variability.

Swarming may often be a better strategy for constraining work in Kanban than numeric WIP Limits, even for similar deliverables or tasks. If the goal is to reduce Cycle Time, it is often more effective to develop a culture in which Team members simply collaborate as needed to complete each item quickly. Collaboration is at the heart of effective Agile processes, and I would rather foster collaboration than focus on the more mechanical structure of numeric WIP Limits.

4.5.4   Flow of a Mix of Tasks and Deliverables

It may seem odd to recommend that one avoid doing what is described in this section, but that is indeed the case. The more focused variants of Kanban discussed in the previous sections are superior for managing work and providing insight. However, there are times when the need in the moment is to provide some structure and insight for a chaotic world that is devoid of both, and the need to get some structure in place quickly is paramount. When facing such a mess, the approach described here can be employed quickly, as a first step, to be replaced later by a set of more finely tailored Kanban variants.

4.5.4.1   Requirements-Definition Artifact

In theory, the various specification types we've reviewed previously provide the best solutions for their different types of work items and should be used appropriately. In practice, the chaotic nature of this scenario likely means that fine-tuning the written format of work items is unlikely to be practical, and we may have to settle for getting anything at all written in any fashion that makes sense.

4.5.4.2   Tracking

In this scenario, we have a mix of all possible types of work and want to provide some visibility into all of them at once. The solution is to provide a mixed Kanban board that displays all possible types of work in the same view.

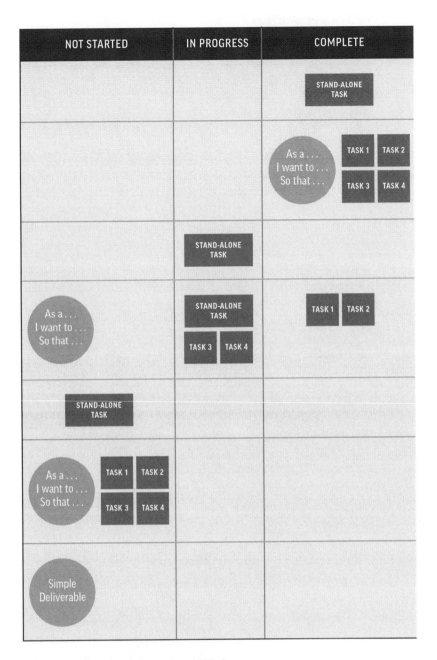

Figure 4.8: Kanban Board for Mixed Work

The mixed Kanban board of Figure 4.8 shows the state of stand-alone tasks, similar deliverables, and dissimilar deliverables with Task Breakdowns. All items on the board move from Not Started, to In Progress, to Complete.

4.5.4.3 Constraining Work in Process

The swarming technique of Section 4.5.3.3 is generally the most appropriate choice for constraining work in process to levels that minimize Cycle Time.

4.6 Metrics

The key metric for Kanban is the Cumulative Flow chart. This chart shows the number of items in different workflow states versus time.

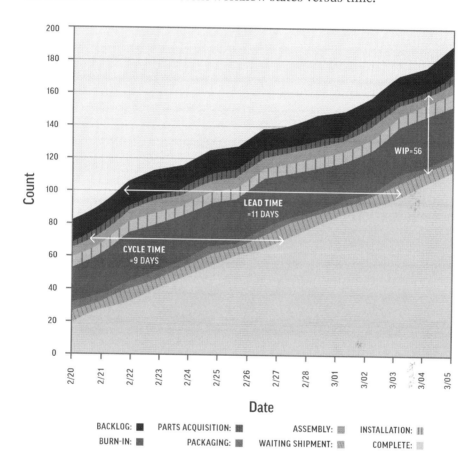

Figure 4.9: Sample Cumulative Flow Chart for Custom-Computer Assembly

Figure 4.9 is a Cumulative Flow chart for the assembly of custom computer orders mentioned in Section 4.5.2.1. An order is taken off of the Backlog and goes through workflow states of Parts Acquisition, Assembly,

Installation, Burn-In, Packaging, and Waiting Shipment. An order moves into the Complete state when the packaged computer leaves the factory.

The vertical axis shows the count of items in each state, for the dates shown on the horizontal axis. All state boundaries go up over time because the Complete state accumulates all finished orders.

One can read key Kanban parameters directly from the chart. The total Work in Process (WIP) on any date is the vertical extent from the top of the Complete state to the bottom of the Backlog state. The time-averaged value of the Cycle Time on any particular date is the horizontal extent from the top of the Complete state on that date to the bottom of the Backlog state at the same height on the graph. The time-averaged value of the Lead Time on any particular date is the horizontal extent from the top of the Complete state on that date to the top of the Backlog state at the same height on the graph.

With experience, it becomes easy to observe not only the parameter values but also trends and bottlenecks. For example, if the Assembly state experiences a major slowdown, the states below it will shrink as they become starved for input and the Backlog state at the top may grow.

With respect to our four flavors of Kanban, the Cumulative Flow chart shows status of tasks, Simple deliverables, or Complex deliverables, but is not applicable to tasks that are linked to Complex deliverables.

5

Agile Program Management

ORGANIZATIONS that use the Scrum framework usually have a number of Scrum Teams that must collaborate to produce products solutions that are too large for any one team to develop alone. Decisions that must be addressed in a multiple-team context include:

- How to divide a large group of people into a specific set of teams

- How many Scrum Masters are needed to support the teams

- How many Product Owners are needed to support the teams

- How to define and allocate deliverables that span many teams

- How to plan, track, and enable successful coordination of work that spans many teams

- How to plan and track work for longer time horizons than one Sprint

- How to balance the competing needs for Product Management for both customer focus and team focus

The above points are not wholly independent. Successful execution of a long-term plan commonly goes hand-in-hand with all of these points. Thus, I will address all of these items as a set in this chapter, and refer to them, collectively, as the fundamentals of *Agile Program Management*. The focus of Agile Program Management is on the concepts and practices required to enable the definition and collaboration of multiple teams in order to achieve business goals of large-scale product development.

Agile Program Management is a style of Program Management that is Agile in the sense that it adapts well to unexpected developments. It requires that the organization's personnel be divided into stable teams who have a known focus but does not require that these teams use any particular process internally. Any one team may work with a Scrum process, a Waterfall process, or some other process that suits their needs. All that we require is that these teams participate effectively in the collaborative effort of Agile Program Management. Teams must assign the appropriate roles and responsibilities to the people involved in this participation, and those people must collaborate via the techniques described in the remainder of this chapter.

For the sake of simplicity, I will use examples of Scrum Teams throughout and assume the obvious modifications will be made for teams that do not use Scrum. For example, a Waterfall Team may have a Project Manager and a Product Manager, instead of a Scrum Master and Product Owner. Other teams, with other processes, may use different language for similar roles but must designate people to fill such roles.

Chapter 3, on Scrum, provided information specific to the development of software and hardware products. While Scrum is equally applicable to both types of product development, the nuances of some of the Scrum practices differ between the two cases, and I addressed those nuances as needed.

The differences between hardware and software development have relatively little impact on the practicalities of Program Management. The largest exception has to do with the logic behind defining Release Cycles, which is addressed below.

5.1 The Release Time Horizon

The word "Release" has become overloaded with meanings. In the context of Scrum and product development, all of these meanings are common:

- A transfer of the product to a department that is responsible for making it available to customers (e.g., "Release to Production" or "Release to Manufacturing")

- The product itself, as made available to customers (e.g., "The new release has these features…")

- A product development cycle, ending with provision of the product to customers

- A product development cycle that is longer than a Sprint

The different meanings resemble and overlap with each other. For my purposes, the last bullet is the appropriate one: a *Release*, or *Release cycle*, is a planning horizon that spans a set of two or more Sprints. (For example, a three-month Release cycle might contain six two-week Sprints.)

In other words, I am defining the Release cycle to be the medium-term planning horizon for Agile product development. It is longer than a Sprint but shorter than a product or Portfolio Roadmap. The intermediate length of the Release cycle is reflected in the granularity of its planning. As we move from Sprint to Release to Roadmap, the granularity moves from Stories and tasks, to Epics and Stories, to large Epics and Initiatives. The techniques used to create these plans all require writing some kind of specifications, and estimating work, but differ in detail from one planning horizon to the next.

The relationship between the Release cycle and the release of a product can vary widely. Examples include:

- The product is released to production at the end of each Release cycle. This practice is moderately common in the software world and introduced Release as both a development cycle and a moment of product production. It is not so common in hardware development.

- The product is released to production at intervals shorter than the Release cycle. A company may release new versions of a software product daily (with a continuous-delivery model) or every few days or weeks but wishes to plan work over a three-month period. This pattern is again not common for hardware development.

- The product is released to production or manufacturing at intervals longer than the Release cycle. It is convenient to have planning horizons of three months in length, but the product will be released to production after fifteen months (and multiple Release cycles). This is a common pattern for both hardware development and software development.

The length of a Release cycle should be based on business considerations. A major driver behind Release length is the customer preference for product-delivery moments, as it is unwise to ship products at rates much higher or lower than customers prefer. Thus, practical Release cycle lengths range from four weeks (e.g., two Sprints) to about six months, with longer periods divided into multiple Release cycles. It is advisable to use the same length for every Release cycle when possible, but this may not always be possible for hardware product development.

5.1.1 Software Releases versus Hardware Releases

The worlds of software development and hardware development have significantly different concepts of what a Release cycle means.

The low cost of change for software development makes it possible for software teams to refine features at any time, to any degree desired. It is desirable for software teams to create a minimal feature that provides a useful solution and then to refine the feature iteratively over time. This refinement takes place in the context of a working software product. Release cycles thus become schedules for internal or external delivery of major new capabilities, within the context of a product that is intended to be functional at the end of each Release cycle.

Hardware development entails a high cost of change that largely precludes rapid feature-level iteration. Hardware products that are in development tend not to be usable or testable as a product until the bulk of development work has been done; that is, until the components and subsystems have been developed and assembled into some concept of the product as a whole. Thus, iterative refinement of the product's design may not be routinely possible at the level of usable features but requires refinement of the product as a whole. This means that the time scale for refinement of product capabilities may correspond very nearly to the time scale of overall product development, which is more often measured in months than weeks.

Thus, the concept of a Release cycle in hardware development tends to align in a natural way with product refinement cycles. We might, for example, have a product development lifecycle that spans three Release cycles whose purpose varies from one to the next in this fashion:

- The first Release cycle produces a full-featured prototype that works and is testable. Product testing, user experience testing, review by manufacturing experts, and other sources of insight feed into the next stage.

- The second Release cycle produces the first attempt at a design that can be manufactured (i.e., a manufacturing prototype). The functionality is now frozen, but it is common to discover issues that make the design not suitable for production.

- The third Release cycle produces the final product design, to be released to manufacturing

Figure 5.1 illustrates the flow of work in these cycles. The amount of time spent in each portion of the flow may vary radically from one cycle to the next, as "define" shifts from developing something for the first time to refining it in a subsequent cycle.

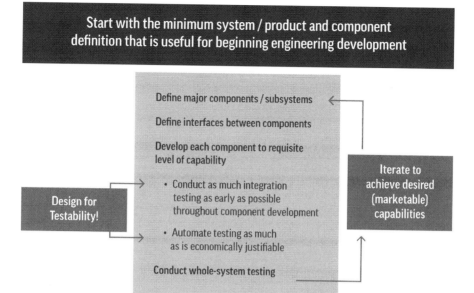

Start with the minimum system / product and component definition that is useful for beginning engineering development

Define major components / subsystems

Define interfaces between components

Develop each component to requisite level of capability

Design for Testability!

- Conduct as much integration testing as early as possible throughout component development

- Automate testing as much as is economically justifiable

Conduct whole-system testing

Iterate to achieve desired (marketable) capabilities

Figure 5.1: Product-Refinement Cycles for Hardware Development

These cycles need not have the same duration, and some might be broken into smaller Release cycles as needed. However, it is commonly the case that each of these product development lifecycle stages ends on the boundary of some Release cycle.

In all cases, it is important to realize that the scope of a long-term plan cannot be guaranteed at a fine level of detail. Scope and effort for product development are only poorly understood up front, which means that the longer the planning horizon, the greater the uncertainty about what can be accomplished. When we consider that scope changes are likely to occur for many reasons, it must be understood that no definition of scope for an interval longer than a few days can be considered reliable. Rather than guaranteeing scope to achieve some concept of success, we must rely more on controlling scope over time, to optimize value delivered.

5.1.2 Managing Quality throughout Release Cycles

The need for high quality is a major goal (and constraint) for every Release cycle. We plan and structure our work to ensure that the quality of our product, or the just-completed portion thereof, is of such a level that potential users of the product would be pleased with the quality. It may be that the product scope is not useful for general consumption at the end of a particular Release cycle, but the quality of what has been built to date should be high.

The development-related practices required to achieve such a level of quality are numerous, and beyond the scope of this chapter, but the following are key concepts:

- For software products, maintaining high quality all of the time requires a high level of test automation (and discipline to maintain that level), coupled with continuous integration and automated test execution on a roughly daily basis. This style of testing is required to detect *regression errors* introduced into previously working features during development of new features.

- For hardware products, a perfect analog of full test-automation and continuous integration may not be possible, but it is still valuable to perform as much in the way of frequent integration and testing of integrated subsystems as can be done to ensure that the quality that can be feasibly tested is always kept at a high level. Test automation is more expensive for hardware than it is for software but is worth pursuing when the benefits justify the investment.

One common technique for ensuring high quality at Release boundaries in software development is that of the Hardening Sprint. A Hardening Sprint focuses not on product development but on regression testing, integration testing, correction of regression and integration problems, and other activities that cannot be done earlier. Thus, we freeze the scope of the product at the start of the Hardening Sprint and perform these activities on a stable product definition.

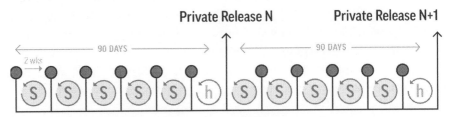

Figure 5.2: Release Cadence with Hardening Sprints

Figure 5.2 shows a Release cadence consisting of five development-oriented Sprints, followed by a Hardening Sprint. Although the product in this example is released to production after the latter of these two Release cycles, we want to keep quality high as we go, and ensure overall product quality at the end of each Release cycle, in order to avoid accumulation of defects.

While the *content* of a Hardening Sprint may be quite different from a normal "Development Sprint," the *conduct* is the same. We define the scope of work to be done in Stories, and then plan, execute (via Swarming), and track work exactly as we do for any other Sprint. The content of the Stories, though, is about integration testing and other work to be done while the product state is frozen. A Technical Story might then define a set of regression tests for a particular functional area or component and have included in its estimate time to fix any regression defects encountered while testing in this area.

Hardening Sprints normally have the same length as regular Sprints, and for the same reason: a standard length simplifies scheduling. If, unfortunately, the Hardening activities require more than a standard Sprint length, then we would have an additional Hardening Sprint (or more) as needed. Obviously, we should do as much as possible to reduce the time dedicated to Hardening over time.

It is possible that the Hardening work might require less than a full Sprint's duration, in which case the question arises as to what else the teams should do. The answer is that they should do whatever makes sense, as long as they plan the work. It is acceptable, for example, for a team to devote the first two thirds of the Hardening Sprint to hardening work, and the last one third to developmental work, provided that they employ strategies (such as branching) to ensure that the new work does not invalidate the hardening work they have just completed.

Viewed in this light, a Hardening Sprint is not so much a Sprint dedicated exclusively to Hardening but a Sprint designated as the one in which Hardening will occur, which is a somewhat different concept.

The concept of a Hardening Sprint makes less sense for hardware products, as hardware products do not accumulate functionality the way that software products do. Instead, integration testing is simply folded into the work of various Sprints over time.

5.2 Overview of Roles and Process

In this section I assume, for convenience, that the Project-level work is accomplished by Scrum Teams. However, any process can be used at the Project level, as long as the required interfaces are maintained. For our purposes, the interfaces are defined by assigning roles analogous to Scrum Master and Team Product Owner for each team, and having those roles participate in the Program-level ceremonies described below. (In classic project management world, the roles might be Project Manager and Product Manager.)

In this conception of Agile Program Management, then, the collaborating teams work in *Release* cycles. The set of collaborating teams has no specific name as such and is most commonly referred to as "the teams," with the understanding that these teams must collaborate in planning and executing work in order to create large-scale products or capabilities.

The *Area Product Owner*[24] engages with customers and stakeholders to understand their needs, develop high-level concepts of solutions, and validate recently completed functionality and plans for next steps in product development. These sessions might be held at monthly intervals and serve to guide future development as much by identifying deficiencies in recent work and plans as by developing new directions.

The Area Product Owner collaborates with *Team Product Owners* in weekly *Product Owner Scrum-of-Scrums Meetings* to clarify how the big-picture needs (in the form of *Epics*) will be distributed across Scrum Teams and to review and revise the status of work and plans. The Team Product Owners then collaborate with their associated teams to write Stories, and to plan and monitor the implementation of deliverables. This ongoing collaboration generates a steady flow of specifications into the Product Backlogs of the different Scrum Teams.

The *Program Manager* facilitates a *Release Planning Meeting* before the start of the next Release cycle, in which the set of Scrum Teams plans the work and schedule of the next release. The Release Plan defines an initial Release Backlog (subset of the Product Backlog) for each Scrum Team, and the teams work through their Backlog Items in rank order throughout the Sprints in the Release cycle.

During the Release cycle, the Program Manager facilitates semi-weekly *Scrum-of-Scrums Meetings*, to maintain a coherent understanding of cross-team developmental work, clarify cross-team impacts, and identify cross-team issues that require assistance to resolve. A representative from each Scrum Team (usually the Scrum Master) attends these meetings.

At the end of the Release cycle, the Area Product Owner facilitates the *Release Review Meeting*, in which the Area and Team Product Owners review the completed deliverables of the Release, make final go / no-go decisions on the Release, and identify modifications to be planned for the future. The Program Manager likewise facilitates the *Release Retrospective Meeting*, in which the Scrum Masters, Area and Team Product Owners, and (optionally) Team members identify how to improve the overall process for future Release cycles.

5.3 Roles

This organizational level adds two roles beyond the basic Team-level Scrum roles: the Area Product Owner and the Program Manager.

In a small organization, the role of Product Owner includes both outward (customer) and inward (team) facing responsibilities. In larger organizations, these responsibilities must be split into separate roles:

- The Team Product Owner writes User Stories, collaborates with Team members to ensure the appropriate Technical Stories are written, ranks deliverables for a Scrum Team, and monitors the development to ensure that the deliverables are as desired.
- The Area Product Owner is responsible for addressing overall customer needs, and the development of big-picture solutions.

Roughly speaking, the former Product Owner can now be considered to be the Team Product Owner, while the Area Product Owner is defined as below.

Team Product Owner: The sole authority over a team's deliverables (definition and sequencing), for up to three Teams. Responsibilities include:

- Writing User Stories for implementation by Scrum Teams
- Collaborating with Team members to ensure necessary Technical Stories are written
- Providing near real-time guidance to team during implementation and testing of deliverables
- Reviewing and approving deliverables

Area Product Owner: The sole authority over product requirements, and the intended content of each Release cycle. Responsibilities include:

- Working with customers and stakeholders to identify needs, solutions, and business value.
- Working with Team Product Owners and Program Managers to develop sufficient detail about requirements and cost (based on development and testing effort) to support useful ROI estimates
- Developing Business Case for Product Releases, for use in Portfolio planning.
- Monitoring changes in business needs, and work with Team Product Owners to revise the planned Product Release content as needed.
- Providing ongoing guidance to Team Product Owners regarding cross-team priorities and tradeoffs.

Program Manager: Works closely with teams' Scrum Masters or Project Managers to ensure that cross-team collaboration is effective in achieving the Product's Release goals. Responsibilities include:

- Enforcing agreements on how cross-team collaboration is done
- Facilitating cross-team meetings

- Monitoring cross-team dependencies, and ensuring that these are planned and addressed effectively
- Assessing impact of development issues and scope changes on cross-team dependencies and overall execution
- Monitoring progress in the Release cycle
- Ensuring that risks are addressed effectively during planning and execution
- Removing obstacles to effective cross-team collaboration

The relationship between roles and the team-oriented structure of the organization is illustrated in the following diagrams. Figure 5.3 shows an example of six Scrum Teams, divided into three pairs of teams that develop three products. In this example, each team has an associated Team Product Owner, and each product has an associated Area Product Owner.

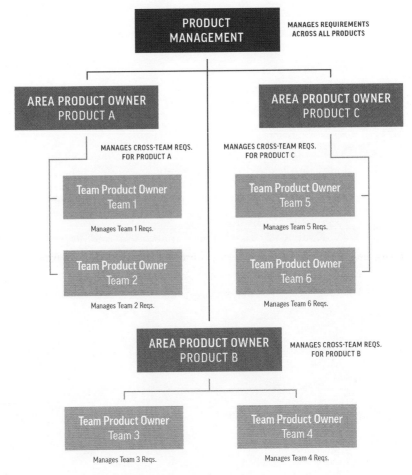

Figure 5.3: Product Owners and Team Hierarchy

Similarly, Figure 5.4 shows the same hierarchy but now focuses on the roles associated with managing execution, namely the Program Manager and Scrum Masters.

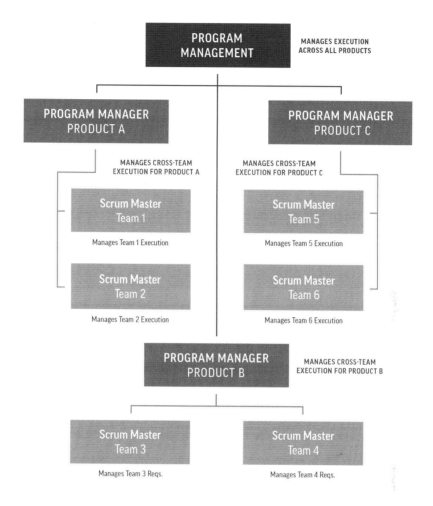

Figure 5.4: Program Manager and Scrum Masters and Team Hierarchy

5.4 Ratios and Rules for Roles

One person can fulfill the role of Scrum Master for up to three teams concurrently, provided all three teams are working on one product. If teams are working in completely unrelated products or areas, then this person can support no more than two teams in the role of Scrum Master. This does not mean that any one person can be Scrum Master for three teams at one time, just that the limit of three should never be exceeded. For example, one person might be Scrum Master for three teams of five people each, but if each team has nine Team members, then a single Scrum Master might be fully loaded with just two teams to handle.

The number of teams supported by a single Team Product Owner is the same as for a Scrum Master, and for the same reasons.

A single Area Product Owner most commonly has overall responsibility for one product, or a subset of a large product, and collaborates with up to five Team Product Owners.

Finally, a single Program Manager likewise collaborates with up to five Scrum Masters.

What	Limits
Team	3–9 people
Scrum Master	Supports up to 3 Teams
Team product Owner	Supports up to 3 Teams
Program Manager	Collaborates with up to 5 Scrum Masters
Area Product Owner	Collaborates with up to 5 Team Product Owners

Table 5.1: Numeric Limits for Scrum Roles and Teams

The above ratios imply that an Area Product Owner or Program Manager will work, through intermediaries, with up to fifteen teams each. Fifteen teams of up to nine people each can encompass a maximum set of 135 development and testing personnel. An organization that has significantly more than 100 Team members will usually have more than one product as well, with each product having its own set of the above roles.

Finally, it is desirable to have each Scrum Master paired with a single Team Product Owner, so that they support the same teams. This practice reduces the communication paths involved in cross-team collaboration.

5.5 Agile Team Definitions

In this section, I will review strategies for organizing people into teams, using Scrum Teams as the example.

While occasional exceptions may exist, teams are generally not interchangeable. Each team has a focus of some kind and performs all of the organization's work that falls into that focus. Each team has its own priorities, plans, and schedule of work, and members of the team can collaborate informally on an as-needed basis.

The membership of a Scrum Team should be stable over time. Exactly how much stability is required is hard to pin down, but I recommend changing membership no more often than quarterly. The creation of Scrum Teams is therefore a strategic decision, as the team definitions are intended to last anywhere from multiple quarters to multiple years.

Why is stability of membership important? The reason is that it takes time for the Team members to become used to working together. The time required for a team to reach maximum effectiveness is on the order of a few months. If we change membership frequently, we disrupt the patterns of collaboration so frequently that the team never achieves high effectiveness.

5.5.1 Hierarchical Organization

Subdivision of a large organization's engineering and testing personnel into teams commonly yields a hierarchical organization. One set of people comprises a team, while a particular product is built by a set of teams, and the organization as a whole may produce many products.

The different groups and people interact with varying degrees of intensity. In a well-structure organization, we hope to see the pattern of Figure 5.5:

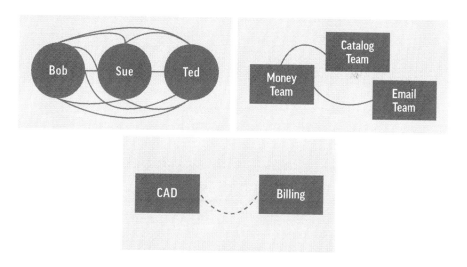

Figure 5.5: Interaction Patterns for Effective Team Hierarchies: Intra-Team, Cross-Team, and Cross-Product Interactions

Coupling decreases as we go higher in the hierarchy.

Interactions within a team are frequent, occurring multiple times per day between Team members, and requiring no special effort for coordination. Team members meet and talk informally, as needed, in real time. They need to interact frequently because they are building small deliverables together, quickly.

Interactions between teams occur less frequently than between members of the same team. While teams need to collaborate to build a product, interactions may occur once a day or less, often on a routine cadence (e.g., twice weekly).

Similarly, interactions between linked products (each produced by a set of teams) are even less frequent. These interactions will occur as needed, but typically on an as-needed basis, monthly or even less often.

5.5.2 Interfaces and Cost of Interaction

The interaction patterns of Figure 5.5 are desirable because they are relatively inexpensive.

Interactions between individuals in the same team have a low cost of interaction because they sit together, and interaction requires no special arrangements or synchronization. The team as a whole has a schedule of work, and team members collaborate informally to get work done, in whatever fashion they need.

Cross-team collaboration crosses an interface between teams. The interface is the boundary between the teams and refers to the division between one team's planned work and another's. Each team has a plan (i.e., agenda, goal, and schedule) for this or subsequent Sprints. Any collaboration across that interface requires effort: effort to schedule, effort to prepare, and effort to conduct. While the actual conduct of the interaction may be no greater than for an intra-team interaction, the effort to prepare is commonly greater, and the effort to schedule the work may be substantial. Moreover, any change to the scheduled interaction requires re-scheduling the work of multiple teams, which costs more effort.

From this observation, I have developed the following guide to team definition:

The key driver for defining optimal teams is the minimization of interaction cost. Thus, we should define teams in a way that minimizes the cost of cross-team interactions, by minimizing the number of cross-team interactions required to develop the product over time.

This principle plays out in different ways for different scenarios, as described below.

5.5.3 Feature Teams

The most common advice for dividing a large group of people into collaborating Scrum Teams is to divide them into groups that satisfy the numeric constraints of Section 5.4 and assign to each team a subset of the product's functionality. These are usually called *Feature Teams*, and this strategy often works well for software-product development. Each team then "owns" its subdomain of the product and contains all of the skills needed to implement and test capabilities in that area, across all types of technology that are required to produce those user-facing capabilities.

For example, suppose we are building a project management product that has three logical categories of user experience: requirements definition, planning, and tracking. If we have fifteen people who develop and test product features, then we might allocate them to three teams of five people each and have one or two Scrum Masters and Team Product Owners for the set of teams. We might call these the Requirements Team, the Planning Team, and the Tracking Team.

Each team would contain all of the skills needed to do that team's work, such as user-interface development, application logic development in some programming language(s), database development, test-plan and test-case development, test automation, test execution, and so forth.

This approach assumes that design and architecture work is done by all teams, and that each team can modify and grow the architecture of the product as needed, as long as they take care not to disrupt dependent teams with unexpected changes.

5.5.4 Client / Server Teams

Feature Teams become less attractive for software products that have multiple clients and one or more back-end services. Clients communicate with the back-end services, but not with each other. Most commonly, the product provides a set of capabilities through multiple clients, such as a Web client and multiple mobile devices. Trying to separate teams along lines of product subdomains requires at least one developer per client type per team, which is costly.

It is often better to have one or more back-end teams, and one client team per client device. This approach requires more cross-team collaboration than does the Feature-Team approach but can be less costly overall.

5.5.5 Component Teams

Another alternative to Feature Teams is to organize people into *Component Teams*. With this model, each team owns a portion of the technical architecture, and it may be that only a subset of the components has a user experience for users of the completed product or solution. (All components have *consumers* of their functionality, but often in the form of other components.) The drawback to this approach is that it requires a higher level of cross-team collaboration and is therefore more costly and prone to errors, compared with the Feature Team approach.

Component Teams are common for hardware products, and products that have multiple client applications and multiple back-end server applications. They are also common for mixed hardware / software environments, such as telecommunications products. In the latter case, customers buy solutions that may contain a large number of components that work together, and do not think in terms of buying products at all.

This model has the highest cost of cross-team interactions, as many user-facing capabilities impact multiple teams, multiple components, and perhaps multiple products. However, it tends to be the only practical solution for these complex scenarios, as attempts to define Feature Teams yield even higher cross-team interaction costs.

In this scenario, a key element for success is the ability to define component interfaces that are flexible and change slowly over time, to minimize the ripple effects of changes in any one component. This "loosely coupled" architecture should always be a focus of development.

5.6 Ceremonies

The Program-level ceremonies listed below in Table 5.2 provide a full range of opportunities for effective collaboration. However, and unlike the Project-level ceremonies presented in earlier chapters, these should not all be considered necessary by default.

Large organizations probably will need all of these ceremonies. Smaller organizations may find that a subset meets their needs, and then introduce others as they grow.

A set of three collaborating teams might require only the Scrum-of-Scrums meetings. If the organization needs to plan over a Release cycle, to avoid frequent problems with unsatisfied cross-team dependencies, then Release Planning becomes necessary. If the organization is large, contains multiple products, and has a Portfolio Management layer, then all of these ceremonies would be needed.

If several teams collaborate to build products or solutions, it is best for all teams to have the same Sprint schedule. For example, five collaborating Scrum Teams should begin their Sprints on, say, Wednesday and end their Sprints on the second following Tuesday. This alignment simplifies planning, tracking, and collaboration, while misalignment complicates and degrades all of them.

Note that alignment of Sprint boundaries does not mean that all teams must have their internal meetings on matching schedules. For example, Teams 1 and 2 might share a Scrum Master, who cannot attend all meetings for both teams if the meetings occur at the same times. Thus, if all teams start Sprints on a Wednesday, then Team 1's Sprint Planning meeting might occur the preceding Tuesday afternoon, while Team 2's Sprint Planning meeting occurs Wednesday morning. Such accommodations to necessity are common, and appropriate, as long as the resulting schedules work for everyone.

Ceremony	Time Box	Input	Output	Value
Release Planning meeting	1–3 days, before start of first Sprint in Release cycle	Epics and PBIs, per Team, with initial ranking	Release Plan: • Epics & PBIs+ estimates • Preliminary Sprint backlogs • Dependencies, esp. Cross-Team	Teams have an initial plan to create the Release Stakeholders have a concept of deliverables planned for the Release
Release Backlog Refinement	1 hr, weekly	Concepts for major initiatives	Scope of specification work to be done by Team Product Owners Consensus on big-picture goals, concepts	Ensures specifications are developed for long-term plans
Product Owner Scrum-of-Scrums meeting	1 hr, weekly	Status of Release In-progress work of Team Product Owners	Impediments raised, follow-up actions identified Modifications to Release Scope	Area, Team Product Owners on same page re: progress and impediments Scope control for Release
Scrum-of-Scrums meeting	1 hr, semi-weekly	In-progress work	Impediments raised Cross-Team issues and impacts understood Follow-Up actions identified and owned	Improved awareness of Cross-Team impacts Cross-Team issues addressed
Release Review	3 hrs, at end of Release cycle	Work completed by end of Release cycle	Go / no-go decision for regarding completed work	Ensures quality and business value justifies is at the level desired
Release Retrospective	3 hrs, at end of Release cycle	Release performance data, e.g., Burn-Up chart	List of improvements for next Release cycle, with owners	Learn from experience, enable continuous improvement

Table 5.2: Program-Level Scrum Ceremonies

SUN	MON	TUE	WED	THU	FRI	SAT	
18	19	20	21	22	23	24	**MARCH**
25	26	27	28	29	30	31	

SUN	MON	TUE	WED	THU	FRI	SAT	
1	2	3	4	5	6	7	**APRIL**
8	9	10	11	12	13	14	
15	16	17	18	19	20	21	
22	23	24	25	26	27	28	
29	30	1	2	3	4	5	

SUN	MON	TUE	WED	THU	FRI	SAT	
29	30	1	2	3	4	5	**MAY**
6	7	8	9	10	11	12	
13	14	15	16	17	18	19	
20	21	22	23	24	25	26	
27	28	29	30	31	1	2	

SUN	MON	TUE	WED	THU	FRI	SAT	
27	28	29	30	31	1	2	**JUNE**
3	4	5	6	7	8	9	
10	11	12	13	14	15	16	
17	18	19	20	21	22	23	
24	25	26	27	28	29	30	

RELEASE PLANNING MEETING: ▓   PO SCRUM-OF-SCRUMS MEETING: ▓   RELEASE REVIEW: ▒
RELEASE BACKLOG REFINEMENT: ■   SCRUM-OF-SCRUMS MEETING: ▓   RELEASE RETROSPECTIVE: ▥

Figure 5.6: Typical Release Schedule

The durations of the Time Boxes are suggestions and should be modified based on experience. They should always be kept to as short a time as will suffice, to minimize overhead.

Ideally, all roles for all teams participate in the Release Planning meeting. This approach becomes more difficult as the number of participating teams grows and as geographic distribution increases. At some point, the concept of a single Release Planning meeting may have to be replaced by a longer Release Planning process, during which the Release Plan is developed incrementally over a few weeks, by the serialized and iterative participation of all teams and roles involved. However, the output (the *Release Plan*) remains the same.

The Scrum-of-Scrums meeting provides a standard forum to address cross-team issues, which occur frequently when teams collaborate to build a product. The Release Review provides a final opportunity to make a go / no-go decision for the product Release, as well as an opportunity to sharpen awareness of the product features. The Release Retrospective captures lessons learned from the Release cycle and produces a list of action items whose purpose is to improve the organization's ability to build products.

When developing integrated systems that contain both hardware and software components, the Scrum-of-Scrums meetings will frequently address integration plans and issues, including hardware-to-hardware, software-to-hardware, and software-to-software integration.

Figure 5.6 shows a typical schedule of the above ceremonies for a three-month Release cycle.

5.6.1 Release Planning

Teams that must collaborate perform Release Planning prior to the start of the next Release cycle. Release Planning is usually scheduled to be done the week before the start of the Release cycle. (The term "Sprint 0" is often used to describe the period in which this planning work is performed.)

The first Sprint Planning meeting of the Release cycle should not follow the Release Planning meeting immediately, as a few days of preparation will be required to get ready for the Sprint Planning meeting. For example, if a three-day Release Planning meeting begins on Monday of one week, the first Sprint Planning meeting to follow might be scheduled for Monday of the following week.

The purpose of Release Planning is to produce a Release Plan, which is an initial map of Epics and PBIs to teams and Sprints in the Release cycle. As always in Scrum, the sequencing of work is driven by value, but constrained by dependencies, and must fit into the estimated Velocity for each Sprint in the Release cycle. The Velocity information comes from the Scrum Masters, who estimate their teams' Velocity values over the course of Sprints in the planned Release cycle.

Release Planning can be done in one large, often two-day, meeting or incrementally. Both approaches are considered here.

5.6.1.1 Single Release-Planning Meeting

The Program Manager facilitates this meeting, while the Area Product Owner provides overall guidance about the product definition and business needs.

The Release-Planning meeting can be quite large, as all members of all collaborating Scrum Teams attend, along with the Area Product Owner, Program Manager, and a scattering of other participants and stakeholders (e.g., executives, user experience, IT, manufacturing, marketing, etc.). Consequently, Release Planning can be an expensive process, as we may need one or two full days of time from all of these people.

The value of the Release Plan must justify the cost of Release Planning, or Release Planning is not worth doing. Common drivers for Release Planning include:

1. Reduction in confusion due to planning cross-team dependencies
2. The need to understand how and when external resources must be engaged
3. The need to plan for customer commitments

Following any introductory presentations desired, the participants meet in one large room, with one team per table. Team Product Owners bring printed Stories and Epics for consideration in the planning session. Some part of the group must also set up the planning board as a grid pattern on a wall, with rows for teams and columns for sprints.

Each team works through a stack of PBIs provided by their Team Product Owner. Each team estimates any PBIs and Epics not previously estimated, identifies and fills gaps, identifies cross-team dependencies, and drafts its part of the Release Plan (as shown in Figure 5.7). Teams notify each other of cross-team dependencies and negotiate how and when to schedule the associated work. They iterate through drafts of the Release Plan until they believe the plan is viable.

It is common for a team to have to estimate around one hundred specifications (PBIs and Epics) in Release Planning meetings. The volume of estimates required precludes careful analysis of each item, so teams commonly use the Affinity Estimation technique (Figure 5.8) to work through these items in a couple of hours.

After estimation has been completed, teams create plans by taping each Epic and Story to the planning board, allocating them to Sprints based on sizing and Sprint Velocity. One wall might display these items five rows (one per team), with cross-team dependencies marked by ribbons or tape from predecessor to successor (see Figure 5.7). Note that PBIs may not cross Sprint boundaries, while Epics (which are placeholders for sets of PBIs yet to be written) may cross Sprint boundaries.

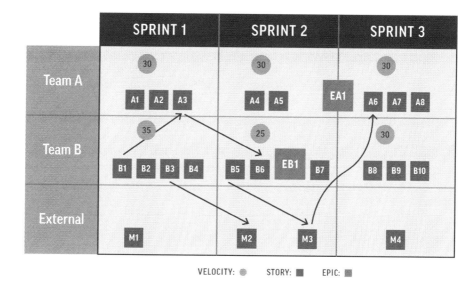

Figure 5.7: A Release Plan, as It Appears in the Release Planning Meeting

Release Planning is applicable for teams that are not using Scrum, as long as they are involved in work related to the product. The row labeled "External," for example, might represent one or more groups that use Waterfall, or some other process that does not plan in terms of Sprints. However, those teams will still have some conception of deliverables or milestones over time and can lay them out on the Release calendar as shown above. Examples of such teams might include marketing, operations, manufacturing, and so forth. It is important that all parts of the organization that need to be involved in planning do in fact participate in the planning meeting, and it is common to have several rows for "non-Scrum" groups.

The Program Manager is response for ensuring that this array of paper is ultimately captured in condensed form as the Release Plan. I normally recommend that the Scrum Team members split the load of data entry into whatever Web-based tool the organization uses for planning and tracking.

All five roles participate in the Release Planning meeting. The teams do the bulk of the work, with Scrum Masters facilitating as needed, and Team Product Owners providing guidance regarding specifications.

The Area Product Owner and Program Manager participate as needed. The Area Product Owner provides the big-picture guidance regarding the product definition and business value and is ultimately responsible for scope tradeoff decisions. The Program Manager focuses on ensuring that cross-team dependencies are identified, as they will be involved in ensuring those dependencies are handled effectively during execution.

Finally, all parties should be aware that the Release scope may change dramatically, if business or technology drivers change. This is normal and expected. Everyone should be aware of this key point:

Success is determined not by implementing the scope of the initial Release Plan, but by managing scope throughout the Release cycle, so that the evolving Release Plan always remains achievable, and delivers the best possible value for the effort expended during the Release cycle.

5.6.1.2 Incremental Release Planning

While the preceding section presents a common way to do Release Planning, alternatives are possible. The various roles may collaborate, formally or informally, in a number of shorter meetings, to assemble a Release Plan in increments. This approach may be more practical for environments where logistical issues make the default approach impractical, such as geographic distribution of Team members. What matters is that the Release Plan be completed in time, and that the teams involved have confidence that the plan is achievable. That said, it is definitely preferable to have the work be done swiftly, with all participants physically present, even at the cost of substantial travel for many.

There are no hard-and-fast rules about how to do incremental Release Planning, but this section gives some guidance. This approach is most commonly driven by the need to collaborate across distributed groups, and often makes extensive use of collaboration tools such as Web meetings, videoconferencing, wikis, and so forth.

5.6.1.2.1 Scope Development and Estimation

Team Product Owners write Epics and PBIs to be used in planning a future Release, weeks to months prior to when the Release Plan must be complete. Team members then provide estimates for these items in Backlog Refinement or Sprint Planning meetings, in addition to estimates for PBIs to be addressed in the Sprint being planned.

Epics and PBIs are critical, but do not provide all required scope information. Architectural guidelines, mock-ups, interface definitions, and other documents are also necessary. These documents may exist to provide general guidance or may (as with mock-ups) be intended to be referenced by specific PBIs and Epics.

5.6.1.2.2 Release Plan Development

Team Product Owners and Scrum Masters collaborate informally to draft their teams' portions of the Release plan. They seek teams' guidance and feedback as required, either informally or in Backlog Refinement meetings. As always in Scrum, the sequencing of work is driven by value, but constrained by dependencies, and must fit into the estimated Velocity for the Release.

The group of Program Manager, Area Product Owner, Scrum Masters, and Team Product Owners hold a series of mini-Release Planning meetings, each of which produces a new draft of the Release Plan that takes into account issues and dependencies identified to date. In between these meetings, the teams review the plans and provide feedback. This sequence completes when the participants agree that the Release Plan is reliable enough to meet their goals.

5.6.2 Release Backlog Refinement

The purpose of Release Backlog Refinement is to ensure that specifications are developed for long-term initiatives, such as for one or more future Release cycles. This meeting provides a recurring opportunity for Area and Team Product Owners to collaborate in developing such specifications. The Area Product Owner facilitates the meeting.

The meeting has no formal agenda, but typically involves these activities:

- The Area Product Owners provide new information about long-term product priorities, new market opportunities, major customer issues that need to be addressed, and big-picture solutions or capabilities to be developed. The Area and Team Product Owners discuss which major deliverables to write up (often as Epics, at this stage), and decide how to allocate deliverables (and the work of developing their specifications) across the Team Product Owners.

- Team Product Owners collect feedback on Epics and PBIs they have developed, primarily from the Area Product Owner, but also from each other, and incorporate this feedback into subsequent revisions of their Epics and PBIs.

5.6.3 Product Owner Scrum-of-Scrums Meeting

The purpose of this meeting is for Area and Team Product Owners to report their personal work status to each other, and to assess progress toward the Release goals. The Area Product Owner facilitates the meeting.

The status information is simple. Each participant summarizes, briefly,

1. What work I've done since our last meeting
2. What I'm planning to do before our next meeting
3. Issues that are interfering with my progress

Unless blocking issues have solutions that can be described quickly (say, in a minute), the standard response to issues is to identify who will meet to address them after this meeting. This approach keeps this meeting acceptably brief.

Next, someone (often the Area Product Owner) shows the Burn-Up chart and describes how well or poorly progress agrees with the plan. If progress is not satisfactory (meaning the planned Release scope may not be attainable), the participants discuss how best to address the problem.

In order of decreasing frequency, the most common responses include:

- Reducing the scope of one or more product capabilities
- Reducing Release scope by dropping capabilities entirely
- Moving the Release date out
- Deciding to request more people be assigned to work on the product

If progress exceeds expectations, then the participants usually decide what to add to the scope and modify plans accordingly.

5.6.4 Scrum-of-Scrums Meeting

The purpose of this meeting is to highlight and address current cross-team issues and impacts so that no such issues linger very long without attention.

The Program Manager facilitates the meeting, which is attended by one or two people from each team. Some teams send Team members, whose technical expertise is needed at the meetings. Most send Scrum Masters, whose attendance at this meeting protects the working time of a Team member who would otherwise have to attend.

Each participant provides two kinds of information, in a quick round-robin fashion:

1. What my team is doing that may affect other teams

2. What issues or impediments my team is experiencing, which may impact other teams or were caused by other teams, and which need to be addressed

Participants identify who will follow up to resolve issues and generally collaborate afterwards to ensure issues are resolved. The Program Manager will typically capture information about issues and follow-up actions, and then track issue resolution or bring in other resources required to ensure resolution. The Program Manager will also review cross-team dependencies in the meeting and work with participants to save threatened dependencies, or to create optimum fallback plans when a dependency fails.

5.6.5 Release Review

This is a very simple meeting of the Area and Team Product Owners, at the end of the Release cycle, facilitated by the Area Product Owner. The purpose of the Release Review is to confirm that the objectives of the Release cycle were met, and, if not, to identify follow-on action. The Area Product Owner has the final authority to decide what actions to take, if any are needed.

Significant failures at this point are rare, as the Team and Area Product Owners have been monitoring progress throughout the entire Release cycle. Nevertheless, it is still a good practice to provide one final time to review what has been done before moving on to the next Release cycle.

5.6.6 Release Retrospective

The purpose of this meeting is to identify ways to improve the entire Release process. The Program Manager facilitates, and the Scrum Masters and Team Product Owners attend. Attendance by others (e.g., Area Product Owner) is optional and decided locally.

Scrum Masters and Team Product Owners should prepare by bringing issues from their teams that are relevant for this meeting, that is, which cannot be handled at the team level. Aside from this bit of preparation, the conduct of this meeting is identical to that of a team Retrospective meeting and will not be repeated here.

Note that recommendations from this meeting often require management or executive approval and action.

5.7 Estimation for Release Planning

The particular challenge for estimation in Release Planning is the number of items requiring estimates. It is not uncommon to require estimates for a few hundred Stories, Epics, and Defects. The Planning Poker technique of Section 3.4.4 is very effective at estimating a single Backlog Item but is too slow for practical use when the need is to estimate 100 items in a couple of hours. This section provides another approach to estimation that is more appropriate for such high-volume situations.

5.7.1 Units for Estimation in Release Planning

Practitioners in the Scrum world often state that each team should be allowed to select its own units for estimating PBIs. This preference is harmless for Scrum Teams that work alone but introduces difficulties when teams must collaborate to develop and execute a Release Plan. Executives and other stakeholders want simple metrics for work completed or remaining in a Release, aggregated across teams, but such aggregation is not meaningful if teams estimate PBIs in different units.

Consequently, an organization may prefer to have some standardization of units across teams that must collaborate, such that a PBI of size "5" communicates a consistent concept of size to all teams. This kind of standardization is provided automatically if teams use time-based units for effort. If teams use relative sizing, standardization is more difficult, and requires developing a common reference scale for Story Points across the teams. My recommendation, therefore, is to adopt time-based units across the organization for all teams, to enable meaningful aggregation of information.

5.7.2 Estimation with the Affinity Estimation Technique

The most convenient method for estimating the PBIs and Epics that will comprise a Release cycle is to estimate them incrementally, over time, prior to Release Planning. However, Release Planning often necessitates estimating the effort of a large number of items in a short time, so I will address that need here.

The *Affinity Estimation* technique is an effective way to estimate many items, quickly. The usual three Scrum roles participate as follows.

The Product Owner prepares by printing out the relevant PBIs and Epics on paper or sticky notes and placing them on a table in the room where the estimation work will be done.

In the first part of the meeting, Team members sort items in order of increasing size from left to right, by taping them to a wall (or laying them on a table, etc.). Some practitioners recommend that this work be done without discussion, on the grounds that it will go faster. I find that some discussion is beneficial, as long as it is not too time-consuming. Either way, each Team member takes an item from the Backlog pile and places it on the sorting wall in the place he or she thinks is appropriate. The Team member also reviews items that have been placed on the wall and moves any that seem to be in the wrong place to the right place. The Team member then picks a new item off the Backlog pile and repeats.

Eventually, the Backlog pile disappears, and Team members focus on resorting items on the sorting wall. Any items that do not stabilize are removed for later consideration. This part of the meeting ends when the Scrum Master confirms with the team that sorting has completed.

In the second part of the meeting, Team members discuss where to draw lines denoting the size bins. I suggest using the pure Fibonacci sequence, rather than literally replicating the numbers from a Planning Poker card deck

(Section 3.4.4). The reason for this decision is that there some Epics may be larger than, say, 13, at which point the usual cards in the Planning Poker deck are not useful.

Any estimation technique that relies on the judgment of a group of people requires that the people have a sense for what the numbers mean. This need is best satisfied by choosing units such that the numbers are in the single-digit to low double-digit range. (For example, it is easier to understand "five person-months" than "8,000 person-hours.") In the context of Release Planning, the person-day unit makes sense. For larger efforts, such as estimation of large business initiatives, "person-weeks" or "person-months" may be more appropriate.

The appearance of a completed exercise in Affinity Estimation is illustrated in Figure 5.8.

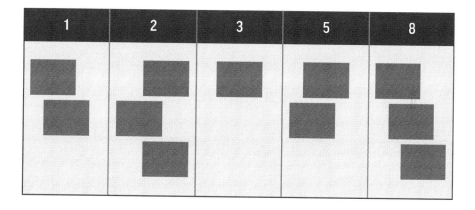

Figure 5.8: An Example of Affinity Estimation

The items grow in size from left to right. Items that are in approximate vertical alignment are about the same size.

If Team members are not all co-located, the fallback options include estimating with a co-located subset of the team or using online collaborative tools that simulate the sorting wall.

5.8 Tracking and Metrics

The key metric for tracking progress for a Product Release in a Release cycle is the Burn-Up chart.

Figure 5.9 is a typical Burn-Up chart, which shows progress toward a goal. The most common goal is the planned scope of a Release or Initiative, whose duration on the calendar spans multiple Sprints. The black scope line shows the effort that has been estimated for the planned scope, which varies over time due to scope changes and revisions to estimates. The bars show the amount of work associated with completed PBIs. The scope line and bars have the same units as the estimates for the PBIs. Ideally, the two curves will intersect at the end of the chart, indicating that the planned scope was completed on the planned end date. In practice, plans and estimates both evolve over time, so the chart is used to guide the scope-change decisions that will be required to meet the business objectives for the Release or Initiative.

A Burn-Up chart may show a single team's progress or show the aggregated progress across all teams working on a Product Release. Both views are useful.

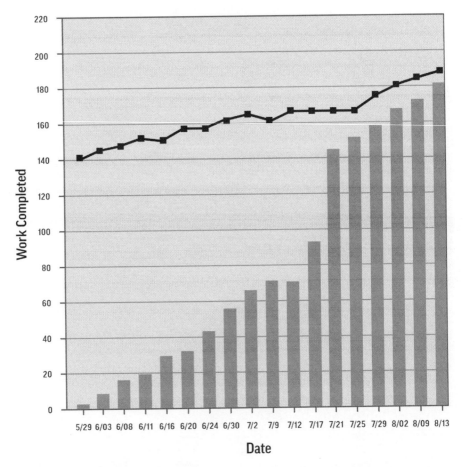

Figure 5.9: A Typical Burn-Up Chart

I look for two things in a Burn-Up chart:

1. Is work proceeding at a reasonably steady and predictable rate? If not, we need to investigate to understand the reasons, and identify appropriate corrective actions.

2. Is the scope achievable? Meaning, does the trend of progress intersect the scope line by the end of the Release cycle? If not, and if work is proceeding as well as can be expected, then the scope needs to be adjusted downwards. (Similarly, if the chart indicates that the planned scope will be completed early, more scope may be added to the Release cycle.)

6

Agile Portfolio Management

PORTFOLIO Management is about making strategic investment decisions for the organization. The Portfolio level is where business strategy informs and is informed by the practical decisions about how to invest the organization's assets to develop products and services. (Large companies may have multiple Portfolios, often associated with different business units.)

Organizations that develop products spend money in many areas. Areas such as accounting, building maintenance, and others may not have a very direct connection to product development but must still be funded. Our focus here is more about Portfolio Management for product development specifically than these other areas. However, as we will see, the finance and accounting functions do connect strongly to product development, and I will examine those links as well.

I consider Portfolio Management to be about defining, evaluating, planning, executing, and tracking the work of major business initiatives. *Agile Portfolio Management* refers to conducting Portfolio Management in an Agile way, using lightweight artifacts and techniques that enable rapid decision-making, enable rapid course changes when business needs require them, and use techniques for tracking that are simple, intuitive, and easy to understand.

Decisions that must be addressed in order for Portfolio Management to be effective include:

- How we define Business Cases for new Initiatives
- How we create Business Cases for new Initiatives
- What factors we consider when making Portfolio decisions
- What the benefits of an Initiative will be
- What the investment required for an Initiative will be
- How we handle risk
- How we decide which Initiatives to implement
- How we decide whether to continue, modify, or terminate an ongoing Initiative
- How we allocate resources to Initiatives over time
- How we handle financial issues (Budgeting and Capitalization)
- How we maintain alignment across Portfolio, Program, and Project levels in the organization

6.1 The Time Horizon for Portfolio Management

I suggest that organizations do Portfolio planning quarterly, for a time horizon of one to a few years. The resulting plan is high-level, coarse-grained, and long-term in nature. In some instances, the plan might be thought of as a product Roadmap, while in others, it is simply the major things the organization has decided to do and that require substantial investment.

I also suggest reviewing the Portfolio-level status of work monthly, rather than quarterly. The intent of monthly review meetings is to identify and select changes in scope or timing of ongoing work. The intent is not to introduce new Business Initiatives, as these are considered in the quarterly planning meetings.

6.2 Alignment and Governance

One of most common problems in Portfolio Management is failure to achieve alignment at all levels in the organization. The strategic vision painfully hammered out by upper management is not understood or executed well by the other layers of the organization. Different departments or development teams work according to local agendas that do not align with the strategic plans.

A common response to alignment failure is to add more governance in the form of additional reports and review meetings. These mechanisms are often burdensome and ineffective because they attempt to address a systemic problem with point solutions. Such attempts rarely work well.

What does work is to build governance into the processes used at all levels, in a way that is organic, lightweight, and perceived as valuable by all of the participants. The last part is crucial: if the people involved see governance as something imposed on them, and of no value to them, they are unlikely to appreciate the request to do more work that provides no benefits to them. However, if they see the value of governance in the course of their own work, they are much more likely to support it.

This line of reasoning brings us again to the concept of Agile governance. Each layer in my model structures its way of planning and working to incorporate governance that is immediately useful to that layer, and also supports interfaces to adjacent layers in a way that ensures alignment without need for additional effort.

Alignment is achieved in large part by having the same people (in the roles of Area Product Owner and Program Manager) participate in the Project, Program, and Portfolio levels, thus bringing awareness and continuity of experience to all three levels. The specific Program and Portfolio ceremonies in which these two roles participate also provide reliable opportunities to enable collaboration in ways that support alignment.

The following sections will lay out these techniques at the Portfolio level.

6.3 Portfolio Concepts

I will start with the concept of an *Initiative*. An Initiative is an endeavor to produce a specific set of deliverables; that is, it is a scope definition.* What distinguishes an Initiative from, say, a User Story or an Epic, is that it is the unit that is evaluated, funded, and planned at the Portfolio level.

At some point, an Initiative must be described in a *Business Case*. A Business Case is a document that provides a short description of the Initiative and includes information about the value and cost of the Initiative that will be used to guide Portfolio decisions. A major goal of Portfolio Management is to select Initiatives that provide an attractive *Return on Investment* (ROI). To make these decisions effectively, we therefore require some concepts of the Investment (cost or effort), and some concept of the Return (value) provided by the completed Initiative. Such information must therefore be estimated and described in the Business Case.

Initiatives that are chosen for implementation enter a Portfolio Backlog, that is, a queue of Initiatives awaiting development or in development. The Portfolio Backlog is similar to a Scrum Team's Product Backlog, with the exception that Initiatives do not leave the Portfolio Backlog to enter some analog to a Sprint Backlog once work on them begins. Initiatives leave the Portfolio Backlog when the work to implement them is completed.

---

* This definition resembles, but is not quite the same as, the classic concept of a project in project management. In project terminology, an Initiative is the scope of the project, not the project itself.

The scope of a particular Initiative may reside entirely within a single Area Product Owner's area of responsibility. In this case, the Area Product Owner will likely write the Business Case, and be responsible for subsequent scope definitions and scope changes throughout the development of the Initiative.

It is not uncommon for a particular goal (e.g., a new product introduction) to span the domains of multiple Area Product Owners. In this case, we need one person to be responsible for the overall definition of the work, and to be the driver for scope decisions over time. I call this person an Initiative Owner.

The role of Initiative Owner is not as standardized as the other roles, but does fill an important need. When an Initiative is not owned by an Area Product Owner, the Initiative Owner must work with multiple Area Product Owners to get Business Cases developed for the different parts of the Initiative that fall in each Area Product Owner's domain. Subsequent development and monitoring of the Initiative then requires close interaction between the Initiative Owner and the Area Product Owners. This interaction is not formalized into specific meetings, but should be maintained at a degree that is useful for the people involved.

Initiative Owners are commonly executives or high-level managers.

The tracking of cross-area Initiative progress can be done by the standard Program Managers, or by designating a single person to aggregate tracking information from each area into an overall measure of progress. In the latter case, we are effectively creating an Initiative Program Manager for the Initiative. This person would then work closely with the Program Managers for the different areas to ensure that dependencies are planned and managed, and to get the tracking data required to understand overall progress on the Initiative.

6.4 Overview of Roles and Process

The overall guidance for Portfolio decisions comes from the *Portfolio Owner*. The Portfolio Owner works in conjunction with a *Portfolio Planning Team*, whose membership consists in large part of Area Product Owners, other Initiative Owners, and Program Managers. The Portfolio Owner sets the overall business objectives at a high level, and these in turn shape the set of Initiatives to be considered in the planning meetings.

An *Area Product Owner* provides a draft Business Case for an Initiative for review in *Portfolio Refinement Meetings*, for general feedback, and to get the necessary effort or cost estimates.* The relevant *Program Manager* is then

---

* There is no rule that other people cannot write Business Cases, and this may happen. However, every Business Case will fall into the domain of some Area Product Owner, who will have to shepherd the draft through refinement and into planning.

responsible for facilitating the estimation work with a group of technical experts chosen to contribute to this effort and for providing the estimates to the Area Product Owner for incorporation into the Business Case.

The Portfolio Owner facilitates review, discussion, and decision-making regarding Initiatives in *Portfolio Planning Meetings*. In these meetings, the Area Product Owners present their Business Cases for group review and discussion. The Portfolio Owner works with the Portfolio Planning Team to approve, reject, or schedule Initiatives for implementation.

The Portfolio Owner also facilitates *Portfolio Review Meetings* to assess what to do with in-flight Initiatives, based on their value, status, and business needs.

Finally, the Portfolio Planning Team conducts periodic *Retrospective* meetings to ensure improvement of their Portfolio-Management process over time.

6.5 Roles

This organizational level adds one role beyond the Program level: the Portfolio Owner. It also involves the two Program-level roles of Area Product Owner and Program Manager. The involvement of these two Program-level roles in both the Portfolio and Program levels is a strong contributor to the goal of alignment across levels. Similarly, the involvement of the Area Product Owner and Program Manager with teams at the Project level likewise contributes powerfully to the goal of alignment across all levels. With respect to roles, the Area Product Owners and Program Managers are the key enablers of alignment.

Portfolio Owner: The authority over Portfolio decisions. Responsibilities include:

- Providing overall guidance regarding business objectives
- Reviewing Business Cases
- Defining the priority or ranking of Initiatives
- Deciding whether to continue, revise, or terminate in-flight Initiatives
- Facilitating the Portfolio Planning and Portfolio Review meetings

Program Manager: The sole authority over cost and effort estimates. Responsibilities include:

- Ensuring cross-team collaboration is done well
- Facilitating effort or cost estimations for Initiatives
- Providing insight into team schedule and capacity information, for Portfolio planning purposes

Area Product Owner: The sole authority over product-scope decisions for approved Initiatives. Responsibilities include:

- Working with customers, stakeholders to define and prioritize product features
- Developing Business Cases for Initiatives
- Estimating the value expected from Initiatives
- Facilitating Portfolio Refinement meetings

6.6 Ceremonies

The Portfolio-level ceremonies listed in Table 6.1 below provide the necessary opportunities for collaborative decision-making, course corrections, and improvement necessary for effective Portfolio Management.

Ceremony	Time Box	Draft Business Cases	Output	Value
Portfolio Refinement	2 hrs, every 2 weeks	Draft Business Cases	Improved Business Cases and effort or cost estimates	Business Case ready for use in Portfolio Planning
Portfolio Planning	1 day, quarterly	Business Cases	Selected Initiatives added to Portfolio Backlog, with appropriate sequencing	New Initiatives are selected and queued for implementation
Portfolio Review	4 hrs, monthly	Status of in-flight Initiatives	Decisions to continue, cancel, or modify Initiatives	Optimize value delivery by addressing cost and changing needs
Portfolio Retrospective	2 hrs, quarterly	Initiative performance metrics, personal observations	List of improvements for the Portfolio Management process	Learn from experience, enable continuous improvement

Table 6.1: Portfolio-Level Ceremonies

The duration and timing of meetings may be adjusted as necessary. Meetings should always be kept to as short a time as will suffice, to minimize overhead.

6.6.1 Portfolio Refinement Meeting

The purpose of Portfolio Refinement meetings is to ensure that Business Cases are ready for use in future Portfolio Planning meetings. These meetings may be held as often as desired, with two weeks being a reasonable interval between meetings. Most Business Cases will require at least two such meetings to achieve the desired state of readiness, and three or four meetings for some would not be unreasonable.

In order for the Portfolio Planning meeting to be effective, these prerequisites must be satisfied:

- Each Business Case's descriptive content must be clear and complete.

- Each Business Case must have well-reasoned numbers for the Return factors.

- Each Business Case must have well-reasoned numbers for the Investment factors.

- Each Business Case must have a clear assessment of risks, and means for addressing the risks.

The Area Product Owner normally facilitates this meeting, which is attended by the Program Manager and other key personnel identified as appropriate. The latter set of people is very much a local decision and often includes senior technical and quality-assurance leads as well as others whose knowledge is relevant.

The Area Product Owner should provide a draft of one or more Business Cases for review prior to the meeting. In the meeting, the other participants ask clarifying questions and provide feedback on all aspects of the Business Case, for use in the Area Product Owner's revisions after the meeting.

A particular Business Case may be provided for multiple refinement meetings, as the Area Product Owner solicits and incorporates multiple rounds of feedback.

The Area Product Owner is responsible for coming up with numbers for the Return factors, but not for the Investment factors. For reasons of both domain expertise and the desire to avoid a conflict of interest, I require that the Program Manager be the person to drive estimation of the Investment factors. Techniques for estimation of both Return and Investment factors are discussed below in Section 6.9.

6.6.2 Portfolio Planning Meeting

The Portfolio Planning meeting is the key decision point for new Initiatives. The purpose of this meeting is to make decisions about whether or when to begin implementation of Initiatives.

The recommended frequency of this meeting is once per quarter. The interval between meetings need not be (and usually is not) the same as the planning horizon, as the latter typically spans a year or more. The quarterly planning meeting enables revision and extension of the current long-range plan.

The Portfolio Owner is the key decision maker and usually the facilitator of the meeting. The Area Product Owners and Program Managers attend the meeting, along with anyone else the Portfolio Owner believes should participate in the discussion.

The Portfolio Owner decides in advance which Business Cases should be reviewed in the meeting, and all participants should prepare for the meeting by reading the Business Cases ahead of time.

In the meeting, each Area Product Owner presents one or more Business Cases, describing the concepts, values, and investment costs. Participants then ask questions and discuss the pros and cons of the Initiative defined by the Business Case. This discussion is important but should be kept brief and to the point.

The discussion is subject to these rules:

- The Portfolio Owner may revise the Value factors of the Business Case, based on personal knowledge and information that emerges in the discussion.

- No one other than the Program Manager can override the estimates provided by the Program Manager. If the decision is made to change the scope of the Initiative, or new issues emerge that were not considered during estimation, then the Program Manager will facilitate an effort to generate new numbers, but otherwise the numbers stand.

After all Business Cases have been reviewed, the Portfolio Owner facilitates the decision process. I look at a variety of techniques used to make the Portfolio decisions in Section 6.11 but can make some general observations about this activity here:

- No decision-making technique is perfect. Their utility is in improving everyone's understandings of the benefits and tradeoffs. They should not be viewed as algorithms that make decisions, but as techniques for generating insights to be discussed in the process of decision-making.

- Not all considerations that impact decisions can be quantified and clarified prior to the meeting. These will emerge and be discussed in the meeting.

- Decisions are always constrained by ability to execute. The Program Manager's insights into teams' work status and capacity will be important considerations for decisions to be made in this meeting.

The main output of this meeting is the set of Initiatives selected for implementation and at least a rough concept of their sequencing. Additional refinement and planning may then be accomplished after the meeting, offline or in working meetings as needed.

6.6.3 Portfolio Review Meeting

The purpose of Portfolio Review meetings is to provide the opportunity to adjust course for Initiatives that are currently in process.

The recommended frequency of this meeting is once per month. Attendance at this meeting is essentially the same as for Portfolio Planning meetings. The Portfolio Owner is again the key decision maker and usually facilitates the meeting. The Area Product Owners and Program Managers attend the meeting, along with anyone else the Portfolio Owner believes should participate in the discussion.

The attendees review the standard progress metrics (primarily Burn-Up charts for each Initiative) and discuss deviations from the previous plans, changes in business environment, and any other topics that are relevant for the purpose of the meeting. Standard agenda items include:

- Area Product Owners' present status of in-flight Initiatives.
- All discussing benefits and drawbacks of continuing, revising the scope of, or terminating Initiatives.
- The Portfolio Owner deciding what to do with each Initiative.

6.6.4 Retrospective Meeting

The purpose and structure of the Retrospective meeting is essentially the same as for other levels. The purpose is to provide an opportunity to review how the process (in this case, Portfolio Management) has been working and to identify opportunities for improvement. The attendance is the same as for the Portfolio Planning and Review meetings, and the conduct of the meeting is identical to that of Retrospectives for the Project and Program levels.

6.7 The Business Case

I define a Business Case to be a document that describes the concept, value, cost, and scope of an Initiative. The purpose of a Business Case is to present the information that is needed in order to make decisions about when or whether to implement the Initiative. In my model, Area Product Owners write Business Cases as the first step along the road to the moment of that decision.

Note that there is no rule against other roles writing Business Cases, and they may. The situation is analogous to Product Owners writing User Stories, while Scrum Team members write Technical Stories. The distinction here is that creation of Business Cases will always be a responsibility of Area Product Owners, and they must become familiar with Business Cases drafted by other participants in the Portfolio Management process in order to understand, or represent, those perspectives.

When writing a Business Case, there is a natural tendency to provide exhaustive details to buttress the argument for supporting the Initiative. However, exhaustive detail is more likely to exhaust the patience of the readers than to benefit the writer. The people who have to read and understand a Business Case often have to read many of them, in a short period of time, and just want to learn the essentials of each, quickly. For this reason, I recommend that a Business Case be short, such as in the two-page template (Figure 6.1).

In the context of Portfolio Management, a Business Case will be presented to two very different audiences.

The first audience is the set of people who will be called upon to provide estimates of effort and cost. These tend to be people who want to dig into the details of the scope and implementation, want more information than can be provided, and have only a small number of Initiatives to consider at any one time. They tend to agonize over the estimates they are producing and worry about being wrong (often due to past experiences with criticism along these lines).

Risks to which this group is subject, when developing estimates, include:

- Underestimating the numbers due to optimism
- Overestimating the numbers in an effort to avoid criticism
- "Analysis Paralysis," or an inability to generate estimates in a reasonable time, due to a combination of fear and excessive focus on too many extreme but unlikely scenarios

These risks are best addressed by having someone who is experienced in such matters (typically, the Program Manager) facilitate the estimation session.

The second audience is the set of people who will review and discuss the relative merits of a set of Initiatives, in Portfolio Planning meetings. These people are typically very busy, have to read and understand a large number of Business Cases in a short time, and want short summary information to enable quick understanding and quick decisions.

Risks to which this group is subject, when engaged in decision-making, include:

- False confidence in the effort or cost estimates. Estimators are usually very aware of the limits on the reliability of their numbers, but other readers may err by assuming high reliability.

- Limited understanding of details. A short Business Case cannot cover all details.

These risks are best addressed by a combination of education, facilitation by someone (the Portfolio Owner) who is familiar with the limitations that are inherent in Business Cases, and the practical limits on our understanding of the Initiatives.

6.7.1 Business Case Format

Figure 6.1 shows a simple but useful format for a Business Case. The example is for a company that develops networked medical devices of various kinds, used primarily in hospital Critical Care Units to monitor patient vital signs in real time for signs of trouble. As costs have come down for these capabilities, the company wants to expand patient-monitoring capabilities into the general hospital population.

Unfortunately, the "quick and dirty" design of the original networked communication protocol is inefficient and uses a lot of network bandwidth by generating a large number of small messages. The result is that no local area network can host more than about fifty of these devices without saturating the network. In order to grow, then, the Agent software modules on the devices must be rewritten to use a richer message format, and a protocol that creates less traffic.

The format is quite different from the common Story / Epic format used at the Project and Program levels. The reason for the difference is that the Business Case is intended not as a specification for a deliverable, but as a summary of the information required to make effective Portfolio decisions. The content and style are therefore different.

The following sections describe the elements of the Business Case in more depth.

6.7.2 Scope Definition and Motivation

ID	1	Title	Upgrade embedded Agents to V2	ROI	2.2

Problem / Opportunity

The large volume of network traffic produced by the Agents in our medical devices means only about fifty devices can be in one network. Thus our three largest customers cannot add more of our devices to their networks. They are unable to provide the benefits of our monitoring services to patients outside of Critical Care Units, and we cannot sell more units to these customers. Also, we can expect to see negative comments in the trade literature if this problem isn't resolved by the end of Q3.

Benefits

This change will enable our large customers to expand monitoring capabilities to patients (typically outside CCUs) who are not well served by current solutions. We will be able to sell up to ten times as many of our medical devices to our large customers and avoid negative press regarding current network limits.

Impact / Opportunity Missed if not done

Our three largest customers will be frustrated with the current limits, and us, and we will not be able to sell more units to these customers. We can expect to be criticized in the press, and by our competitors, in Q3 and Q4 this year.

Description

This upgrade will allow customers to tailor device parameters (through the remote Administration console, or locally) to optimize performance. Even with no customization, default configurations should allow at least ten times the number of devices per site than is currently possible.

This upgrade requires major changes to the Agent, and smaller changes to the MMS Administration and Monitor applications.

The upgrade addresses these top requests from major hospitals

- Reduce average startup connection time from three minutes to thirty seconds, which shortens down time due to restarts
- Replace fixed polling intervals (typically 1 ms) with user-selected intervals. The new default of 500 ms will reduce the number of messages 500-fold.
- Provide for richer and more customizable information transmission via customizable XML encoding, with expanded metadata
- Enable System Administrators to tailor polling intervals, message content (including debug levels), and other parameters to optimize performance
- Maintain backward compatibility with previous communication protocols

Acceptance Criteria

- System works with at least 500 active devices, 50 monitors, and 5 administrative stations
- Upgraded monitor and admin stations support mix of V6 and earlier Agents in networked devices
- SysAdmin can set new parameters (polling intervals, logging levels, content of device reports)
- Agent connection time < 30 seconds after restarts (is now 3 minutes)

Decision Factors					
	Return		**Investment**		
Factor	NPV	Urgency	Effort	Tech. Risk	Standard
Weight	1	0.5	1	0.5	Standard
Factor	8	8	5	1	Per BC

Risk Management		
Risk	**Response (Avoid, Transfer, Mitigate, Accept)**	**Owner**
Developmental delays may make planned scope unachievable in required time frame.	Mitigate the risk by surveying largest customers to see which devices are most critical, and update agents for those first. This approach maximizes the value we can deliver and reduces risk of being unable to meet the most urgent customer needs.	C. Baker
We don't know if the desired connection time is achievable, and it may not be possible.	Accept the risk, since we will implement whatever improvement is achievable, and the result will be better than current performance.	N/A
Bendix Medical has threatened to sue us for lack of performance, if our next Agent upgrade doesn't meet their specs.	Transfer the risk to our Legal department. They will prepare for a possible suit and investigate insurance and other relevant options to mitigate the risk.	D. Fraser, in Legal
The TinyTime timer we'd planned to use for controlling transmission intervals has proven unreliable.	Avoid the risk by using JemTime, which S. Larkin has just finished testing and confirmed to be suitable.	S. Larkin

Figure 6.1: Sample Business Case for Agent-Upgrade Initiative

The *Title* is a short phrase or sentence that conveys the essence of the Initiative.

The *Problem / Opportunity* section provides the business context or motivation behind the Initiative. This section contains a short statement of the problem to be resolved, or the business opportunity to be presented.

The *Benefits* section explains the benefits to customers and the organization.

The *Impact / Opportunity Missed if not done* section clarifies the negative impacts of not pursuing the Initiative.

The *Description* section presents the scope of the Initiative. This is perhaps the most difficult part to write as a short, condensed summary, but it is also critical to have a short and understandable description. This section is analogous to the Narrative portion of a Story or Epic.

The *Acceptance Criteria* are specific criteria that must be validated as part of the implementation of the Initiative. This section has the same format and purpose as the Acceptance Criteria for a Story or Epic.

The remaining portions of the Business Case represent major topic areas and are addressed below.

6.8 Introduction to Decision Factors

Many different factors could, in principle, be addressed in making Portfolio decisions. One of the challenges in Portfolio Management is to identify the set of factors that must be considered, and to keep that set to a reasonable size. While it may be tempting to identify a comprehensive set of factors, the practical reality is that more is generally not better, and the most useful strategies focus on a small number of truly critical factors.

Some Portfolios use the concept of *category* or *investment theme* to group Initiatives in ways that guide decisions. Possible categories or themes might include:

- Business Value
- Architecture
- Infrastructure
- Technology Development
- Regulatory Compliance
- Profitability Improvement
- Risk Reduction
- Operations
- Research

Categories may be used in a very loose sense, as an aid in understanding the focus of an Initiative, or in a stricter sense, as when an organization wants to ensure that at least some of the budget goes to (for example) Infrastructure development. In the latter case, we might fund each category to some level, and use the techniques described in the following sections to select the Business Cases to be implemented for each category.

Ultimately, the decisions about whether to use a categorization scheme, or which categories to use, should be made based on how useful the categorization will be.

What is required is some scheme for assessing and describing the value proposition of Initiatives, to enable the Portfolio Planning Committee to make educated decisions. The following section provides a simple but informative example, whose principles will shape the more elaborate variations that follow.

6.8.1 Simple Example of Portfolio Decision Process

Let us say that some concept of Return on Investment (ROI) can be estimated for each Initiative. Taken literally, ROI can be defined as

$$ROI = \frac{R}{I}$$

where R is the Return (some measure of value), and I is the Investment (some measure of cost).

The benefit to the organization increases as ROI increases. The challenge, of course, is estimating the values of R and I.

We might think of the Return in monetary units, such as dollars, representing a lump-sum payment, or the results of a Net Present Value calculation. Similarly, we might estimate the Investment as the monetary cost, or the total effort expended in the implementation of the initiative.

Given these values, the estimate of ROI is straightforward.

Unfortunately, it is very commonly not possible to estimate the monetary value of the Return at all.

6.8.1.1 The Limitations of Knowledge

Suppose we are considering five Initiatives, each of which adds a major capability to a specific product or solution that the organization sells. We can fund and execute three of these Initiatives prior to product delivery and need to decide which three to implement. In this example, customers do not purchase the output of any one Initiative as a single product or line item but purchase a solution that is enabled by multiple Initiatives.

In this example, then, *it is not possible to forecast the monetary value of any one Initiative* in any meaningful way because customers do not purchase the delivered scope of any one Initiative as a separate item. Instead, they purchase the next product or solution, leaving us no way to predict in advance, or discover after the fact, the financial contribution of each Initiative to the total.

The example illustrates an important limitation on what is possible for us to know. In general, the Return reflects the contribution of multiple factors, as does the Investment. Many factors often cannot be tied to real-world numbers at the time of Initiative approval, or even measured after the results of the Initiatives go to market.

6.8.1.2 Working within the Limitations

Fortunately, it is not necessary to know, or be able to estimate, the real-world value of Return or Investment factors in order to make decisions about Initiatives. What is necessary is to be able to assess the relative desirability of different Initiatives, *compared with each other*, and this can be done.

Returning to our sample Initiative, let's say that we want to consider these factors: Net Present Value (NPV), Urgency, Effort, and Technical Risk.

- NPV represents the value of the revenue stream over time generated by delivery of the Initiative, in the form of a single number.
- Urgency reflects the existence of a window of opportunity, meaning that the value of the Initiative decreases as the Initiative is increasingly delayed.
- Effort is the total effort to implement the initiative.
- Technical Risk reflects the impact of uncertainty around our ability to deliver the Initiative's scope, due to unknowns that may increase cost or effort significantly beyond the estimate.

We create a rating scale for each factor, used to compare different Initiatives. Each factor's estimate is drawn from a pool of predefined numbers of modest size, such as the Fibonacci sequence.* We look at a set of Initiatives, consider the NPV for each, and select larger or smaller numbers from the set based on how each Initiative's NPV is likely to be smaller or larger than other Initiatives in the set.

We proceed in a similar fashion for the other factors and assign each factor a value from the set of Fibonacci numbers: 0, 1, 2, 3, 5, 8, 13, and 21.

The factor values denote the relative size of each of the Initiative's factors relative to other Initiatives' values, but we also need a sense for how much each factor contributes to the overall assessment of the Initiative's desirability. For example, we might estimate the NPV and Urgency both as 8 but conclude that Urgency is half as important as NPV. Thus, for each factor, we also define a weight to indicate the significance of that factor's value to the overall assessment.

Return Factor	Weight	Investment Factor	Weight
Net Present Value	1.0	Effort	1.0
Urgency	0.5	Technical Risk	1.0
Regulatory Compliance	1.0		

Figure 6.2: Factor Weights for Portfolio Containing the Agent-Upgrade Initiative

Now the Return can be computed as the weighted sum of the Return-Factor values, and the Investment as the weighted sum of the Investment-Factor values. If, for example, we assign the following values to the factors

---

* The Fibonacci sequence provides numbers spaced far enough apart to be meaningfully different but close enough to allow for a useful set of values.

Factor	Value
Net Present Value	5
Urgency	3
Regulatory Compliance	1
Effort	8
Technical Risk	1

Figure 6.3: Factor Values for Agent-Upgrade Initiative

then the ROI is computed as

$$ROI = \frac{1.0 \times 5 + 0.5 \times 3 + 1.0 \times 1}{1.0 \times 8 + 1.0 \times 1} = 0.83$$

This ROI value can be compared to the ROI values of other Initiatives to guide the selection and scheduling of Initiatives over time. Higher values are better (more desirable) than lower values.

In this example, a value of "1" as the weight for a factor denotes the maximum possible impact, with less significant factors having smaller weights. This convention is not the only possible one. For example, one could normalize the set of weights for Value factors such that the sum of all weights is one, and likewise for Return factors. The choice of normalization is less important than simply getting agreement on the relative contribution of factors.

The example is a simple one, and real-world scenarios tend to be more complex. However, the approach to identifying numeric values for use in comparing Initiatives applies to these more complex scenarios as well.

6.9 Decision Factors in Depth

The concept of Return on Investment (ROI) introduced in Section 6.8.1 provides a simple way to consider the contribution of multiple decision factors with a single composite value. This approach is not the only way to evaluate the desirability of an Initiative, but it is a powerful one. The ROI concept is useful enough that it provides a convenient way to organize our thinking about decision factors into two basic categories: Return-related factors, and Investment-related factors.

In this and following sections, I look at a variety of Return and Investment factors that are often useful in evaluating Initiatives for Portfolio-level decisions.

6.9.1 Return-Related Factors

The Return of an Initiative is a measure of its value, that is, the benefits that follow from the Initiative's implementation. Thus, the Return-related factors are numeric values that reflect some kind of motivation for selecting the Initiative for development.

There is no reason to assume that the factor values remain constant over time. For example, an "Urgency" factor might have a high value in the present, due to the timing for a particular marketing or sales opportunity, and a value of zero six months later, after the opportunity has passed. When making Portfolio decisions, we should use values that reflect the reality at the time of the decision.

While it is possible in principal to have factor values that are less than zero, the calculations can become peculiar if this happens. If a factor under consideration represents a disincentive to implement an Initiative, I would generally prefer to address it as an Investment factor, rather than a Return factor with a negative value.

The set of possible Return factors is quite large. Examples include:

- Net Present Value
- Importance
- Urgency
- Total Revenues
- New Market Revenue
- Upgrade Revenue
- Customer Satisfaction Score
- Customer Acquisition
- Customer Retention
- Cost of not Doing
- Regulatory Compliance
- Enabling Infrastructure
- Enabling Technology Development
- Risk Reduction
- Market-Share Growth
- New Market Development
- Cost Reduction
- Time-to-Market Reduction
- Margin Improvement
- Publicity
- Tax Benefits
- Brand Development
- Product Line Diversity

The wealth of options can easily overwhelm and lead to analysis paralysis, so it is best to pick a small number of factors (e.g., 2–3) that are most critical.

The goal is not to ensure complete coverage of all possible decision criteria. The goal is to select the smallest number of distinctly different factors that will most often yield reasonable decisions. No factor should be added to the set under consideration unless its inclusion is likely to yield decisions that are frequently and substantially better than those that would have been obtained without it.

In other words, if a possible factor's contribution does not materially improve the Portfolio decisions, it should be omitted.

Finally, note that factors should be defined so that larger values imply greater benefits or desirability.

Examples of some common Return factors follow.

6.9.1.1 Importance

Perhaps the simplest possible Return factor is "Importance," which is nothing more than a single number that reflects how beneficial an Initiative's deliverables are likely to be for the company. The Importance of an Initiative depends on a common understanding of how value, revenue, or other considerations of interest lead to the factor's value.

Importance is often too simple to be an effective factor, but its simplicity is a virtue.

The benefit of Importance is that it is easy to define, and intuitive to many people. The drawback is that its highly subjective value may be hard to justify.

The table illustrates a simple definition of values for Importance

Range	Value
Lowest	0
	1
	2
	3
	5
Highest	8

Figure 6.4: Sample Values for an Importance Factor

6.9.1.2 Urgency

"Urgency" indicates how time-critical an Initiative is. Two Initiatives that have equal value by some measures may not have the same urgency associated with them.

For example, suppose that either of two Initiatives would yield $1,000,000 in profit if launched now, but one of them would yield substantially less profit if started six months from now. All else being equal, we should implement the more urgent Initiative sooner, and the other one later, in order to maximize our benefits.

The numeric value of an Urgency factor reflects general understanding of the impact of timing, and of known milestones (e.g., a dominant trade show's dates, a competitor's announced product launch, etc.).

The benefits of an Urgency factor are that the degree of Urgency is often obvious, and timeliness is both easy to understand and commonly of interest.

The drawback of Urgency is that subjective assessments of the impact of timing may be hard to justify.

The table illustrates a simple definition for values of Urgency. The numbers indicate windows within which the Initiative must be launched (relative to the timing of the Portfolio Planning meeting) in order to achieve maximum value.

Range	Value
0 months	8
1–3 months	6
4–6 months	4
7–9 months	3
10–15 months	1
>15 months	0

Figure 6.5: Sample Values for an Urgency Factor

6.9.1.3 Total Revenue

"Total Revenue" represents a single monetary value that represents the total financial benefit to the organization. It is most appropriate when the financial benefits occur as a single lump-sum transaction rather than as a continuing series of payments over time. The benefit may be defined as total payment, net profit, or any other concept of monetary benefit of interest for planning purposes.

The benefit of a Total Revenue factor is that it provides the simplest possible description of a monetary benefit and is easy to understand.

The major drawback of a Total Revenue factor is that it assumes a single payment, and so does not represent the value of a revenue stream very well.

The choice of numeric values depends on the extent to which the monetary benefits can truly be quantified in monetary units. If this kind of assessment is feasible, then we can define a mapping of factor values to monetary values. If not, then we proceed as for the Importance factor, using the best insight we have to assign a number to each of multiple Initiatives, based on how we believe their Total Revenue compare with each other.

Figure 6.6 shows an example of mapping monetary values to factor values.

Range	Value
$0	0
$1–100,000	1
$100,001–200,000	2
$200,001–300,000	3
$300,001–500,000	5
>$500,000	8

Figure 6.6: Sample Values for a Total Revenues Factor

6.9.1.4 Net Present Value

"Net Present Value" represents the value of a revenue stream over time. It addresses the accumulation of value from multiple expenses and payments over time and the impact of the time value of money on the total. It is, simultaneously, the most meaningful concept of value for a product whose sales and development costs are spread out over time, and the most complex factor we consider here. While the complexity of the calculation may appear daunting, we will see that the "bottom line" of NPV as a practical factor is not so difficult.

First, some definitions. If I have a sum of money now, with a "Present Value" (PV) of $1,000, I can invest that money in a fund, stock, bank account, or by other means. If that investment yields an annual interest r, then the "Future Value" of the investment after n years is

$$FV = PV(1 + r)^n$$

If the interest rate is 5 percent (= 0.05), then this formula gives the value after ten years as $1,629.

We can also reverse the calculation to compare possible investments. Suppose I can choose to receive $900 two years from now or $1,000 five years from now. Which is better? We can answer the question by computing the Present Value implied by those two investments:

$$PV = \frac{FV}{(1 + r)^n}$$

where r is now referred to as the *discount rate*. If we again assume $r = 5$ percent, then these two options yield the following Present Values:

	Future Value	Years Out	Present Value
Option 1	$900	2	$816
Option 2	$1000	5	$784

Table 6.2: Present and Future Value of Money

While we don't actually have any money at the present time, the Present Value numbers give us a way to compare money that arrives at different times. In this case, the first option ($900 in two years) is the better choice because its PV value is higher. Over time (say, at the five-year mark, when Option 2 becomes possible) we will have more money for having chosen Option 1. Computing the value of Option at that five-year mark yields $1,042, which is indeed higher than the $1,000 we'd have at that point from Option 2.

This logic can be extended to define the Present Value for a series of financial transactions that occur over time. Suppose the amount of each year's transaction, for the next five years, is represented by the values $C1$, $C2$, $C3$, $C4$, and $C5$. Suppose the discount rate (the term used in NPV calculations, in the place of the interest rate we've been using) is r. Then the Present Value for this series of transactions is

$$PV = \frac{C_1}{(1 + r)} + \frac{C_2}{(1 + r)^2} + \frac{C_3}{(1 + r)^3} + \frac{C_4}{(1 + r)^4} + \frac{C_5}{(1 + r)^5}$$

As we go further out in time, each year's total contributes relatively less to the Present Value because of the additional factor of $(1 + r)$ in the denominator. Thus, future-year contributions are discounted relative to the first year (hence the term *discount rate*).

The Net Present Value is the difference between the Present Value and the Cost of the Initiative (C_0), namely,

$$NPV = PV - C_0$$

It should be clear that the NPV values depend strongly on the value of the discount rate, r. While much has been written about how to generate appropriate values for the discount rate, that subject is not important for our purposes. It is enough to note that the computational utility of the NPV formula deteriorates dramatically if the uncertainty about the annual revenue figures greatly exceeds the value of r.

As we are addressing the case where high uncertainty is the norm, and it is frequently impossible to compute a meaningful value of NPV in monetary terms, the details of the NPV calculation become unimportant. What is important is simply awareness that the value of future revenues is negatively impacted by their distance in the future, and that NPV is, conceptually, a measure of the monetary value of an Initiative for the entire stream of revenues for which it is responsible. This more qualitative concept of NPV is what I consider here.

The benefit of NPV as a factor is that it describes the monetary value of an investment that generates a revenue stream over time, which is, conceptually, what we typically wish to know. It is useful for comparing benefits of different initiatives to different costs and revenue streams.

The drawbacks of NPV are that the revenue stream over time often cannot be estimated, in monetary values, for an Initiative whose scope is not delivered as a stand-alone product.

With all the above said, the actual factor values may be defined in exactly the way as they were for the Total Revenue factor. The difference is not in the value definitions but in our understanding of what they represent.

The choice of numeric values depends on the extent to which the monetary benefits can truly be quantified in monetary units. If this kind of assessment is feasible, then we can define a mapping of factor values to monetary values. If not, then we proceed as for the Importance factor, using the best insight we have to assign a number to each of multiple Initiatives, based on how we believe their Total Revenues compare with each other.

Table 6.3 shows an example of mapping monetary values to factor values.

Range	Value
$0	0
$1–100,000	1
$100,001–200,000	2
$200,001–300,000	3
$300,001–500,000	5
>$500,000	8

Table 6.3: Sample Values for a Net Present Value Factor

6.9.2 Estimation of Return-Related Factors

The Return-related factors I have reviewed may or may not be tied to a meaningful conception of real-world numbers. In the event that any one factor can be related to real-world values, and can be estimated meaningfully in those terms, then it makes sense to map those values to modest numbers as we've illustrated above.

For many factors, such estimation is not possible. Instead, we may have to estimate, say, Importance without reference to a source of quantitative information. The comparison method of Section 6.8.1.2 is appropriate for such cases.

6.9.3 Investment-Related Factors

The Investment for an Initiative is a measure of cost, although not necessarily in purely monetary terms. The most common conceptions of Investment are Cost and Effort, or other parameters that can impact cost and effort.

As for Return-related factors, Investment-related factors need not be constant over time. The cost, say, estimated for an Initiative now might be X, but an estimate of that same Initiative's cost a year later might yield a different number.

The set of possible Investment-related factors tends to be smaller than the list of possible Return-related factors. Examples include:

- Effort to Implement
- Cost to Implement
- Technology Uncertainty

Here again I recommend selecting the smallest practical set of factors to consider in order to reduce confusion in decision-making.

Examples of some common Investment factors follow.

6.9.3.1 Effort

Effort has been described multiple times in this book. It is the aggregated time spent (or estimated to be required) to implement the Initiative, summed across all people working to implement the Initiative. At the Initiative level, Effort is most commonly estimated in units of person weeks (5 person-days), person-months (defined as 22 person-days here) or person years (250 person-days).

If effort is estimated directly in person months, and the numbers are one-digit or low two-digit numbers, then the numbers can be used directly. If the numbers or units are such that the numbers are much larger, then it is a good idea to map the raw numbers to numbers of more modest size, such as in Table 6.4.

Range	Value
0	0
1–100	1
101–200	2
201–300	3
301–500	5
>500	8

Table 6.4: Sample Mapping Person-Days to Small Numbers

Table 6.4 assumes that estimates were provided in person-days, and the typical numbers found when estimating Initiatives are such that the mapping shown in the table yields values of convenient size. A similar mapping can be created for any situation where the raw estimates are of inconvenient size.

6.9.3.2 Cost

Cost refers to the monetary cost of the Initiative's implementation, meaning the total amount of money spent to develop and deliver the scope of the Initiative.

For types of work for which the cost of labor is virtually all of the monetary cost, then effort may be used as a proxy for cost or converted to cost by multiplying effort by an appropriate burn rate (e.g., dollars per day).

In the somewhat more complex case where the cost of labor is dominant but varies widely across different people, then cost may be computed by summing the individual labor costs across all of the people (i.e., summing the product of each person's effort and burn rate).

The above scenarios are common for software product development, due to the low material cost involved. For hardware development, or other types of work, materials and other costs may be large, or dominant. In these cases, the total cost includes the cost of internal effort, materials, goods and services purchased, and all other costs incurred. This more complex case may have to address the differences between capitalized and operational costs, at which point the appropriate financial expertise should be involved.

As usual, we want to map the large monetary values to a more convenient range of numbers, such as in Table 6.5.

Range	Value
$0	0
$1–100,000	1
$100,001–200,000	2
$200,001–300,000	3
$300,001–500,000	5
>$500,000	8

Table 6.5: Sample Values for Total Initiative Cost

6.9.3.3 Technology Uncertainty

It may be the case that estimates of effort or cost can be obtained but are considered highly unreliable due to unknowns in technology. When cost is highly uncertain, it may be preferable to account for the uncertainty in cost separately from cost itself.

One example of estimating the impact of uncertainty in cost estimation is given in Figure 6.7. We would probably apply a relatively low scale factor for this table (e.g., 12.5 percent) so that the highest value represents a potential doubling of the cost due to technology unknowns. The factor itself would be estimated by the comparison technique of Section 6.8.1.2.

Range	Value
Lowest	0
	1
	2
	3
	5
Highest	8

Figure 6.7: Sample Mapping of Technical Uncertainty Values

6.9.4 Estimation of Effort and Cost

At some point after introducing a new Initiative in Portfolio Refinement meeting, the Area Product Owner will need estimates for the work required to implement the scope of the Initiative. For the sake of concreteness, I address estimates of effort specifically, but the same logic applies to estimates of Cost as well.

6.9.4.1 Scope Definition and Decomposition

The Business Case describes the scope of the Initiative. Initiatives are typically much larger than the scope definitions encountered at the Project or Portfolio levels, and it is not usually practical to estimate the effort of an Initiative as a single, monolithic item.

Instead, we must first decompose the scope of the Initiative into smaller deliverables to be implemented by different teams. This is necessary because our capability for estimation is very much dependent on team-specific expertise, and because we require an estimate of each team's effort in order to support any subsequent planning exercise.

The usual approach to scope decomposition in classic Project Management is to develop a Work Breakdown Structure of the deliverables. This attempt produces a tree structure, whose leaf nodes (at the bottom of the tree) represent the specific pieces of scope (smallest deliverables) to be estimated and developed.

The approach in Agile processes such as Scrum is very similar. We decompose larger pieces of scope (Epics) into smaller pieces, and likewise produces a tree structure. When developing plans for individual Sprints, the Epics are decomposed all the way to Stories, which will be implemented in Sprints. For our purposes here, we do not carry the decomposition of the Initiative scope all the way down to the Story level because fine granularity is not needed at this time. Instead, we decompose to the level of Epics that are large but can be estimated.

Using the Agile terms, then, we decompose the Initiative scope into a set of major Epics, each of which is chosen to be implementable entirely by a particular team. It is necessary that the Epics to be estimated be aligned with teams because this is how we estimate each team's effort.

The work of this estimation is done by a Technical Planning Team assembled by the Program Manager. This team includes engineering leads, test leads, and others who have good insight about the work that will have to be done by the different teams.* Also included are the Team and Area Product Owners, Scrum Masters, and other people whose expertise is required. The Program Manager facilitates, and other participants contribute as needed. This work may be done in pieces, over time, or in a single estimation meeting. In the latter case, one or two all-day sessions may be required.

Consider the example of the upgrade of Agents embedded in the networked medical devices. The Initiative is "Agent V2 Upgrade," and the decomposition into Epics for teams might resemble Figure 6.8.

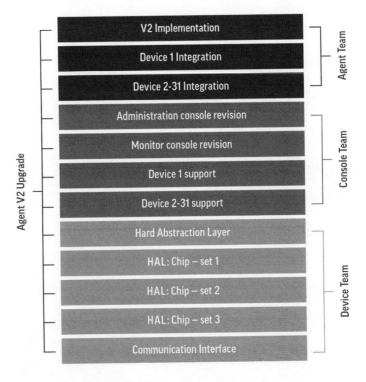

Figure 6.8: Decomposition of Initiative for Estimation Purposes

---

* This group often contains technical managers.

The members of the Technical Planning Team collaborate as needed to write each Epic in the list, in our standard format for Epics (Title, Narrative, Acceptance Criteria). This work can be done prior to the meeting, or in the meeting, as circumstances dictate.

The example shows twelve Epics, which is a small number. More realistic examples might contain 50 to 100 Epics, not all of which are of critical importance. Decomposition of an Initiative frequently yields child Epics whose importance ranges from "must have" to "nice, but not important." A convenient way to represent the priority as well as definition of the Epics is to use a tabular structure such as in Figure 6.9.

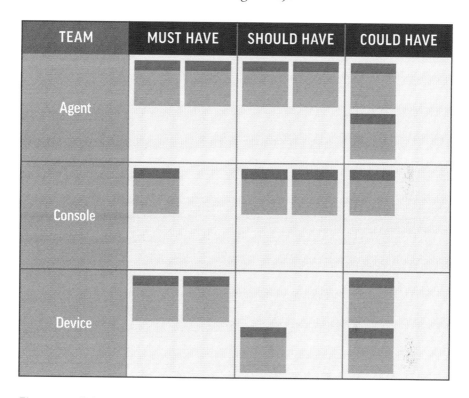

Figure 6.9: Prioritized Decomposition of Initiative

For example, we might decide to put all of the "Must Haves" and one of the "Should Haves" into a specific Initiative and defer others for later consideration.*

---

* "Tabular layouts" developed by several people in a room almost always involve taping sheets of paper to a wall. This is an effective practice for the purpose.

6.9.4.2 Estimation of Effort

Estimation is performed after the Initiative's scope decomposition is completed.

The first step is to select the units to be used for estimation. A key principle in this decision is the understanding that single-digit to low two-digit numbers are much easier to understand than large numbers. Thus, we should select units that yield estimates are in this numeric range.

As described in Section 5.7.1, organizations that contain multiple interacting teams often standardize on time-based estimates. While it is not impossible to work around the challenges of relative sizing and unique units per team, doing so becomes a constant and frustrating headache at higher levels of the organization. For this reason, I will use time-based units here.

A common choice of unit for Portfolio-level estimation is the *person-month*, or *man-month*. As calendar months vary in size, there is no unique definition of these terms, so I will define a person-month to be twenty-two person-days here. The usual caveats around making the distinction between effort (what we are seeking) and duration (not what we are seeking) apply. (If person-month is too large, a *person-week* of five person-days might be a better choice.)

As always, the total effort estimated for an Epic must include all work, including testing and defect-resolution, required to deliver the scope of the Epic in a form that functions as intended. It is therefore important to make sure that the people on the Technical Planning Team have all the engineering, testing, and other skills required to estimate all aspects of the work to be done.

For estimating the effort of Epics in an Initiative, and thus the effort of the Initiative itself, I recommend the Affinity Estimation technique of Section 5.7.2. It is simple, quick, and reliable enough for the current purpose.

It is sometimes useful to provide skill-oriented estimates to guide specific resourcing decisions. For example, different Epics in a software-oriented Initiative might require different levels of software development skills and Quality Assurance skills, and we may want to assess whether we have enough people who specialize in, say, the QA skill set. For a hardware context, we might need to get a sense of effort spent across Mechanical Engineering, Electrical Engineering, Firmware, and other skill sets.

One quick way to estimate the division of labor between skill sets is as follows.

Using the software example, let us estimate the QA skill set, in particular. First, complete the total effort estimation, as above. Then select fractions of the total to be used in estimating the work that must be done by QA specialists. My preference is to select the coarsest meaningful scale, which I take as "less than half" or "more than half" of the total work. This scale can be represented numerically by 0, 33, 66, and 100 percent. Thus, we ask the Technical Planning Team members to annotate each Epic with a QA fraction drawn from this set, which takes very little time. A similar approach can be taken to other combinations of skills as well.

Finally, the Program Manager should record all of the Epics and estimates for later use.

Epic	Device Team	Agent Team	Console Team
Agent v2 implementation		270	
Integration of Agent with Device 1		13.5	
Integration of Agent with Devices 2-31		279	
Revision of Administration console			120
Revision of Monitor console			120
Support for Device 1			6
Support for Devices 2-31			124
Base Hardware Abstraction Layer (HAL) capability	90		
HAL for chip-set 1	30		
HAL for chip-set 2	30		
HAL for chip-set 3	30		
Interface for Agent communication	60		
Total Effort	**240**	**562.5**	**370**

Figure 6.10: Effort Estimates for Agent Upgrade Initiative

Figure 6.10 shows the estimates for the Epics in the Agent Upgrade Initiative, in units of person-months. This information can be used for planning work on a schedule, or as input to subsequent cost calculations.

As previously described, cost estimation is an extension of effort estimation. One converts the effort figures into cost by use of a known burn rate, and then adds other developmental costs to get a total cost.

6.9.4.3 Additional Estimation Techniques

I have discussed two estimation techniques (Planning Poker and Affinity Estimation) in considerable detail. While these are widely used because they work very well, other techniques do exist and may be useful in some circumstances. I will review those techniques here.

Like Planning Poker and Affinity Estimation, these techniques can be used to estimate anything that can be quantified, in any units desired. They can be used to estimate each of the Epics generated by the Initiative's scope decomposition, or the entire Initiative, as appropriate. I believe they are most likely to be useful for estimating costs other than those related to effort, based on expenses incurred in previous development efforts.

6.9.4.3.1 Parametric Estimation

Parametric Estimation is perhaps the most attractive technique. It is useful when an organization has historical or other information that enables development of a parametric model, into which one can plug parameter values that define the current item in order to generate the estimate.

Some examples of parametric estimation include:

- One painter can paint 1,000 square feet in one workday (8 hours). How many painters are needed to paint 10,000 square feet in two workdays?

- One person in the sandwich shop can make 20 sandwiches per hour. If we have five workers, how long will it take to make 1,000 sandwiches?

Parametric estimation works well when we can build these kinds of quantitative models.

6.9.4.3.2 Analogous Estimation

Analogous Estimation is done by comparing the item to be estimated to a similar one that has been completed, and for which the information (cost, time, etc.) is known. Examples include:

- Building our second data center cost $10,000,000 and took 9 months. Our third data center should have the same cost and take the same time to build.

- The last 10 three-bedroom houses we painted cost $3,500 to paint. The next three-bedroom house will also cost $3,500 to paint.

6.10 Risk Management

A *risk* is any known or potential problem that may have a deleterious impact on our concept of success for an Initiative. Areas frequently impacted by risks include:

- The effort or cost to implement an Initiative
- The value provided by the implementation of the Initiative
- The schedule on which value is realized

Some types of risk are assessed by our ROI calculations (e.g., Technical Uncertainty, which impacts cost and schedule). Others should be addressed in the definition and scheduling of Initiatives. I will consider these types of risk below.

The Area Product Owner should provide an assessment of major risks as part of the Business Case, and a proposal for how to manage each of the risks. The description of risks and strategy for managing them should be brief, containing only a few sentences.

The Project Management Institute defines four basic Risk-Management strategies: Avoid, Transfer, Mitigate, and Accept. Another variation sometimes seen is Resolve, Own, Accept, and Mitigate.

Strategy	Description
Avoid / Resolve	Adjust plan to eliminate possibility of the risk
Transfer / Own	Shift ownership, impact of risk to another party (e.g., buy insurance, negotiate warranties, use cost-plus contracts)
Mitigate	Plan, act to reduce probability or impact of risk
Accept	Decide to take no action now, and accept that risk may occur later, at which time decisions will be made as to how best to deal with the problem

Figure 6.11: Risk-Management Strategies

Figure 6.12 shows some common risk types.

Type	Description
Market	Market needs, drivers, competition may change
Value	Value of Initiative scope may differ from expectation
Legal	Risk of lawsuits, patent violations, contract issues, etc.
Regulatory	Regulations may change, or be hard to satisfy
Personnel	People unavailable due to layoffs, job changes, contention for resources
Process	Process may be ineffective in delivering results
Deferral	Value realization requires meeting specific window / date
Technical	Risks to ability to implement scope on estimated schedule

Figure 6.12: Common Risk Types

Technical Risks may be accounted for in estimates of ROI, as we've seen, but strategies to deal with them should also be listed in the risk section of the Business Case.

Mitigation is only one of the four Risk-Management strategies, and so is not always possible. However, when risks can be mitigated, we often see impacts and mitigation strategies as shown in Figure 6.13.

Type	Impact Type	Description
Market	V	Revise scope on discovery
Value	V	Revise scope on discovery
Legal	C, V	Conduct legal review, incorporate relevant work in scope of Initiative
Regulatory	D, C, V	Conduct legal review, incorporate relevant work in scope of Initiative, revise scope on discovery
Personnel	D, C, V	Hire, promote, retain as possible. Schedule to minimize resource contention.
Process	D, C	Identify, implement process changes needed
Deferral	V	Schedule for window of opportunity
Technical	D, C, V	Incorporate time and scope into the schedule to address technical issues that may arise

- **D:** Delay in revenue realization
- **C:** Cost increase
- **V:** Value reduction

Figure 6.13: Some Common Risk Impacts and Mitigations

The Business Case in Section 6.7.1 provides some practical examples of risks and their management.

6.11 Techniques for Making Portfolio Decisions

Portfolio decision-making cannot be reduced to an algorithm. We develop quantitative techniques to assist us in generating insight about the desirability of different Initiatives, but the purpose of these techniques is just that: to develop insight. Ultimately, the decisions that we make should be informed by these insights, but not adhere slavishly to the results of any one analytical technique.

In this section, I will look at several different techniques for making decisions about which Initiatives to approve for execution. I suggest that a Portfolio Planning Team use two or three different methods in order to provide different insights, talk through the various pros and cons identified in the discussion, and then work toward a consensus decision. While the Portfolio Owner must make the final decision, the discussions are highly informative, and the consensus that arises from the discussion is beneficial in many ways.

All decision-making techniques assume a particular time horizon for planning purposes. For example, we might hold the Portfolio Planning Meeting every three months and plan for the next three months. Or we might meet every three months but plan for a six- or twelve-month horizon in each meeting, with the intent of revisiting some of this meeting's decisions in the next meeting. My default recommendation is to plan for a one-year horizon, every three months, but the timeline should be adjusted as appropriate for the organization.

To start the decision-making process, the Portfolio Planning Committee assembles a set of candidate Initiatives worth consideration, but which, all together, will take significantly more time to implement than the planning horizon. The reason for looking at more Initiatives than can be implemented in the planning time frame is because we want to optimize the chosen set to best fit our business goals.

6.11.1 Comparison Methods

Comparison methods work by comparing individual Initiatives to other Initiatives. The result of the comparison is a ranking, or sequence, for the Initiatives in the set. This ranking may then be used as a guide to planning work over time, with the highest-ranked (lowest number) Initiatives started soonest.

6.11.1.1 Multi-Column Sort

The simplest technique is the Multi-Column sort. We list the various Initiatives and decision factors, and then define a sort order based on primary, secondary, tertiary, etc. columns.

	Factor	Net Present Value	Urgency	Effort	Rank
Initiative	D	5	2	2	1
	C	5	3	5	2
	B	3	8	2	3
	A	3	1	2	4

Figure 6.14: Decision by Multi-Column Sort

The example of Figure 6.14 reflects a sort first by decreasing Net Present Value, second by increasing effort, and third by decreasing urgency. While the composite factor of ROI could, in principle appear in this table, in practice we tend to use this type of sorting as an alternative to defining and computing ROI.

This method may be too simple to use as a primary guide to Portfolio decisions, but, precisely because it is so simple, it is a good one to have in the set of methods commonly used. Sometimes simple techniques yield insights that sophistication can obscure.

6.11.1.2 Decision Matrix

The Decision-Matrix technique offers perhaps the most convenient mix of sophistication and ease of use available. With this technique, we typically do define and compute an ROI value based on our selected decision factors, and then rank the Initiatives based on ROI.

	Factor	Net Present Value	Urgency	Regulatory Compliance	Effort	Technology Uncertainty	ROI	Rank
	Weight	1	0.5	1	1	1		
Initiative	B	3	8	3	1	2	3.3	1
	D	8	2	1	2	3	2.0	2
	C	5	3	2	5	5	0.9	3
	A	1	1	5	8	0	0.8	4

Figure 6.15: Decision by Decision Matrix

Figure 6.15 uses NPV, Urgency, and Regulatory Compliance as Return Factors, and Effort and Uncertainty as Investment Factors. With the factor weights as shown in the table, the ROI values, and therefore the ranking, are as shown.

6.11.1.3 Pros and Cons and Combinations

The Multi-Column sort is the easiest to set up but is difficult to use for more than a few factors. The Decision Matrix handles more factors, and incorporates an intuitive concept of ROI, but is more difficult to set up because of the need to define and compute ROI.

A reasonable approach is to start with a Multi-Column sort, review the results, and then try the Decision Matrix. If both approaches yield essentially the same results, then the pair may be redundant. If they show different results, it is advisable to understand why, and use the resulting insight to improve the decisions.

Finally, it is possible to combine the two approaches. Set up the Decision Matrix, and add additional factors that may not be well-suited for an ROI definition, but which are important in making the best decisions. One can then use the Multi-Column sort with ROI as one of the columns, and the additional factors as the other columns.

6.11.2 Grouping Methods

Grouping Methods focus less on ranking Initiatives, and more on selecting the best subset of Initiatives under consideration, based on balancing factors across the set. As for the Comparison methods, the Portfolio Planning Committee assembles a set of Initiatives to review, and then selects a subset. Sequencing decisions may then be made based on any criteria the Committee considers appropriate, including, but not limited to, ROI.

6.11.2.1 Portfolio Balancing

To employ the Portfolio Balancing technique, the Portfolio Planning Committee must do the following:

1. Define categories of investment criteria to be considered.

2. Set target values for each category, to be met by the set of Initiatives to be chosen.

In the Portfolio Planning meeting, the Committee then reviews how each candidate Initiative contributes to the category targets and considers various possible subsets of the Initiatives under consideration in order to define the optimum set.

This approach involves a significant amount of "What-if" analysis and consideration of alternatives but does achieve the goal of the set-based optimization.

For example, we might define the following criteria for planning, say, one year out:

- At least 50 percent of Initiatives must have *Time to First Revenues* under six months, to ensure cash flow every quarter
- No Initiatives can have *Time to Break Even* over two years
- At least one Initiative to have *Cost Reduction* Factor >5
- Highest NPV, after other factors are addressed

This example relies on these specific factors:

- **Time to First Revenues:** interval from start of Initiative to revenues realized for its deliverables

- **Time to Break Even:** interval from start of Initiative to when the total revenues realized equals the Cost of the Initiative

- **Cost Reduction Factor:** the factor by which the cost of some activity is reduced if the Initiative is implemented

6.11.2.2 Structured Group Prioritization

This concept parallels the Planning Poker estimation technique, in that it uses a structured approach to tap the expertise of a group of people to make the Portfolio decision. The Portfolio Planning Committee would use this technique to tap the expertise of a different, and usually much larger, group of people who have insights to offer.

In other words, the Portfolio Planning Committee convenes a focus group, and uses a particular technique to gain insights from the group. The group provides a set of recommendations for the best set of Initiatives, along with the reasoning behind those decisions. The Portfolio Planning Committee then uses this information as a key input into the Committee's decisions. While there is no expectation that the Committee will simply adopt the recommendations in toto, the recommendations will carry a great deal of weight, and strongly influence the Committee's decisions.

Focus group membership can be whatever the Committee desires, including:

- Executives, Upper-level Managers, Technical Leads
- People from Sales, Marketing, Support, Services, Engineering
- Outside stakeholders or industry experts

It is critical to choose participants so as to provide a wide variety of perspectives and deep knowledge of relevant factors.

6.11.2.2.1 Multi-Voting Method

Sometimes called "Dot Voting," Multi-Voting is perhaps the simplest possible technique for structured group prioritization.

The simplest version requires that the focus-group participants be in the same room. A facilitator posts a set of Initiatives on a wall or whiteboard (e.g., with sticky notes, or pages with tape). The facilitator also gives each participant three (or any other number of) stickers.

The facilitator begins the session by providing whatever information the participants are likely to need, in order to do the work. This information includes the purpose of the meeting and the information that is known and useful for decision-making.

Next, the facilitator provides the statement that the session is intended to address. It is important to phrase the statement with care. Statements such as "Vote for what we should do" are so open-ended as to make many interpretations possible. More effective statements could include the following:

Vote for Initiatives that:

- Most improve customer retention
- Have the highest ROI
- Best leverage our strategic investment in additive manufacturing

Next, the participants vote on the Initiatives. Each participant places his or her votes (stickers) on the posted Initiatives, based on a personal understanding of values, costs, and tradeoffs. A participant may put one vote on each of three Initiatives, all three votes on one, or any other combination.

Many possible variations exist:

1. The facilitator may ask people to vote in silence (useful for large groups) or feel free to discuss the tradeoffs with each other (more appropriate for small groups). I favor allowing discussion when feasible.

2. The number of votes may be larger than three.

3. A person's initials may be used instead of stickers (useful when the facilitator forgets to bring stickers).

4. The process may be done online, via Web interface, for a distributed group meeting conducted by teleconference. It can be done with a shared document, or with a product intended for distributed Multi-Voting.

The key to this approach is to enforce scarcity by giving each person much fewer votes than there are Initiatives to consider. Thus, no one can vote for all Initiatives, and participants must make tradeoff decisions.

The output of this exercise is a set of Initiatives with varying numbers of stickers on them. The most highly decorated Initiative is the one the group considers to be the most urgent, most valuable, or otherwise best addresses the facilitator's request. The number of stickers then indicates how far down the list each Initiative appears (i.e., the Initiatives are sorted in decreasing order of sticker count).

This simple technique is very useful and can be used in many contexts that involve selection or prioritization of a set of items by a group of people. Because it is simple, it is easy to do, with minimal setup or infrastructure required. It is, therefore, highly recommended not only for its usefulness, but also because of its simplicity and low cost.

6.11.2.2.2 "Buy a Feature" Method

Perhaps the most widely known example of this technique is the "Buy a Feature" or "Decision Engine" product from Conteneo.[25] This product provides a Web-based interface for the participants to use in making decisions about a set of items (such as Initiatives). Each item has a cost (intended to reflect the actual cost estimate), and each participant has a budget. The participants' budgets are such that participants can only 'buy' items by pooling resources. The product enables participants to discuss (via written chat sessions) the pros and cons of various items, and to decide how much of their own budgets to allocate toward the purchase of the various items.

Key elements of this technique include:

1. Enforcing scarcity, so participants must make tradeoff and prioritization decisions

2. Enforcing collaboration, so that participants must make decisions as a group

3. Capturing the discussions for later review

The Portfolio Planning Committee should review the discussion logs generated by this technique for useful insights that emerged in the discussions.

6.11.3 PARRIKA Method

PAPRIKA—an acronym for "Potentially All Pairwise RanKings of All Possible Alternatives"—is a method for multi-criteria decision-making that involves users answering a series of simple questions based on their expert knowledge and judgment. This method was developed by Hansen and Ombler[26] and has been incorporated into the 1000minds[27] product by the company of the same name.

The PAPRIKA method does not start by asking users to provide estimates for decision factors but to identify criteria or attributes that are relevant for decision-making.

Each question posed by the PAPRIKA method requires the decision-maker to choose between two hypothetical alternatives defined on just two criteria or attributes at a time and involving a tradeoff. Each criterion has at least two "levels of performance," which can be quantitative or qualitative, such as:

Criterion A: Likely effectiveness of the proposed solution
Levels (lowest to highest ranked): <40%, 41–60%, 61–80%, 81–100%.

Criterion B: Fit with the organization's strategic priorities
Levels (lowest to highest ranked): Low, Medium, High.

An example of a pairwise-ranking question appears in Figure 6.16. From the decision-maker's answers, weights on the criteria (see Figure 6.17), representing their relative importance, are derived using mathematical methods.

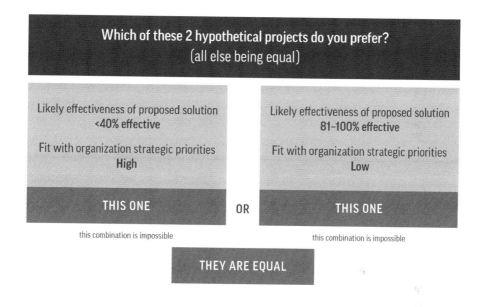

Figure 6.16: Example of a PAPRIKA / 1000minds Question

Instead of guessing the relative importance (weights) of the criteria, or assuming they're all equally important (a common fallacy), the PAPRIKA method determines and reports them, based on the decision-maker's expert knowledge and judgment. Figure 6.17 shows an example of this kind of evaluation.

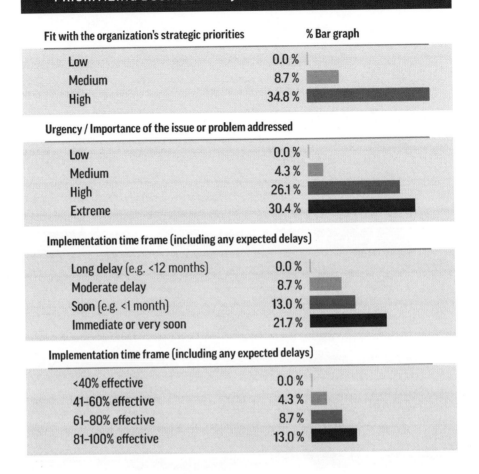

PRIORITIZING BUSINESS PROJECTS & ALLOCATING BUDGET*

Fit with the organization's strategic priorities	% Bar graph	
Low	0.0 %	
Medium	8.7 %	
High	34.8 %	

Urgency / Importance of the issue or problem addressed		
Low	0.0 %	
Medium	4.3 %	
High	26.1 %	
Extreme	30.4 %	

Implementation time frame (including any expected delays)		
Long delay (e.g. <12 months)	0.0 %	
Moderate delay	8.7 %	
Soon (e.g. <1 month)	13.0 %	
Immediate or very soon	21.7 %	

Implementation time frame (including any expected delays)		
<40% effective	0.0 %	
41-60% effective	4.3 %	
61-80% effective	8.7 %	
81-100% effective	13.0 %	

Figure 6.17: Preference Values for PAPRIKA Example

Finally, the software uses the preference values to rank the Initiatives, as in Figure 6.18.

The PAPRIKA method is the most mathematically sophisticated technique considered here. It replaces the concept of factor estimation previously described with a process that derives the numerical values of a somewhat different conception of "factors" (criteria and weights). The sophistication comes at a cost (no such products are free as of this writing) but is worth considering when many millions of dollars are at stake.

	ALTERNATIVE click to open	CRITERIA				RANK	TOTAL SCORE	TOTAL SCORE	OTHER CONSIDERATIONS		
		Urgency / importance of the issue or problem addressed	Likely effectiveness of the proposed solution	Fit with the organization's strategic priorities	Implementation time frame (including any expected delays)				Confidence in cost estimates; 1=LOW 2=MED 3=HIGH	Environmental externalities	Likely political support
☐	New Business Development Push	Extreme	81-100% effective	High	Soon (e.g. < 1 month)	1st	91.3%	400	1	no	yes
☐	Desktop Platform Refresh	Extreme	61-80% effective	High	Moderate delay	2nd	82.6%	400	1	no	no
☐	Recruitment Campaign	High	41-60% effective	High	Soon (e.g. < 1 month)	3rd	78.3%	300	3	no	yes
☐	Back-Up Generator	Medium	81-100% effective	High	Immediate or very soon	4th=	73.9%	450	3	yes	yes
☐	Hire New Programmers	Medium	81-100% effective	High	Immediate or very soon	4th=	73.9%	600	3	no	no
☐	Renew Oracle Software License	High	41-60% effective	High	Moderate delay	4th=	73.9%	50	3	no	no
☐	Upgrade System X	Extreme	61-80% effective	Medium	Immediate or very soon	7th	69.6%	1,800	1	yes	no

Figure 6.18: Sample Ranking of Initiatives for PAPRIKA Method

Exactly who answers the questions is another decision to be made. I favor involving the entire Portfolio Planning Committee, and having the members discuss and decide the answer to each question, with the Portfolio Owner able to break deadlocks when necessary. The discussions among the members as to which criteria take precedence is itself a useful exercise in building a consensus understanding of the Portfolio-decision tradeoffs.

6.12   Scheduling and Resource Planning

The selection and sequencing of Initiatives should be driven primarily by business goals but will always be constrained by availability of resources. In this section, I address the tightly coupled issues of scheduling and resource allocation.

Our goal is easily described: create a plan for implementation of Initiatives over a specified planning horizon. The plan should address the duration of each Initiative's work, the availability of resources, and the schedule of the Initiatives' work.

6.12.1   The Beginning of Planning

Let's begin by focusing more closely on the process of Portfolio Refinement, as these efforts feed directly into planning.

The Area Product Owner facilitates Portfolio Refinement meetings on a regular cadence. The other attendees are as described in Section 6.9.4.1.

Let's say the Area Product Owner has introduced a newly drafted Business Case in a Portfolio Refinement meeting. He will likely leave the meeting with a list of changes to make to the Business Case, based on feedback.

In the next Portfolio Refinement meeting, everyone agrees that the revised Business Case is clear, well-written, and ready for estimation.

Estimation of Effort, Cost, or other Investment factors will be facilitated by the Program Manager and accomplished by a Technical Planning Team of domain experts who can provide the required information. Often times, the Technical Planning Team is the same group that attends the Portfolio Refinement meetings.

In the estimation sessions, the Area Product Owner collaborates with the Technical Planning Team to decompose the Initiative scope into smaller (but still large) deliverables. The more and smaller the deliverables are, the better the estimates will be, but also the longer the process will take. In practice, the "sweet spot" is usually between twenty and one hundred deliverables. If we assume that the implementation work will be done by a known set of teams, with known areas of responsibility, then the decomposition must yield deliverables that align with specific teams. In other words, none of the deliverables to be estimated can require work from more than one team.

The Program Manager facilitates the Technical Planning Team's estimation work using the techniques we've discussed (most commonly, Affinity Estimation), as illustrated in Sections 6.9.4.1 and 6.9.4.2.

All told, typical sessions for scope decomposition and estimation usually require a day or two to complete.

6.12.2 Resource Planning and Scheduling

Resource Planning and Scheduling for the work of an Initiative, or set of Initiatives, cannot be separated. Any existing understanding of resource availability will constrain possible schedules, and if the best schedule is not acceptable, it may be necessary to increase resources. A certain amount of iteration is commonplace, during which we modify resources to see how schedules are affected.

The techniques used for resource planning and scheduling vary. I will refer to two standard models as "Classic" and "Agile," and consider each below.

6.12.2.1 Classic Resource Planning and Scheduling

In this well-established model, we typically have a set of Project Managers for various connected projects. The projects roll up into a program, which is managed by a Program Manager.

The Project Managers know the scope for their projects and gather estimates for the work to be done by any of a variety of methods already described. Such estimates often resemble the following:

Resource	Estimate
Electrical Engineer	1,300 hours
Peter, our only Antenna Expert	1,700 hours
Firmware Engineer	1,100 hours

Figure 6.19: Example of Classic Resource Estimation

In an organization of modest size, the Project Manager may work through the scheduling for a particular project. In a larger organization, the Project Managers will provide the work estimates to the Program Manager, who is then responsible for generating the overall plan across all of the projects and personnel.

Assuming the larger scenario, the Program Manager will create draft schedules for a set of projects, with candidate resource allocations. This work always involves a lot of "What-if" explorations, to understand how variations in resource planning and sequencing of work impacts the schedules.

The process is easier to show than to describe. I will use Planview PPM Pro[28] to show how this kind of resourcing is done in practice.

In this example, our Program Manager will create a first draft of allocations of people to projects. Figure 6.20 shows an example of how one person (Scott) is allocated across multiple projects. The columns at the right show how his allocation per project varies over the coming months.

ALLOCATIONS: TOWNSEND, SCOTT							
Actions							
Resource	Role	Project	Start Date	End Date	Headcount	Feb '18	Mar '18
Townsend, Scott	R&D Engineer	Capital Investment Project	5/1/2018	2/28/2019	0.25		
Townsend, Scott	R&D Engineer	Enhance Cardiac Rhythm Products	12/17/2017	11/28/2018	0.20	0.20	0.20
Townsend, Scott	R&D Engineer	Expand OTC Healthcare Offerings	11/14/2017	2/27/2018	0.21	0.08	
Townsend, Scott	R&D Engineer	Expand into Spine Market	11/1/2017	5/17/2018	0.10	0.10	0.10
Townsend, Scott	R&D Engineer	Expand into Spine Market	1/2/2018	5/18/2018	0.75	0.75	0.75

Figure 6.20: Sample Project Allocation for One Person

Given this kind of information per person, it is possible to show how everyone in the pool of resources is allocated across projects for each of the following months.

MY RESOURCES (ALL)													
Name: Last, First	Feb '18	Mar '18	Apr '18	May '18	Jun '18	Jul '18	Aug '18	Sep '18	Oct '18	Nov '18	Dec '18	Jan '19	Feb '19
Laird, Peter	145%	114%	45%	35%	30%	25%	25%	25%	11%	10%	11%	10%	10%
Snipes, Courtney	200%	105%	100%	100%	100%	100%	100%	100%	70%	0%	0%	0%	0%
Szrejter, Tim	152%	152%	150%	150%	150%	129%	100%	100%	70%	0%	0%	0%	0%
Tayler, Zachary	151%	151%	151%	129%	79%	68%	65%	65%	65%	65%	42%	0%	0%
Townsend, Scott	113%	105%	105%	96%	45%	46%	45%	45%	45%	43%	25%	25%	25%

Figure 6.21: First Draft of Program Schedule via Resource Pool Analysis

The draft of the plan in Figure 6.21 has serious problems. Many people have their time allocated at levels beyond what they can possible sustain in standard work weeks. Many of the worst areas show allocations well over 100 percent.

The over-allocations are eliminated by changing how people are allocated to projects over time. Figure 6.22 shows a more reasonable scenario.

MY RESOURCES (ALL)													
Name: Last, First	Feb '18	Mar '18	Apr '18	May '18	Jun '18	Jul '18	Aug '18	Sep '18	Oct '18	Nov '18	Dec '18	Jan '19	Feb '19
Laird, Peter	91%	72%	45%	35%	30%	25%	25%	25%	11%	10%	11%	10%	10%
Snipes, Courtney	100%	81%	80%	80%	80%	80%	80%	80%	56%	0%	0%	0%	0%
Szrejter, Tim	100%	100%	98%	98%	98%	77%	50%	50%	35%	0%	0%	0%	0%
Tayler, Zachary	97%	97%	97%	93%	76%	68%	65%	65%	65%	65%	42%	0%	0%
Townsend, Scott	99%	90%	90%	87%	45%	46%	45%	45%	45%	43%	25%	25%	25%

Figure 6.22: Second Draft of Program Schedule via Resource Pool Analysis

Several parameters can be modified to generate a viable allocation of people to projects over time. These parameters include project start dates, resources allocated to projects (often expressed as fractions of one person's time), and which projects to attempt, defer, or exclude.

This approach to resourcing makes intuitive sense and is effective when the pool of resources contains a modest number of people. Unfortunately, the difficulty of this approach increases rapidly as the number of people and projects grows. The problem is not with the tool (Planview PPM Pro, for example, provides excellent capabilities), but with an approach that does not scale well with large numbers.

6.12.2.1.1 Issues and Challenges with Classic Resource Planning

The classic approach to scheduling and resourcing has multiple issues, all of which become onerous as the size of the resource pool and project count increase:

- The biggest, and most obvious, issue is that this plan, which took hours or days to develop, is invalidated as soon as any one resource has a future that deviates significantly from the plan. If someone schedules a vacation, is given urgent work to do that overrides the program priorities or has any other issue that changes how the person's time is spent, the plan promptly breaks. For a group of, say, fifty people, such cases will arise frequently, forcing the Program Manager to update the plan at least weekly. The impact analysis and replanning tend to be laborious and time-consuming.

- No Program Manager (or Project Manager) will be happy at the need to change the plan constantly. No stakeholder or executive who needs a reliable plan will be happy with the constant changes. No person whose name appears in the plan will be happy at the constant sense of uncertainty about what he or she is going to be asked to do over time.

- It may not be possible to achieve business goals with the existing resource availability. One approach to addressing this problem is to negotiate with other projects or programs for the availability of certain key people. This, too, can take a great deal of time, with no guarantee of success, and often with no guarantee that anyone truly has the authority to make a decision, and stick to it.

- The common practice of sharing people across multiple projects is problematic. Table 3.1 (page 34) shows the dramatic loss in productivity that people experience when forced to change context frequently. The loss of productivity is much greater than people typically assume, and the experience of frequent context switching can be demoralizing.

The long list of issues may give the impression that this approach to resourcing and scheduling large Initiatives is unsatisfactory. I believe that it is, indeed, often unsatisfactory at large scales, and cannot be improved

significantly with better tools or more stringent attempt to "get things right."
I will look at a simpler alternative below.

6.12.2.2 Agile Resource Planning with Teams

Perhaps the single biggest obstacle to success with the classic style of resource planning is that it attempts to plan the future for too many individuals at one time. The approach can work if we are planning how to allocate time for ten people, but it becomes impractical when we try to do this for eighty people at once.

The classic model of a "Project Team" assumes that a set of people is drawn from a larger resource pool in order to execute a project. The Project Team is formed, performs its work, and then disbands. The degree to which a Project Team has a formal definition may vary greatly across organizations, but the idea of drawing on people from a pool is commonplace. The competition for resources across projects, and the time variation in each person's membership in various Project Teams, greatly complicate planning.

It is easier to perform resource planning if we use teams rather than individuals as the unit of planning. A team should contain people with the required skills. Following the Scrum practice, I will define a team of contributors (who do the hands-on work) as consisting of three to nine people. Each such team will have a well-defined association with product and project management personnel (e.g., Team Product Owner and Scrum Master).

Each team is a persistent structure, whose membership evolves slowly over time. Teams should have definitions that last at least for three months, and commonly up to several years, albeit with some changes in membership over time.

Each team has a domain, or area of expertise, meaning that each team implements certain types of valuable deliverables that are intended to be used by people outside the team. Thus, all requests for a particular type of deliverable (e.g., a module in a software product, or an avionics package) are directed to the team that works in that area.

The persistence of teams, and the definition of each team's focus, means that the work of a specific Initiative will flow to whatever teams are required to do the work of the Initiative. The patterns of collaboration between teams will then change over time, based on which Initiatives require work from which collaborating teams. Figure 1.1 (page 12) illustrates how these patterns vary from one Initiative to the next.

This approach to mapping work to resources essentially invalidates the concept of a "Program" in the context of classic Project Management. Since we have no individual Projects (just persistent teams), and we have no standard pattern of relationships between Initiatives and teams, the concept of a Program as an entity disappears. The discipline of Program Management remains, albeit with an Agile flavor, but the concept of a Program itself effectively vanishes.

Resource planning with teams, instead of individuals, offers a variety of benefits:

- Teams are resilient in the face of vacation time and other time-off events. Individuals may be away, but the team continues to function. The team's rate of work may decrease, but it can still get work done.

- There are far fewer teams than individuals. Resource planning for twelve teams is much easier than planning for one hundred individual people.

- Resource contention is handled not by reserving time from individual people, but by our standard techniques for scheduling work for a set of collaborating teams.

In essence, this approach turns resource planning into an exercise in scheduling. I will look at how to conduct this kind of team-oriented resource planning below.

6.12.2.2.1 Duration

In Section 6.9.4, I discussed how to estimate the effort of Initiatives in a way that aligns scope definitions with specific teams. Figure 6.10 provides an example of the decomposition of Initiative scope, and the estimates for different Epics assigned to different teams.

The estimates for effort may suffice for understanding cost considerations but are not sufficient to address scheduling needs. We now require a way to derive duration from estimates of effort.

The concept of Velocity (Section 2.4) provides the answer. Recall that I define Velocity to be the amount of work a team can perform in a standard period of time. In the context of a Scrum process, this period is most commonly a Sprint (usually two weeks in length).

Velocity has an analog in Kanban in the form of throughput. Given a number of work items, and an average throughput, we can forecast the average time required to complete that set of items. This approach, however, has limitations. It does not address how the variation in size affects the throughput. While it is true that the averages are computable, and it is true that over a long enough period the averages will provide a reasonable approximation, this may not suffice for specific periods of interest. (Perhaps more importantly, Kanban is not often used in a context where work *must* be planned against time, for the simple reason that Kanban does *not* plan against time. Thus, the question is seldom encountered in practice.)

Velocity has no direct analog in the world of classic project management, where schedules are built from tasks, task durations, knowledge of dependencies, and resource limits.

Returning to the Scrum perspective, if we divide each team's working time into Sprints of known duration (most commonly two weeks), and we estimate each team's Sprint Velocity, then we can map effort to duration in Sprints via the simple formula

Duration = Effort / Velocity.

The concept of Velocity greatly simplifies estimates of duration, relative to the methods of classic project management.

Using our Agent-upgrade example, then, we can forecast the duration of each team's involvement with the Initiative via Figure 6.23:

Agent V2 Upgrade	Device Team	Agent Team	Console Team
Total effort per Team	240	562.5	370
Team Velocity (Person-Days per two-week Sprint)	30	45	40
Number of Sprints required	8	12.5	9.25

Figure 6.23: Example of Duration Forecasting for Agent-Upgrade Initiative

In this example, the Agent Team is the "long pole in the tent." If all teams start at the same time, the Agent Team is the last to finish, and so the overall duration of work for this Initiative cannot be less than 12.5 Sprints, or 25 weeks. In practice, however, there is no reason to assume that all teams will begin the work of this Initiative at the same time, and the overall bounds of this Initiative's work may encompass more than 25 weeks.

6.12.2.2.2 Scheduling

Let us now consider the practical case of scheduling work for multiple Initiatives that draw on the same teams. We will consider the four Initiatives in Figure 6.24:

Initiative	Duration (Sprints)		
	Device Team	Agent Team	Console Team
Agent v2 Upgrade (AU)	8	12.5	9.25
Support for Gelco Cardiac Monitors (GC)	0	5	5
Support for Belden Cardiac Monitors (BC)	0	3	3
Vascubot Controller (VC)	9	0	0

Figure 6.24: Duration Information for a Set of Initiatives

The approach to scheduling these Initiatives as a set is iterative, but much simpler when we base the schedule on teams, rather than individuals. Our first attempt at a schedule might resemble the following:

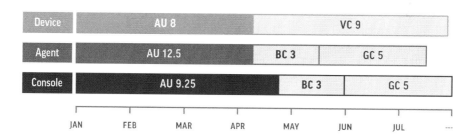

Figure 6.25: First Attempt to Schedule Initiatives

The duration of each team's contribution to each Initiative is denoted by the length of the bars in Figure 6.25. The patterns and acronyms in the bars correspond to specific Initiatives.

This first attempt shows that all Initiatives can be completed in eight months, if the schedule as shown can be achieved. However, this schedule is not actually achievable because the Agent team needs the Device team to finish the device interface, and so cannot start in parallel with the Device work.

Our second attempt looks like this:

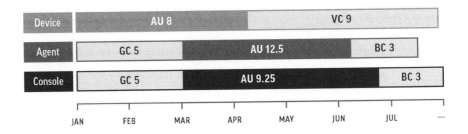

Figure 6.26: Second Attempt to Schedule Initiatives

Moving the start of the Agent-upgrade work out gives the Device team enough time to establish interface standards and stubs so that the Agent team can work productively. The support work for Belden and Gelco Cardiac Monitors can be done in parallel between the Agent and Console teams because the interface is well understood. However, the Console team cannot start work on the Agent upgrade until after the Agent team has developed some interface standards, which means that this schedule will not work for the Console team.

Our third attempt looks like this:

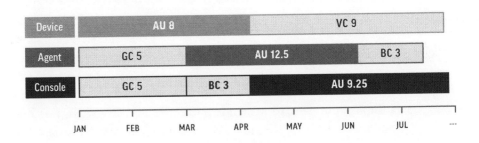

Figure 6.27: Third Attempt to Schedule Initiatives

Moving out the start of the Console team's Agent-upgrade out gives the Agent team enough time to lay the groundwork required by the Console team. This schedule should work.

In reality, previous commitments to other Initiatives means that it is unlikely that all teams will begin new work on new Initiatives at the same time. The logic, however, still applies.

6.13 Tracking and Managing Initiatives

The Portfolio Review meetings are held more frequently than Portfolio Planning meetings (e.g., monthly instead of quarterly). In each Portfolio Review meeting, the Portfolio Planning Committee reviews Initiatives that are in development in order to make appropriate decisions about whether or how to adjust the scope of remaining Initiative work.

The Committee will take into consideration all relevant qualitative and quantitative information, such as market conditions, changes in the competitive landscape, and so forth. One thing that is always of interest is information about the progress and status of the in-flight Initiatives.

6.13.1 Tracking with Burn-Up Charts

One useful metric for tracking each Initiative's progress is the Burn-Up chart. Burn-Up charts resemble Earned Value charts of classic Project Management, in that both measure progress toward a goal. Burn-Up charts align more easily with the measurement techniques of Agile processes and will be considered in more depth here.

Section 5.8 describes Burn-Up charts in some detail. The example of a Burn-Up chart in Section 5.8 shows progress toward the goal of a Release cycle, but a Burn-Up chart can be used to show progress toward any quantitative goal over time.

For our current purposes, we want to see the progress toward planned Initiative completion for each team. It is possible to aggregate the numbers across all teams into a single view, but this view can be hard to interpret when the teams' involvement with work on an Initiative does not have the same start and end dates. Thus, it is generally more useful to look at each team's Burn-Up chart for their work on the Initiative of interest, individually, in order to assess whether the rate of progress is likely to lead to completion of the intended scope on the planned date.

Suppose, for example, that we have the following progress information for a particular team's work on the XYZ Initiative:

Date	Scope	Completed	In Progress	Not Started
Apr	400	0	0	400
May	400	25	125	250
Jun	440	125	75	240
Jul	440	250	100	90
Aug	500	350	75	75
Sep	500	450	50	0

Figure 6.28: Progress Data for an Initiative

The Burn-Up chart might then be represented in this fashion:

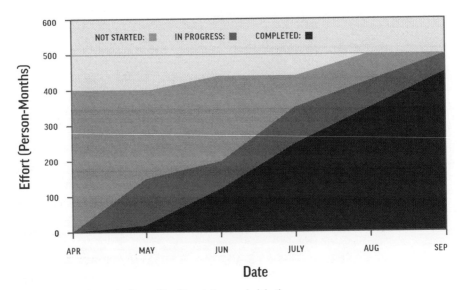

Figure 6.29: Sample Burn-Up Chart for an Initiative

If we had intended for this Initiative to complete by September 1, then this chart is disappointing. On the positive side, the trend that was visible on June 1 predicted that we might well not achieve the desired goal, and every additional data point confirmed the unfortunate trajectory. Thus, we should have had advance notice of the need to take corrective action.

6.13.2 Managing Initiatives

What should we do with the Initiative represented in the Burn-Up chart of Figure 6.29? More information is needed to assess the tradeoffs, but we might decide to reduce scope, or accept a slip in the completion date. The trends visible in the Burn-Up chart will be key factors in making such decisions.

More generally, we typically make one of the following decisions for the Initiatives under review.

- Does this Initiative represent the right use of our resources? If not, then perhaps we should cancel it.

- If work is ahead of schedule, then we may choose to

  - Add scope to the Initiative.
  - Finish this Initiative work early, and start work on another Initiative.

- If work is behind schedule, we may choose to

  - Reduce the scope of the Initiative to hit the target date.
  - Accept the slippage in the completion date and defer other work accordingly.

- If our understanding of how to deliver the maximum value has changed, we may choose to

  - Change the major deliverables to be implemented in the remainder of the Initiative.

These decisions are not necessarily exclusive. We might choose to both slip the schedule and revise the remaining deliverables. If the desire is to increase the rate of progress, this can be done by adding people to teams provided that the organization can afford a few weeks of slowdown while the new people come up to speed.

The cancellation of an Initiative can be a fairly traumatic occurrence for organizations that organize Project teams around Initiatives. It is less traumatic when Initiative work is parceled out to persistent teams because the teams remain after the Initiative is terminated and people continue to work with their colleagues as before. The work that is funneled to the team will change from what had been planned, but the team itself is not generally threatened by the cancellation of an Initiative.

6.14 Budgeting and Capitalization

Budgeting refers to the planned allocation of funds within an organization. Capitalization refers to how we classify or record the spending of money, specifically with respect to how we define assets versus expenses.

6.14.1 Classic Budgeting

The classic perspective on budgeting is that each project has a budget, out of which personnel and other expenses are paid. The approval process for a project incorporates cost estimates and allocation of funds for the project. Organizations often perform this kind of budgeting on an annual basis.

The difficulties that arise from this approach to budgeting commonly include the following:

- The plans (and project budgets) become obsolete soon after the annual budget has been defined.

- Project-based budgeting makes it difficult to re-allocate resources and funds to address changing customer needs and business drivers.

- Desire for accuracy leads to exhaustive analyses and highly detailed plans that give the illusion of understanding and control, without the reality.

- The common assumption of high availability of resources for productive work (e.g., 100 percent) is not matched by the reality (e.g., 50 percent), and leads to unrealistic plans.

The results are often found to be unsatisfactory, but organizations continue to budget in the same fashion because they lack knowledge of more effective alternatives.

6.14.2 Agile Budgeting

The Agile world is team-oriented rather than project-oriented. We do not budget projects at all, as such, but allocate long-term budgets to a small collection of stable teams, which simplifies the process.

Each Portfolio is given its own budget. Depending on the size of the organization, there might be one such Portfolio, or many (e.g., one per Business Unit).

While organizations may be funded on an annual basis, we allocate budgets to Portfolios on a quarterly basis, in order to provide flexibility to allow for change as business needs dictate. It is not an accident that this frequency matches that of Portfolio Planning: both activities are done on the same cadence, and for the same reason.

Given a known budget for the Portfolio in a quarter, we then plan Initiatives that maximize value over time. We do not allocate funds per project at all. We allocate funds to this part of the organization and leave the allocation of investment (effort and other costs) to the Portfolio Management process.

6.14.3 Capitalization

From an accounting perspective, the money spent to develop a product must be *expensed* or *capitalized:*

- The cost may be expensed or declared as an expense in the current year.

- The cost may be capitalized, or recorded as an asset in the current year, and depreciated over some period (often five years) as a series of smaller expenses.

The need to declare the money spent as expensed or capitalized is driven by regulatory requirements, such as from the United States Securities and Exchange Commission. These accounting standards are needed in order to provide an "apples to apples" comparison of financial statements from different companies. Without standardization in this area, it would be very difficult to compare financial statements from two different companies.

The decision to record cost as an expense or capitalized asset can affect perception of how well a company is doing. Since an organization has some flexibility about how to categorize costs, a particular choice may make a company look more (or less) appealing to potential investors or customers at a particular point in time.

The Profit-and-Loss figures a company computes depend significantly on the capitalization versus expense decision. At a minimum, a poor ability to track how money is spent can render P&L statements unreliable.

Money spent on long-term product development efforts can be capitalized if the products are intended to produce revenue or cost savings. Money spent on related infrastructure may or may not be capitalizable, depending on details that are generally understood by Finance departments. Money spent in other ways is most commonly not capitalizable.

The following types of cost can generally not be capitalized:

- Planning meetings
- Fixing defects in a released product, while also developing new features
- Product localization effort to support multiple languages
- Data conversion efforts
- Training people to use the product
- Operations activities beyond deployment, such as monitoring, reporting, configuration
- Routine Sarbanes–Oxley (SOX) or security reviews [15 USC 7211]
- Product customization efforts to support individual customers

Unfortunately, the type of work that can be capitalized is often intermixed with work that cannot be capitalized and is even performed by the same people. Thus, an accurate picture of the cost of work that can be capitalized depends on knowing which type of work contributes directly to product development, which in turn may require fine-grained knowledge of what our teams are doing with their time.

If fine-grained capitalization knowledge is required, the information can be obtained easily in organizations that employ Agile project management techniques such as Scrum and Kanban. The fine-grained deliverables that teams produce in Scrum and Kanban are usually recorded in a Web-based tracking system. If required, we can even tag each deliverable with a flag to indicate if it contributes to capitalization, if it should instead be considered an operational expense, or categorized in some other fashion.

Story	Person-Days	Capitalized
1	2	Y
2	3	Y
3	5	N
4	3	Y
5	8	Y

Figure 6.30: Example of Story Capitalization

In the context of a Scrum process, the estimates for Product Backlog Items that have been completed, for capitalizable deliverables, can simply be summed and multiplied by an appropriate factor to convert these estimates into monetary values. The process is not quite as simple in Kanban, where work is not estimated, but the addition of an "actual work" field to the Kanban deliverables can be used in a similar fashion.

Value	Description
16	Total Capitalized Person-Days
$500	Avg. Salary / Day
$8,000	Capitalizable Cost

Figure 6.31: Sample Capitalization Calculation

In summary, capitalization calculations are simple in a process such as Scrum, which estimates and tracks every deliverable produced by the teams. All that is needed is to note whether each deliverable should or should not be capitalized, and then to sum the effort estimates and convert to monetary equivalents.

7

Adaptations for Geographically Distributed Organizations

THE Scrum framework for teams was developed with the assumption that all of the people on the Scrum Team are co-located, meaning physically close to each other (e.g., seated at adjacent workstations, offices, and so forth). While co-location is highly desirable, Scrum is commonly used in large organizations that have offices in multiple locations around the world. I will provide guidance here for how to implement a Scrum process in distributed organizations.

A Scrum process is not unique in facing issues due to geographic distribution. Similar issues arise in any process for which the people involved do not work in close proximity. Thus, the adaptions described in this chapter, while presented in the language of Scrum, will be useful in other contexts as well.

I look at possible scenarios and adaptations below.

7.1 Case of Multiple Scrum Teams, Each Co-Located

The best scenario is to have Scrum Teams that are individually co-located (all three roles in the same building), with different teams in different places. This is by far the best scenario, and organizations should strive to achieve this scenario as much as possible.

The reason this scenario is desirable is because it is relatively easy to implement because only the cross-team interactions are distributed. As described in Section 5.5.1, cross-team interactions are much less intense than intra-team interactions.

In this scenario, the most difficult challenge is with Release Planning. It is best if the complete set of collaborating Scrum Teams travels to one location to do this work. For some organizations, this may be too costly, in which case we may fall back to Incremental Release Planning and develop a Release plan over the course of several weeks. This is basically a slow-motion version of the process described in Section 3.3.1, with the iterative revisions of the plan done in via many small meetings, and via email or other asynchronous messages. (See Section 3.3.1 for details.)

While the idea of addressing geographic separation in Release Planning with videoconferencing technology may be appealing, it tends to be ineffective in practice. The physical act of placing Stories and Epics on the planning board cannot be replicated sufficiently well with videoconference technology, at least at the time of this writing.

This is not to say that videoconferencing has no value for distributed organizations and Release Planning. What such technologies can offer is assistance with estimation and prioritization decisions for each team individually, when not all Team members can be physically present. This is useful, even if it isn't sufficient for the overall planning exercise.

The Release Backlog Refinement meetings, Team and Product Owner Scrum-of-Scrums meetings, Release Review meeting, and Release Retrospective involve a much smaller group of people than does Release Planning and can normally be accomplished in reasonable fashion via videoconference.

7.2 Case Where Individual Scrum Teams Are Split Geographically

This scenario is less productive due to increased communication latency and the inevitable shift to written communication over real-time discussion. No process adaptations can make these problems vanish.

Splitting one Scrum Team across two locations introduces two levels of difficulty:

1. The first level is a shift in the approach to communication and collaboration. Real-time communication that would otherwise be done in person must now be done via telecommunications technology. This shift increases the cost

of collaboration but to an extent that is not related directly to the physical distance between people. As the cost of interaction increases, the frequency goes down and the length of the interactions increase (i.e., quick pairwise conversations are replaced by group meetings). More communication is done in writing and less is done by talking.

2. The second level is due to the difficulty of collaboration due the time-zone separation between people, which increases as the time-zone separation increases.

Adaptations required for this particular scenario follow.

7.2.1 Adaptations for Roles

The Scrum Master and Team Product Owner roles are affected.

7.2.1.1 Scrum Master Adaptation

The Scrum Master's core responsibility is to do whatever is necessary to make the team as productive as possible. Fulfilling this responsibility requires that the Scrum Master maintain good situational awareness of what all the Team members are doing, how well they are doing, and so forth. This situational awareness enables the Scrum Master to identify problems early and ensure that they are addressed before they become big problems.

The Scrum Master's responsibilities require physical presence with Team members and cannot be carried out remotely. When one Scrum Team is split into two pieces, the Scrum Master can only maintain good situational awareness for the local portion of the team because the day-to-day or hour-to-hour activities of the remote portion are not visible. A common consequence of this reality is that the remote portion is less effective than the local portion because the Scrum Master cannot identify and address the numerous little issues that crop up daily. The remote team members tend to forget to attend meeting, forget to update task status for tracking purposes, get into various kinds of trouble without realizing they are in trouble, and generally neglect aspects of the development process other than creating and testing their deliverables.

The practical result of this scenario is that the team's overall productivity is poor, due to large number of little problems that never get better.

The adaptation for this scenario is to designate someone to be a *Scrum Master Proxy* for the remote portion. The Proxy does 80 percent of the work of a Scrum Master relating to situational awareness. The Proxy works closely with the remote portion to ensure that little problems are fixed quickly, and that people are following the process correctly.

The Scrum Master and Proxy must talk daily, as well as provide other information in writing, to ensure smooth handoffs and overall awareness of Sprint status.

7.2.1.2 Team Product Owner Adaptation

The Team Product Owner does not have to be physically present with Team members to be effective, although such presence makes the interactions easier. As long as the Product Owner is highly available via chat, voice, video, and screen-sharing applications, Team members can query the Product Owner for real-time guidance as needed.

The challenge for this role is not geographic separation as such but time-zone separation. If the time zones of the portions of the teams are too far apart, the Product Owner cannot provide the real-time guidance Team members need. When spread across eight or more time zones, for example, one portion of the team may have no ability to get real-time answers to questions about their current Stories. As a result, they must either wait a full day while blocked, or guess and risk implementing something that will have to be discarded and re-implemented following clarification the next day.

The adaptation here is to designate someone to serve as a *Product Owner Proxy* for the remote portion of the team. The Product Owner Proxy provides then real-time guidance that is needed.

The Product Owner Proxy represents the Product Owner's perspective but cannot do so perfectly. The risk is that the Proxy provides erroneous guidance that the Product Owner will correct the next day, leading to rework. However, the risk of getting wrong real-time guidance 20 percent of the time, which requires rework, is still much better than getting no real-time guidance 100 percent of the time. Everyone involved simply needs to realize that this solution cannot be made perfect.

The Product Owner and Proxy must talk daily, as well as provide other information in writing, to ensure smooth handoffs and overall awareness of Sprint status.

7.2.1.3 Rules for Proxy Roles

The rules about who can fulfill Proxy roles are less stringent than for the standard roles because the Proxies do not have the same level of authority as the Scrum Master and Product Owner, who can override decisions made by their Proxies. Basic guidelines include:

- A functional manager can be a Scrum Master Proxy or a Product Owner Proxy.

- One person can serve as both Scrum Master and Product Owner Proxy at the same time, provided the workload is manageable.

I do recommend that Proxies not be part-time Team members because the context-switching problem of Section 3.2.2 still applies, but the emphasis for Proxies is primarily on whether they can do the necessary work.

7.2.1.4 Analogous Adaptations to Contexts Other Than Scrum

In more classic language, the above role adaptations speak to the need for project and product management personnel to be aware of and accessible to other project team members on a near real-time basis. This need is generic, and not limited to Scrum. While the product management responsibilities can be carried out remotely, via real-time electronic communications, the project management responsibility requires physical presence.

7.2.2 Adaptations for Ceremonies

I will discuss how to adapt each Scrum ceremony for a split team below, primarily with respect to the impact of time-zone separation between the portions of the team.

7.2.2.1 Backlog Refinement Meeting

Team members who can readily participate in real time with the Team Product Owner should do so, whether in person or by teleconference. Team members who cannot participate in real time should provide their feedback on the PBIs being reviewed by email, prior to the meeting. The Product Owner should them summarize the agreed-on changes in a message to all Team members after the meeting.

While estimation of PBIs is common in Backlog Refinement meetings, it is not appropriate to do this for planning purposes if some Team members cannot attend due to time-zone separation. All Team members must participate in estimation, in real time, if the estimates are to be used for Sprint Planning.

7.2.2.2 Sprint Planning Meeting

Part 1 of the meeting creates the initial scope definition for the Sprint, based on the ranking of the PBIs, the PBI estimates, and the team's estimated Velocity. If PBI estimates are done in this meeting, then all Team members must be present in real time for this purpose, even if some must work late or get up early. Full-team presence for estimation is a requirement because we need everyone to provide insight and gain understanding at the same time.

Part 2 of the meeting develops the Task Breakdowns and revises the Sprint scope as needed based on the finer-grained task estimates. This work does not require real-time participation of all Team members, if that participation is painful due to time-zone separations.

In the latter case, it is sufficient for the portion of the team that can continue a normal workday (following Part 1 of the meeting) to draft Task Breakdowns and estimates and begin work on top-ranked PBIs. On the next day, the second portion of the team can review the Task Breakdowns and estimates and request any changes they consider important. The Scrum Master will then review these requests with the local portion of the team the following morning and make adjustments the latter consider sensible.

This strategy may not achieve perfect consensus, but it usually works well enough for practical purposes. It also requires that part 1 of the planning meeting occur the day before the start of the Sprint, so that the completion of part 2 officially begins the Sprint (and provides information required to begin drawing the Burndown chart).

7.2.2.3 Daily Stand-Up Meeting

The purpose of this meeting is to get everyone on the same page regarding what is happening in the Sprint and to identify issues that require swift corrective action. We can accomplish those goals by splitting the meeting into pieces.

There is usually no need to capture meeting minutes for this meeting when everyone attends in real time, as the information is not of long-term interest. However, when this meeting is split into two regional meetings, the Scrum Master and Proxy should both facilitate local meetings and capture the content by taking minutes or recording the session. Each then provides the captured information to the full team, and the Scrum Master or Proxy will present the information from the other half of the team at the start of the local Daily Stand-Up meeting.

7.2.2.4 Sprint Review

The Sprint Review meeting has the simplest adaptation. The portion of the team that can meet in real time with the Team Product Owner participates in the meeting and presents all of the completed deliverables. The Product Owner Proxy should also attend, if possible, to maintain awareness of the deliverable's degree of acceptability.

7.2.2.5 Retrospective

The Retrospective meeting's adaptation resembles that of the Daily Stand-Up meeting. The Scrum Master and Scrum Master Proxy facilitate and take notes from local Retrospectives with their portions of the team and create a document with the combined findings and recommendations. The Scrum Master should then work with both portions of the team to generate a set of consensus decisions about policy revisions and follow-up actions over the next few days. This asynchronous approach works because the Retrospective findings, while important, are not usually time-critical (unlike the work of a Sprint Planning meeting, which is time critical).

7.3 Final Thoughts about Adaptations for a Distributed Organization

The patterns presented in this chapter have been presented in the language of Scrum, but the same basic needs exist in any distributed organization, and the adaptations described will be relevant to other contexts that do not resemble Scrum.

The key insights are these:

- It is important to have Product Management (requirements-oriented) and Project Management (execution-oriented) perspectives available in real time for every team or portion thereof. While real-time Product Management can be done to a useful degree via teleconference technology, the same is not true for Project Management. The latter requires physical presence. The adaptations for Proxy roles reflect these realities.

- Whole-team estimation of work, which is required for near-term planning, requires real-time participation of Team members.

- All other activities can be done in pieces over time, using the patterns provided above.

8

Requirements Development

THE preceding chapters have focused on the flow and patterns of decision-making and collaboration. In this chapter, I shift the focus from how and when decisions are made to the content and motivation of important decisions.

8.1 Needs of Business Success Drive Agile Practices

One way of describing the elements of successful product development is to say that we need to succeed in two ways:

1. Building the right things (product definition and development of specifications)

2. Building things effectively (execution)

Unfortunate choices in product definition yield a product that has little appeal to customers. Failure to execute product development successfully will lead to excessive cost or schedule creep and can bring a product too late to market to matter or fail to deliver a product at all.

As I have already examined how to *build things effectively*, from the perspective of planning and execution, I now address the concept of *building the right things*.

8.2 Building the Right Things

The product must have the features and components to appeal to customers, and at a price that customers consider affordable.

A classic model of requirements-definition has been to write the "Big Up-Front" (BUF) approach, sometimes referred to as "Big Design Up-Front" or "Big Requirements Up-Front." The BUF concept is to invest time in thinking through the product's usage, architecture, and overall definition in a holistic sense and generate a lengthy and detailed requirements specification to drive the subsequent development of the product.

While the concept of thinking through the product's definition and design is laudable, the attempt to capture a high-level detail prior to initiation of development work is generally ineffective. Product development of any kind contains such a high volume of "unknown unknowns" that the detailed scope of work cannot be created reliably in an up-front planning exercise. The attempt to proceed with a BUF approach yields a lengthy specification that contains numerous errors and omissions. During subsequent development work, we typically find requirements that cannot be implemented as described, that turn out to be poor choices, or that contradict each other. We also discover important items that must be addressed but that appear nowhere in the documentation.

I have already addressed part of the solution to the limitations of the BUF approach by introducing the concept of Stories in Section 3.5.1.1. These artifacts provide medium-level summary specifications for small deliverables, in a way that leads to effective implementation.

What the Story concept does not do, by itself, is provide guidance around what requirements to write. I will address this issue now.

Two key concepts that guide our decisions about what to build are *Minimum Viable Product* (MVP) and feedback loops.

A product's MVP is the set of features that must be present in order for the product to be worth consideration by customers, while feedback loops are used to optimize product definition over the span of the product's development period.

The concepts of Minimum Viable Product and feedback loops differ significantly between software and hardware products, and I will consider these variations below.

8.2.1 Scope versus Time for Software Products

For software products, we need to provide some conception of the first version of the product that will be provided to our customers (the MVP).

However, the MVP concept has much less utility when defining features sets for future versions of a software product. By definition, we achieved the MVP by selling an initial version to customers, so application of the MVP concept to future versions tends to produce more confusion than benefit. It is normally preferable to define a cadence of product upgrades, and to optimize the content of each upgrade by maximizing the value of our investment for each.

For example, we might choose to produce new versions of our software product every six months and divide each such delivery interval into Release Cycles for planning purposes. We then define and estimate a rough sequence of high-level product features and components and select the highest-value items for implementation during the two Releases.

Implementation of any concept of "feature" is seldom an all-or-nothing proposition. Each such feature may be represented by a large Epic, whose decomposition into smaller Epics and Stories yields items of varying significance. An Epic titled "Administrator sets parameters for networked monitors" may have a logical decomposition into 200 Stories. Although some conception of the feature as a whole is important, it is unlikely that all of the Stories that appear in its logical decomposition are critical. Some of them will be critical, but some will be nice-to-have capabilities that can be omitted from a new version of the product without great impact.

We exploit the varying levels of importance across Stories to develop plans that are robust in the face of uncertainty. We put the most critical items into, say, the first two-thirds of our six-month development period, and the nice-to-have items into the second third. The nice-to-haves then comprise a *Feature Buffer* whose Stories may be removed from the product upgrade if the work on required items expands beyond their original estimates.

8.2.2 Tuning Software-Product Scope over Time via Feedback Loops

Experience suggests that any concept of initial scope of the next version of a software product is unlikely to deliver an optimum set of capabilities for customers. No Product Owner should be expected to define the perfect set of features for a product shipment that requires six months of work to produce. More likely, any such attempt will include elements that are very useful, elements that could be useful but are not implemented in a very usable way, and elements that will turn out to have negligible appeal or utility to customers.

Thus, while an initial conception of product definition is useful to have at the start of a long development cycle, we should not rely on that conception to guide our work completely over time. We should avoid or minimize our investment in unproductive choices by creating frequent feedback loops that inform our decisions over time.

For example, a Product Owner (Area or Team) could meet with key customer representatives and stakeholders once per month. The Product Owner would demonstrate recently developed features, show mock-ups of features in development, and describe plans for features to be developed in the next few months. (This review could be as short as a one-hour meeting, or as long as a two-week hands-on test period of a product's current state at customer sites.)

The participants in this review process will then provide feedback on the accomplishments and directions. Some features might be declared as desirable and well-done, others salvageable with effort, and still others actively undesirable. Equipped with these insights, the Product Owner can then change course to optimize the value of the ongoing development work, and thus optimize the value of the product upgrade over the course of multiple feedback cycles.

The example of a monthly meeting may not be possible for all product development scenarios. However, while the nature of the feedback loop can differ from the example (e.g., soliciting feedback from many customers through online "early access" programs, Question-and-Answer sessions, and so forth), the concept of implementing some kind of feedback loop is important.

8.2.3 Scope versus Time for Hardware Products

The work of software development creates the software product. The work of hardware development creates designs for a product to be manufactured at a later date. Software products accrete functionality over time, by making small and synchronized changes to multiple components or technology layers to enable the increments of functionality, but hardware products cannot accrete functionality over time in a similar fashion.

The inability to accrete functionality in hardware development is driven largely by the high cost of change that is innate to hardware development. Another important factor is that one cannot decompose the scope of usable functionality into narrow vertical slices that result in small updates to numerous components or technology layers. Instead, one must create components (e.g., power supplies, cooling systems) that support the range of needs required and shape the remainder of the product around these components' capabilities and limitations. Any change that impacts multiple components commonly requires replacing all of those components with new ones, which is costly and time-consuming.

For the above reasons, most hardware products *do* require a definition of Minimum Viable Product, as future "versions" of the product are actually new, physical products that do not simply represent accretions of new capabilities onto a previous physical product. Thus, the new "XL22" successor to the "XL21" cardiac monitor is not simply the previous box with more pieces added, but a new device with a new internal design and different physical components than were found in the XL21.

Much as for the software model, it is useful to divide a long-term (e.g., two-year) product development lifecycle into intermediate-length Release cycles, for the purpose of planning work, tracking status, and revising product concepts over time. However, each Release cycle's scope and goals are more likely a reflection of physical realities than simply convenient checkpoints.

For example, the product development lifecycle of a cardiac monitor might consist of three logical phases:

1. Develop an engineering prototype. This prototype performs essentially all of the desired functions, but its design contains enough custom work and expensive components that it cannot be manufactured and sold in any practical sense.

2. Develop a manufacturing prototype. This is the first attempt at designing the product in a way that can be manufactured, using affordable components. The resulting product design is likely to contain enough minor to modest issues that it is not practical as a manufacturable design at this point.

3. Develop the final design. This design will be provided to the manufacturing facility for production of the product.

Each of these phases maps logically to one or more Release cycles of modest length. For example, the first phase might be represented as two Release cycles of four months, while the next two consist of Release cycles of three and two months, respectively. We may, therefore, have to replace the concept of uniform Release cycles of the software world with Release cycles of varying length that better fit a hardware-development process. That said, the mechanics of Release Planning and Sprint Planning remain the same for both worlds.

We might begin our product development lifecycle by writing high-level Epics that cover all areas required to create the design and construction of an engineering prototype. The bulk of the deliverables for this work would not relate directly to the different user interactions with the product but to underlying design, circuit board elements, temperature control systems, power supply, chassis and mold design, environmental test results (vibration, shock, heat, electromagnetic interference, etc.), and so forth.

The planning for the Release cycle would then proceed as described in preceding chapters. The major differences in this planning exercise, compared to software products, will likely consist of more early work on technology and design issues, which are needed because the higher cost of change of hardware development implies a need to reduce the number of later design changes.

That same cost-of-change concept impacts how scope decisions evolve over time. As for software, we do want to front-load the Release cycle with highest-value items and allocate the latter third, say, to nice-to-have items than can be dropped if needed to hit the end date of the Release cycle with a viable product. However, we have less ability to change direction, once started, if business or market conditions indicate a change is needed. Such changes will likely require starting over (or close to it) and slip the completion date. This behavior contrasts with that of software development, where shifts in plans can be accommodated more easily in most cases, without necessarily changing target dates.

8.2.4 Tuning Hardware-Product Scope over Time via Feedback Loops

Perfect forecasting of desired features is no more achievable in hardware products than it is in software products. The same issues with impacts of changing business environments, competitive landscape, and internal discoveries and challenges apply to both worlds. What differs is the response.

While feedback loops with customers and stakeholders are still desirable, they are harder to conduct in a meaningful way for hardware products. This is because we do not accrete functionality that can be demonstrated on, say, a monthly basis, to enable course changes on such a time scale.

We are left with some combination of these options for feedback:

- Hold feedback sessions less often than for software (e.g., quarterly versus monthly).

- Rely more on mock-ups and concepts, and less on demonstrable capabilities.

- Iterate more on a Release-cycle or prototype-cycle basis rather than on a Sprint basis.

As always, we want useful feedback as early and often as possible, and should incorporate what we learn as soon as possible, but "often" will be less often for hardware products than for software products.

8.2.5 Scope versus Time for Combined Hardware–Software Products

Most hardware products of relevance to our world in this book either contain embedded software or work with external software. All comments about the creation and evolution of product requirements described above apply without modification to the combined world, for each portion thereof.

The major point to be made here is that "the product" is neither hardware nor software but some combination of both. Planning should be for the integrated product as a whole, not for "the software" and "the hardware." The historical separation of these worlds masks the practical reality that "the product" incorporates both, and people buy "the product," not its components. We should no more develop the hardware and software independently than we should develop two modules of the same software product independently. The different growth paths (accretion of features versus components) may complicate planning but do not excuse its omission.

Product planning occurs at all levels: Portfolio, Program, and Project. Hardware and software planning should be conducted in an integrated fashion at all of these levels. As software development has fewer hard constraints than hardware development, it may often be the case that the pace of hardware development constrains software development activities in unfortunate but unavoidable ways. Hardware emulation, software stubs, and other techniques are useful to reduce the impact, but some impact is unavoidable.

Other points worth mentioning include the following:

- If hardware and software development is done, at least to some extent, by different teams, then Sprint boundaries should be aligned across those teams. If two different teams truly must have different Sprint lengths, then align Sprint start dates as often as possible.

- All of the Program Management concepts described in this book apply without modification to the combined hardware–software environment.

8.2.6 The Planning and Evolution of Complex Solutions

My language has been product-oriented throughout, meaning that I have described how to develop products in an Agile manner. This orientation is directly applicable to many companies, but contexts exist that blur the usefulness of the word "product."

The world of telecommunications companies provides good examples of this issue. An organization that purchases mobile telecommunication services purchases a solution, not a product. The system includes a variety of individual products (handheld radios, mobile relay stations, fixed relay stations, central control and communication facilities) that contain both hardware and software. In this context, purchasing a "product" makes sense only with respect to adding another one (say, a handheld radio) in a context where the others are already present.

The mobile communication system that we purchase is both highly customized (so many of each component, with certain software-controlled features activated or used for each) and drawn from a base of many standard components.

The customers' needs for such solutions drive vendors to think about systems of components that can be combined in a very wide variety of ways and over scales that vary by orders of magnitude. One company's products may provide a solution for a small police department with five portable radios or an Army division in the field with thousands of distributed users.

In this world, the concept of planning the *product* moves up a level to planning an *ecosystem of interacting products*. A new customer request may ultimately impact ten different components. Many components are products that have no direct human users but interact only with other components.

The definition of standard but flexible interfaces becomes critical, and the evolution of these interfaces is a strategic necessity, not just a convenience.

In summary, I see these shifts from the product-oriented world:

- The solution is a configurable system of configurable components that interact via standard and critically important interfaces.

- Solution-oriented thinking and planning drives component development over time.

- Complex solutions are driven by Portfolio-level decisions that are themselves strongly dependent on each other.

The Scrum Teams themselves are likely to be organized as component teams, mirroring the organization of the various categories of components.

8.3 Techniques for Scope Decomposition

I introduced the concept of an Epic in Section 3.5.2. An Epic is a description of a deliverable that is too large for a team to implement and validate in a few days' time. Either the Epic requires more than the allowed amount of time to complete, or it requires two or more teams to implement different portions of the Epic.

In the lifecycle of product development, a Product Owner (for example) may identify a desirable feature that will require substantial time and / or multiple teams to develop. The Product Owner will commonly begin the work to define the desired capability by writing an Epic to describe it. Over time, the Product Owner and Team members will collaborate to decompose this feature definition into a set of User and Technical Stories whose implementation will yield the completed feature that was summarized in the Epic. This decomposition will produce the kind of tree structure shown in Section 3.5.2.

Often omitted in discussions of Epics is just how to proceed with the decomposition of Epics into Stories. This process of decomposition, which is sometimes referred to as "Story slicing," can be done in a variety of ways. I will look at slicing strategies for software and hardware development below.

8.3.1 Scope Decomposition for Software Products

I will now look at a number of common techniques for scope decomposition in software products, using four examples related to a travel-reservation system:

1. As a Traveler, I want to look at possible itineraries, so that I can understand my options.

2. As a Traveler, I want to search for a flight, so that I can build an itinerary.

3. As a Traveler, I want to purchase a flight reservation, so that I can fly to and from my destination.

4. As a Traveler, I want to manage my account, so that it works according to my preferences.

These examples are referred to as the Itinerary, Search, Purchase, and Account-Management Epics below.

Many of the decomposition patterns provide different ways to achieve specific goals. In these cases, all of the variations are useful but may involve different levels of effort. This is an extremely common situation, and we often choose to implement the simplest or least costly form out of a set of multiple possibilities first in order to produce a usable product as soon as possible. Afterwards, we can then add the other variations in future versions of the product.

Note that the "Quantitative Increments" and "Incremental Functionality" patterns are essentially the same. Both are presented here because both terms are in use.

8.3.1.1 Workflow Steps

We can decompose the Itinerary Epic into smaller Epics or Stories that relate to finer-grained workflow steps associated with itinerary definition.

1. Search for flights matching criteria.
2. Specify sort order for departing flights.
3. Select departing flight.
4. Specify sort order for returning flights.
5. Select returning flight.
6. View pricing and details of itinerary.

8.3.1.2 Business-Rules Variation

We can decompose the Search Epic into smaller Epics or Stories that relate to different "rules" or modes for searching.

1. Find flights for any time of day.
2. Find flights before specified time.
3. Find flights after specified time.
4. Find flights between specified times.

8.3.1.3 Major Effort

We can decompose the Purchase Epic into smaller Epics or Stories that provide different options for the base functionality, but for which implementation of the first option also develops much of the infrastructure required for the other options. The other options then require significantly less effort to implement.

1. Pay with a Visa card.
2. Pay with a MasterCard.
3. Pay with American Express card.
4. Pay with a Diners Club card.
5. Pay with PayPal.

8.3.1.4 Simple / Complex

We can decompose the Search Epic into smaller Epics or Stories that represent different levels of complexity and implement them in the order of increasing complexity.

1. Search with minimum data.
2. Search with specified number of stops.
3. Search with "airports near" for origin and destination.
4. Search with "dates near" for departure and return.

8.3.1.5 Variations in Data

We can decompose the Search Epic into smaller Epics or Stories that provide different types of data which produce logically equivalent results.

1. Search with source and destination as airport codes.
2. Search with source and destination as airport names.
3. Search with source and destination as city names.

8.3.1.6 Data-Entry Methods

We can decompose the Search Epic into smaller Epics or Stories that accept input data through different mechanisms.

1. Search with dates typed in and parsed.
2. Search with populated by calendar control.

8.3.1.7 Defer Performance

We can decompose the Search Epic into smaller Epics or Stories that represent a progression of performance improvements for a particular capability. We would implement the simplest (and slowest) option first, and upgrade to the faster and more complex versions when the need for them becomes clear.

1. Implement simple search algorithm.
2. Interleave departure and return searches with UI updates.
3. Improve search algorithm.
4. Reduce JavaScript footprint and execution time for display of search results.

8.3.1.8 Operations (CRUD)

We can decompose the Account-Management Epic into smaller Epics or Stories that operate on (change) the state of a user's Account. Perhaps the most common pattern is the "CRUD" pattern, whose name is an acronym for basic database operations (Create, Read, Update, and Delete).

1. Create account.
2. Edit account settings.
3. Cancel account.

8.3.1.9 Break Out a Spike

We can decompose the Purchase Epic into smaller Epics or Stories that address the common problem of having a need to accomplish some goal, but not having the knowledge of how to proceed. We need to implement a credit-card billing capability, but the people involved have not done this kind of work before, and do not know how to proceed, or even how to write the relevant Stories.

In this kind of situation, we allocate a Technical Story to conduct research to find the answers to questions which are needed before we can proceed with the work. (Stories for research are sometimes referred to as "Spikes," hence the section title.)

For the example, we might create a pair of Stories such as:

1. Research credit card gateways for pricing, capabilities, development tools.
2. Create simplest proof-of-concept to validate techniques.

After completing these Stories, we have the knowledge that enables us to write and estimate the Stories that implement the desired capabilities.

8.3.1.10 Partition by Subsystem or Product

For this pattern, I consider the Epic:

Refactor existing code to use Enterprise Java Beans 3.1 instead of EJB 2.0.

Assuming backward compatibility (or, at least, the ability to coexist) of the newer version with the older version, we can refactor portions of the software in succession.

1. Refactor Billing Module.
2. Refactor Catalog Module.
3. Refactor Subscription Module.

8.3.1.11 Quantitative Increments

For this pattern, I consider the Epic:

Support 10,000 concurrent users.

We approach this goal in stages, over time, as it is not necessary to achieve the goal immediately.

1. Support 1,000 concurrent users.
2. Support 3,000 concurrent users.
3. Support 10,000 concurrent users.

8.3.1.12 Incremental Functionality

For this pattern, I consider the Epic:

Improve reliability by eliminating single-point-of-failure scenarios.

We approach this goal in stages, adding more robustness over time as we implement each stage.

1. Implement load balancing.
2. Implement application server clustering.
3. Implement database clustering.

8.3.2 Scope Decomposition for Hardware Products

Fewer patterns are available for scope decomposition in hardware products than for software products. Such scope decomposition is primarily component and subsystem oriented, rather than oriented toward user interactions, which is quite different from the software model.

Four of the Epic-decomposition patterns from the preceding list do apply to hardware development. They are listed below, for examples relating to the development of unmanned aircraft.

Note that the "Quantitative Increments" and "Incremental Functionality" patterns are essentially the same. Both are presented here because both terms are in use.

8.3.2.1 Defer Performance

For this pattern, I consider the Epic:

Propulsion system should provide 20,000 pounds of thrust.

The example decomposition is:

1. Use the off-the-shelf solution that provides 10,000 pounds of thrust.
2. Develop new engine that produces 20,000 pounds of thrust.

We can start work on the overall aircraft sooner if we use an existing engine rather than wait for a new one to be developed.

8.3.2.2 Break Out a Spike

For this pattern, I consider the Epic:

Investigate dependence of high-speed aerodynamics on proposed sensor-package geometries

The example decomposition is:

1. Conduct computational fluid dynamics assessment of geometry 1.
2. Conduct computational fluid dynamics assessment of geometry 2.
3. Conduct wind-tunnel test of the geometry predicted to be most suitable by the computational fluid dynamics calculations.

The results will pave the way to writing and estimating Stories for implementation of the sensor-package housing, based on what we've learned.

8.3.2.3 Quantitative Increments

For this pattern, I consider the Epic:

Airframe must support a 2,000-pound sensor package

The example decomposition is:

1. Design for a 1,000-pound sensor package.
2. Design for a 2,000-pound sensor package.

The goal is to support 2,000 pounds for the commercial product, but we can start flying and testing much sooner if we start with a 1,000-pound sensor package. We expect lower risk and cost growth if we develop this capability incrementally over time rather than all at once.

8.3.2.4 Incremental Functionality

For this pattern, I consider the Epic:

Environmental-control system must keep sensor package within its operating limits for temperature

The example decomposition is:

1. Use conventional techniques for thermal control to keep temperature in -40 to 80 degrees C range.

2. Use cryogenic cooling with liquid nitrogen to 77 K for advanced sensors.

We create a basic and generally useful capability first and extend the capabilities when the need for lower temperature materializes.

9

Practicalities

THIS chapter addresses some common practical issues that arise in the course of planning and executing work in Agile ways.

9.1 The Troubles with Time Boxing

A key concept in Scrum is that Product Backlog Items should be completed in the same Sprint in which they are started. We never plan to start an item that we believe cannot be finished in the same Sprint, and we never start a particular item in a Sprint unless we believe, at that time, that we can finish it in the Sprint.

The reasoning behind this practice is threefold:

- There is no guarantee that the unfinished work in a Story that did not complete in the previous Sprint will be picked up and completed in the next Sprint. The choice to do this is the Product Owner's, and there will be times when a Product Owner identifies a need to change direction in ways that are incompatible with completing the unfinished Story. Depending on how the work of the uncompleted Story impacts the product at the moment, the impact can range from negligible to serious, and may require substantial corrective action to address.

- The consequences of allowing Stories to be started and not finished in the same Sprint include an inability to know whether we are on a path to success. While tracking progress at the task level in Burndown charts is valuable for identifying issues that threaten to cripple our plan, it is completion of Stories, not tasks, which contribute value. An inability to start and finish Stories in the same Sprint destroys our ability to know whether we are going to achieve business goals, or to provide useful insight about when specific capabilities (on which others depend) are likely to be completed.

- If Team members receive the impression that it is acceptable to start a Story and not finish it in the same Sprint, discipline can erode quickly. The result can be an increase in the number of Stories started but not finished in each Sprint, to the point where it is no longer possible to understand what progress means.

The requirement to finish Stories in the same Sprint in which they are started is sometimes misinterpreted or seen as a challenge that cannot be met. I will look at common situations of this kind in the following sections.

9.1.1 Feature Completion versus Story Completion

One protest I have heard many times is some variation on this statement: "Most of our features take a few weeks to complete. We can't finish any of them in a Sprint, so we can't use Scrum."

The issue here is the confusion between a "feature" and a Story.

The term "feature" is common but has no standard definition in Scrum. The common understanding of a feature is that it is a set of behaviors or elements in the product that provide a useful capability. For example, one feature might be the ability to pay for a purchase with a credit card, while another might be to search a product catalog, say, for a collapsible umbrella that is pink and decorated with stars.

A Story is defined to be a specification for a deliverable that can be created, tested, and confirmed to be developed and working as intended in a few days' time. A feature that takes substantial time must then be decomposed into a number of testable deliverables, which, together, yield the desired feature in the product. In Scrum language, we often say that the feature is defined (documented) as an Epic, which is then decomposed into Stories.

Another misunderstanding, if not objection, which comes up in the discussion of feature decomposition into Stories has to do with the nature of integration testing. If an Epic represents some kind of useful feature, and is decomposed into five Stories that produce smaller deliverables, then don't we need a Story about integrating the small deliverables into the whole feature and doing integration testing for the feature as a whole? And would that Story be part of the Epic or outside of the Epic?

The short answer is that we avoid integration Stories as much as possible, inside or outside the Epic. Instead, we conduct whatever integration testing is needed as soon as it can be done. For example, if each Story's deliverable adds functionality in its own right, and more functionality when used in conjunction with deliverables from the previous Stories in the same Epic, then we incorporate integration testing of the second Story into the scope of work for that Story. By continuing this pattern, we complete integration testing of all deliverables of the Epic when we finish the development and testing of the last Story in that Epic.

9.1.2 The Problem of Latency

Latency refers to a gap of some kind, in the middle of some logical stream of work.

Latency is a common problem in software development, and even more so in hardware development. One example might be the development of a molded-plastic part. From the perspective of the engineer who wants to develop a successful part, the goal is, of course, a part that meets the needs. The overall process of getting a suitable part has a logical sequence of steps, which I might summarize as:

1. Develop the design for the part.
2. Order ten samples of the part from a vendor.
3. Wait for the parts to come back from the vendor, who will make the mold and create the parts as specified.
4. Test the parts for acceptability.

If the parts are acceptable, then there is no more work needed in this area. Otherwise, we proceed as appropriate on a second attempt.

The issue here is not that the work takes some weeks to complete. We've addressed that point in the preceding section by dividing the overall sequence into a set of smaller deliverables. The problem is that we have to wait for something in the third step.

The latency in the third step is sometimes seen as a deal-breaker. "We can't finish our Story about getting the part because the vendor needs four weeks to fill the order. This means we can't use Scrum."

Here again is the confusion between completing a feature (getting the right part made) and completing Stories (small deliverables to be completed along the way). The confusion is worsened because of the delay encountered in the middle.

The solution is a simple one: write and implement Stories for the work done by the team. The sequence of such Stories pauses at the time the order is placed. We resume with the next Story in the sequence (test the parts for acceptability) after the parts arrive. The set of Stories that comprise the entire feature (develop a plastic part that meets the need) defines the work that the Scrum Team needs to do. The latency in the middle of the sequence affects the timing of these Stories, but not the ability to plan work as a set of small Stories.

In other words, latency begins after a Story ends, not in the middle of a Story.

Software examples are common as well. One Epic might require Team A to do some work, followed by some work by Team B that depends on Team A's work, followed again by more work from Team A that depends on Team B's work. Team A experiences some latency in the middle of the Epic, and simply works on other things until Team B's related work is completed.

Latency most commonly occurs as a consequence of external dependencies, meaning dependencies of one team on resources outside the team. We should plan these dependencies as well as reasonably possible and manage them as well as we can. Aside from that, we address them by planning and implementing work before the start of latency as a set of Stories, and resume work at the end of the latency period as another set of Stories.

9.2 The Patterns of External Dependencies

Scrum Teams develop products but not all of the work associated with bringing products to market is done by Scrum Teams. From the Scrum Team perspective, there are always "external dependencies" on people and organizations that reside outside the Scrum-Team boundaries. Different patterns of external dependencies are reviewed below.

9.2.1 Continuous Dependencies

The first pattern involves frequent and ongoing interaction between two groups. When that interaction occurs between Scrum Teams, the details are handled as previously addressed in our program-management content. When the interaction is between, say, a Scrum Team and another organization that does not use Scrum, different techniques may be needed.

A good example is the common need to provide technical documentation for products. The users, administrators, technicians, maintenance personnel, and the vendor's internal support staff all require some form of technical documentation. These audiences have different needs, but what they all have in common is that a Technical-Publications group usually creates the documents.

The major challenge in creating technical documentation is in managing the knowledge transfer from the development teams to the technical writers. The difficulties are twofold, relating to the timing and completeness of the transfer.

In old-school Waterfall–style development shops, the knowledge transfer tends to occur late in the development cycle, when the product's feature set has stabilized. The motivation behind this strategy is that technical writers can be confident that the product's state will not change dramatically while they are writing their documents. The problem with this strategy is that the knowledge transfer is very large and must happen very quickly. This puts a burden on the writers to create their documents under great time pressure and requires the Team members to transfer a lot of information which, commonly, they must struggle to remember at this point.

When development teams use Scrum, the Sprint cadence provides a natural and obvious opportunity to perform the knowledge transfer to the technical writers frequently, in pieces of manageable size. Not only is this approach easier on the writers, but it engages the development-team members at a time when the knowledge of recently completed features is fresh in their minds.

The downside to a Sprint cadence of knowledge transfer is that the product's functionality is not stable at the time of transfer and continues to evolve over time. However, the benefits of this approach usually exceed the cost of occasional revisions to the documentation caused by product evolution.

The mechanism by which Scrum Teams and Technical Writers conduct knowledge transfer remains to be defined. Different models are possible.

9.2.1.1 Technical Writer as Scrum Team Member

The simplest model has a Technical Writer being a member of the Scrum Team. The writer attends all of the meetings, participates in the planning work, and has deliverables that are defined in Stories.

This model is appealing but has some drawbacks. On the plus side, the close integration with Team members makes the knowledge transfer easy for everyone. On the down side, the writer's work is not something that is a team responsibility the way the product development work is a team responsibility. It is the work of one person, working roughly a Sprint behind everyone else, and feels odd to everyone when performed in this fashion.

9.2.1.2 Technical Writer as External Dependency

In practice, we usually have a Technical Publications department with multiple writers, who support multiple products, and making any one writer a

Scrum Team member is a practical impossibility. A more practical approach is to maintain the separation between the Scrum Teams and the Technical Publications group, and to manage the relationship effectively over time.

Now the challenge is to engage the right writer, at the right time (as needed), Sprint by Sprint, for different Scrum Teams and products. A reasonable way to make this happen is by having weekly or biweekly meetings with the Product Owners and the Technical Publications lead, to provide visibility into near-term knowledge-transfer needs.

When specific needs have been identified, follow-up meetings between the writer and Team members can be arranged, as desired. However, since the goal of the collaboration is to generate effective written documentation, I strongly recommend that the work of drafting useful descriptive text be done by Team members, as tasks in the relevant Stories (or, occasionally, as entire Stories, for larger items). The follow-up meetings should then focus on clarifying the written descriptions provided by the Team members. The writer can then use or revise the Team members' text as appropriate.

The inherent cadence of a Scrum process for product development provides a natural opportunity to transfer knowledge and build technical documentation incrementally, an approach that brings to technical documentation many of the same benefits that it brings to product development. The Technical Publications department typically does not use Scrum internally, however, as its schedule of work is largely driven by the work of product development. The key mechanism for planning and executing knowledge transfer from developers to writers is the recurring meeting with the Product Owners and the Technical Publications lead, which provides the insight needed to perform that transfer effectively. A major element in making that transfer easy is having Team members write a first draft of the required text and provide the text to the Technical Writers for review, discussion, and revision.

9.2.1.3 Conclusion

The detailed example of technical writing contains lessons that are generally useful. As the Product Owner is responsible for the product's definition and usability, the Product Owner is commonly the liaison for product-related development in general. The means by which ongoing interactions are managed is by maintaining a continuous interaction with the Product Owner over time, typically on some kind of Sprint cadence.

9.2.2 Milestone-Driven Dependencies

By "milestone-driven dependencies," I mean dependencies that do not happen on a recurring or continuous basis but relate to specific and scheduled milestones. Such dependencies are commonplace and involve specific Stories that belong to Scrum Teams. In this situation, a particular Story may be a predecessor or a successor in the dependency relationship.

Examples of predecessor–successor dependencies include:

- A Scrum Team's first attempt to connect to a credit-card transaction sandbox for testing connectivity requires that the IT department create an opening in the company's firewall.

- A Scrum Team cannot evaluate the quality of a plastic part that was ordered from a vendor until the part arrives.

These intermittent dependencies were addressed in Section 5.6.1.1, with respect to Release Planning. Management of these dependencies generally falls more to a Program Manager or Scrum Master than to a Product Owner. They appear on one or more rows on a Release Planning board. The rows may be associated with departments, or other categories of convenience.

9.2.3 Schedule-Driven Dependencies

Some dependencies relate to phases or dates within the product development lifecycle rather than to specific Stories. Examples include the involvement of a Release-engineering team, or a Manufacturing engineer. These people should be involved in Release Planning meetings but may not need to engage with the Scrum Teams until the product has reached a certain level of maturity.

For example, consider the case of a hardware product that goes through three Release cycles prior to the handoff of the design to the Manufacturing division. The intent for the second Release cycle is to create a manufacturing prototype, meaning the first attempt to create a design that can be manufactured within reasonable cost, reliability, and other constraints.

The ideal time at which to begin engagement with the Manufacturing perspective might be one month (two Sprints) after the start of the second Release cycle. Prior to that moment, the Manufacturing engineer's perspective was not needed and could not be used, but from now on, we must address the manufacturing realities in the product design.

The subsequent pattern of engagement of the Manufacturing engineer is likely to be cadence-based. This could consist of a once-per-Sprint meeting of the Scrum Team(s) with the Manufacturing engineer, to discuss potential manufacturing impacts of decisions that are currently under study. It might also entail some time per Sprint for the Manufacturing engineer to review the teams' current Stories and attend Backlog Refinement meetings.

Whatever the cadence may be, the intent is to ensure sufficient engagement between the development engineers and the source of manufacturing expertise to ensure that the product's design is compatible with the manufacturing necessities.

9.3 Estimating the Whole Product or Project

In classic project management, one creates a project plan that includes schedule, resources, and cost. The intent is to deliver the planned scope on time and within budget.

In the Agile approach to product development, we aren't planning and estimating *projects* at all, but we still have to define the scope of some aspect of a *product*, and estimate the work and costs required to create it.

Much of the content of this book has focused on defining, estimating, and implementing small specifications over time, whose accumulated deliverables yield some meaningful product. The Agile emphasis on planning and managing this work incrementally over time is important but can obscure the reality that we do need some concept of whole-product effort or cost estimates at times.

Our product might, for example, be a cardiac monitor. The definition of the product includes its physical hardware, firmware, and internal software, and the requirement that it must work with a set of other networked devices and associated monitoring and management software. The product design must address requirements around manufacturability, supportability, serviceability, installibility, and other "-ilities" as well as user experience and functionality.

Prior to starting development on this cardiac monitor, we need a basic conception of what it is, and some sense of the resources and time required to create it, along with the associated costs.

I have described the techniques required to generate these estimates in Chapter 6. The difference between providing these estimates for an Initiative and a product is mostly a matter of size. The techniques do not change.

In brief, then, we take the product concept and decompose it into a set of major product aspects. The decomposition will usually contain some combination of components, and features or modules, which can be documented as large Epics.

Each of these major Epics contributes to the cost and effort estimates. Some of the work for each will consist of activities that directly contribute to the product or its design. Some activities will be oriented toward research, engineering infrastructure (i.e., test facilities), and a variety of other things that must be done, but that are not themselves parts of the product in any sense.

We typically estimate effort using the Affinity Estimation technique previously described. The effort estimates translate into labor cost in a fairly direct fashion that is based on the salaries of the people who do the work.

Estimation of other costs, such as engineering infrastructure and test facilities, parts, and prototypes will come not from the Affinity technique but from historical data and knowledge of existing suppliers and their pricing.

Finally, the timeline is determined from a combination of team Velocities and knowledge of supplier lead times that cannot be absorbed simply by sequencing work in a clever fashion.

9.4 Framing Documents

One of the many challenges of product development is in maintaining an appropriate focus across a large group of people for a long span of time. This kind of focus requires defining and maintaining a variety of norms across all of the people in the group, to shape product decisions in effective ways.

In this section, I look at ways of shaping and bounding, or *framing*, the content or conception of work to be done, rather than the mechanics of decision-making (which has been addressed in depth in previous chapters). I will look at some key artifacts that provide a useful focus for our decision-making by putting appropriate boundaries around the decisions to be made.

9.4.1 Product Vision

A *Product Vision* is a short description of the product that serves multiple purposes. A Product Vision:

- Promotes a common understanding of the product across the organization
- Keeps everyone focused on the critical aspects of the product
- Informs tradeoffs during development
- Provides motivation, and enhances morale, for those working to develop the product, by providing a clear understanding of the purpose and benefits of the product

Product Visions are useful for any kind of product but perhaps most acutely so for software products. The malleability of software makes it relatively easy to add features that may be attractive individually but detract from the product's value as seen by potential purchasers. For example, there is no technical reason why software for controlling networked medical devices cannot also provide capabilities for purchasing video games or online dating services. However, any product that contains all three of these capabilities is likely to be considered inappropriate by anyone who seeks any one of those capabilities in a product.

Thus, a Product Vision serves the important purpose of keeping everyone focused on development work that contributes to the purpose of the product. An eager Marketing intern, for example, might be very excited about the potential of social-networking capabilities and advocate the addition of social networking to a company's products based solely on the market potential of that capability. However, the Product Vision exists to describe a product that customers will find useful, and the addition of that focus could dilute the product's definition enough to make the product as a whole unattractive.

An alternate possibility is that the addition of some of the characteristics of social-networking software might indeed add value to the medical software. For example, real-time chat might enable rapid and effective communication between widely separated people in the event of a patient's medical emergency. In this case, the Product Vision might help us see the value of some aspect of social networking in the context where the product will be used.

In the end, the main benefit of a Product Vision is not that it ensures the right decisions about product features. The main benefit is that it forces us to pause and think carefully about whether a particular proposal is a good idea.

9.4.1.1 Developing a Product Vision

The ideal time to develop a Product Vision is during the initial effort to figure out what the product should be and should do. However, one can and should develop a Product Vision for any product in active development, if it does not already exist. The lifecycle of a Product Vision typically starts with a flurry of revisions, followed by less frequent revisions, which is followed by a fairly stable definition that might be revised every few years.

The person driving the Product Vision's creation usually represents a business perspective of some kind, but can have any of a wide variety of job titles or roles. In our language, Area and Team Product Owners may often act as the drivers, but so, too, can Product Marketing Managers, Vice Presidents of Product Development, and numerous other titles.

The product-definition effort generally receives inputs from Portfolio investment themes, customer requests, the capabilities of competitor's products, industry analysts, development personnel, and technical support departments (who hear a great deal about customers' areas of dissatisfaction).

The activity of developing the Product Vision can be as simple as having one person draft it and incorporating feedback from various reviewers. More structured techniques for eliciting ideas include the "Buy a Feature" technique of Section 6.11.2.2.2, Story writing workshops, and so forth.

9.4.1.2 Format

One common format for Product Visions comes from Geoffrey Moore's book, *Crossing the Chasm*.[29] Moore suggests that a Product Vision should provide answers to these questions:

1. Who will buy and use the product?
2. What customer needs will the product address?
3. What category is the product in?
4. Which attributes must the product have to address key customer needs selected, which are critical for the success of the product?
5. How does the product compare against existing products? What are the product's unique selling points?

Moore provides a paragraph template into which the answers to these questions can be inserted in order to produce a short and meaningful summary:

For a (target customer) who (statement of the need or opportunity), the (product name) is a (product category) that (key benefit, compelling reason to buy). Unlike (primary competitive alternative) our product (statement of primary differentiation).

An example:

> For medium to large hospitals that must monitor patients' vital signs in Critical Care Units, TelCorp's CardiNet 3000 cardiac monitor provides real-time and highly configurable status information. Unlike cardiac monitors from Gelco and other competitors, the CardiNet 3000 integrates fully with TelCorp's network-monitoring software to enable custom monitoring and emergency-response plans to be defined for every patient, and to notify doctors and nurses of emergencies on a policy and per-person basis.

9.4.2 Agile Charter

An Agile Charter is an extension of the Product Vision concept that addresses a wider range of needs than the Product Vision alone.

While there is no unique definition of an Agile Charter, I favor a version that has these three components:

- Product Vision
- Mission
- Success Criteria

The Product Vision is a description of the product, as described above. The Mission is a short description of what the business will do with the product, while Success Criteria are criteria by which we evaluate the degree of our success (or failure) with the product.

The Agile Charter may be revised more frequently than the Product Vision, especially for software products whose vision may be stable across multiple product releases but whose mission or success criteria evolve over time as the product features, customer base, and market evolve over time.

For our cardiac monitor of the previous section, the Mission and Success Criteria might be written as:

- Mission

    - Produce our first network-configurable cardiac monitor, to be sold to our largest hospital clients. The CardiNet 3000 will be the pioneer and trendsetter for network configurability in our product line, as well as the industry at large.

- Success Criteria

    - First product shipment by end of Q2
    - 50 units sold by end of Q3
    - 200 units sold by end of Q4

9.4.3 Organizational Strategy

Organizational Strategy is most commonly applied at the level of the overall organization, or (in larger companies) at the level of Business Units. That said, the concept is a generally useful one for any organization.

Unfortunately for us, the terminology of Organizational Strategy overlaps with that of the Product Vision, but with somewhat different meanings. I will say that Organizational Strategy addresses these key questions:

1. What is the purpose of our organization? (This is the Mission.)
2. Where do we want to go in the next few years? (This is the Vision.)
3. What specific things do we want to accomplish? (These are the Strategic Objectives.)

Organizational Strategy is normally the province of the C-Level executives, as it goes right to the heart of the purpose of the entire organization.

For our fictional TelCorp company, the pieces of the Organizational Strategy might look like this:

9.4.3.1 Mission

The Mission statement describes why the organization exists.

TelCorp develops, sells, supports, and provides training for medical devices that support surgical procedures and patient monitoring in hospitals. TelCorp is dedicated to enabling the best possible medical care for patients, by producing networked medical devices whose integrated management provides benefits that far exceed the sum of the individual products.

9.4.3.2 Vision

The Vision summarizes where the organization hopes to go in the next few years.

TelCorp will add support for leading third-party devices in 2015. The rollout of TelCorp's new vascular-surgery robot in 2016 will expand the company's capabilities from monitoring surgery to performing surgery and lead the way to additional surgical devices in 2017.

9.4.3.3 Strategic Objectives

The Strategic Objectives are statements about specific accomplishments to be achieved (conceptual definition) and how the objectives will be measured (operational definitions).

Objective	Success Criteria	Date
Third-party support	Cardiac monitors from Gelco and Belden	30 Jun 20XX
Third-party support	MRI imaging from Gelco, Nukim, and Tesloc	31 Dec 20XX
VascuBot	Ship 20 by target date	31 Dec 20XY
Additional surgical device (TBD)	Ship 1 by target date	31 Dec 20XY

Table 9.1: Example of Strategic Objectives

9.4.4 Portfolio Charter

An organization may have multiple Portfolios, each with its own funding. Each Portfolio should have a clear focus and definition. The definition of a Portfolio puts boundaries around content that is or is not appropriate for the Portfolio.

A Portfolio's content must align with the objectives of the Organizational Strategy. For example, TelCorp's "Medical-Management System" Portfolio should contribute to the organizational goals in some reasonably straightforward fashion. Thus, an Initiative about cardiac monitors would be appropriate, while one about setting up an internal ERP system probably would not.

A Portfolio Charter defines and documents the intended characteristics of a particular Portfolio. I prefer to define the parts of a Portfolio Charter as:

1. Purpose
2. Alignment with Organizational Strategy
3. Objectives of the Portfolio

   a. Major accomplishments that reflect the Strategic Objectives

4. Portfolio-management roles and responsibilities
5. Anything else considered relevant

A Portfolio Charter is commonly defined at one level below that where the Organizational Strategy is defined. The person who has the role of Portfolio Owner will be a participant in this definition. The right time to create the Portfolio Charter is right before setting up the Portfolio-Management structure in which the Portfolio is managed.

I will look at elements of TelCorp's "Medical-Management System" Portfolio below.

9.4.4.1 Purpose and Alignment with Organizational Strategy

This portion describes the purpose of the Portfolio; i.e., it describes what we are trying to achieve with this Portfolio. We also address how this purpose aligns with our Organizational Strategy.

Medical-Management System Portfolio

This Portfolio's focus is to enhance MMS software, in alignment with these company objectives:

- Improving patient care through better monitoring and reporting of patient health
- Reducing cost of ownership through

  - Improved monitoring and control of networked devices
  - Making installation and configuration of devices easier

- Expanding the list of supported devices, from TelCorp and third parties
- Increasing revenues through market expansion and retention of current margins

9.4.4.2 Portfolio Objectives

This portion lists the principal objectives of our Portfolio.

Portfolio Objectives

- Add installation, configuration, control, and real-time monitoring capabilities for new TelCorp and selected third-party devices.

    - Includes new surgical robots.

- Redesign user interface for monitoring and reporting of patient data.
- Validate new PC-based monitor stations.
- Upgrade device-resident Agents for more data and better performance.
- Support monitoring and controlling device-resident Agents (V2 and up).
- Expand reporting for devices with V2 Agents.
- Enhance fault-tolerance of system.

9.4.4.3 Roles and Responsibilities

This portion identifies the roles needed to manage the Portfolio effectively. We will have to map these roles to specific individuals at some point.

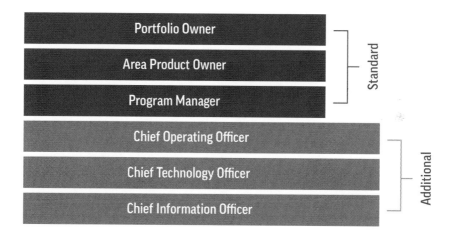

Figure 9.1: Portfolio Management Roles

The first three roles appear in our definition of Agile Portfolio Management, and we may have multiple Area Product Owners and Program Managers.

The remaining roles are not standardized across Portfolios but are selected as appropriate to each Portfolio. In this case, these roles happen to be job titles in this organization and are associated with people who have valuable contributions to make to the Portfolio decisions and governance.

Conclusion

I N this book, I have tried to provide guidance around decision-making for product development work at multiple organizational levels. Much more can be written on the subject of product development, for both software and hardware products, and doubtless will be.

In particular, I have not tried to present a comprehensive introduction to the process by which the definition of product scope proceeds from initial conception to high-level requirements, although much of what is in this book is certainly relevant to that subject. Product definition is itself a process, with its own structure and concepts, and the details of a product definition process can vary widely across different product domains.

The decision to omit product definition as a domain is a conscious one. Part of the reason for this choice was the desire to keep the scope of the book to a more modest level. Another part was to preserve the focus on certain kinds of decision-making practices, in ways that are generic and applicable to a variety of contexts. And a final part was to enable an equal focus on both software and hardware products, as the details of how requirements evolve differ between these two types of products.

As always in the Agile world, it is important not to over-specify the processes and practices. I have tried to keep to the Agile philosophy by providing a minimal set of roles, ceremonies, and other elements, which is sufficient to meet the most common needs. Every organization will have to incorporate additional practices to address its specific needs. Such customization is always necessary.

Over-specification is a perennial problem for process definitions, Agile or otherwise. The desire to cover all possibilities leads to huge process definitions that never do cover all of the possibilities but that are too big, too rigid, and too full of irrelevant material to be practical and accessible. Whether, or how well, I have avoided this problem is something readers will have to decide.

My final note is to encourage readers to keep the concept of Agile governance in mind whenever devising solutions for collaboration in product development. As per Section 1.1,

Agile governance is an Agile style of governance that emphasizes rapid decision-making based on lightweight artifacts that are developed with minimum effort and that are part of the natural flow of work.

With that note, I wish you well on *your* journey to rapid and effective decision-making.

Acknowledgments

LIKE most books, this one involves the efforts of too many people for me to acknowledge adequately. I would like to single out a few for special recognition.

Paul Hansen of 1000minds not only provided permission to use screenshots of this excellent product but went above and beyond duty to improve the corresponding section in this book (that's *improve* in the sense of *rewrite*).

Jane Kovacs and friends from Planview created a resourcing model and screenshots in Planview PPM Pro to illustrate my discussion of resourcing.

James Kolozs of Syncroness gave freely of his time to read the book and provide insights, especially with respect to hardware development.

John Carter of TCGen, colleague and partner of surprisingly many years now, has offered both encouragement and deep insight into the mechanics of hardware-product development.

Next is an absolutely huge acknowledgment to cPrime, where it has been my pleasure to work for many years. cPrime has given me a home and space to develop these ideas, and the chance to put them into practice for our clients.

And speaking of clients—I've had the honor and privilege to help well over a hundred clients in their Agile transformations over the years. I am very grateful for the opportunity to work with so many wonderful people, and to make a difference in their lives.

Last, but never least, I express my lifelong gratitude to my wife, Elaine, my daughter, Helen, and my parents, William and Inez Thompson, whose encouragement has always sustained me.

Endnotes

1   Henrik Kniberg. *Scrum and XP from the Trenches*. Toronto: C4Media Inc., 2007.

2   Kevin Thompson. "Recipes for Agile Governance in the Enterprise: The Enterprise Web." cPrime, Inc., 2013. Referred to as RAGE throughout.

3   Kevin Thompson. "Agile Processes for Hardware Development." cPrime, Inc., 2015.

4   Kent Beck with Cynthia Andres. *Extreme Programming Explained: Embrace Change*. 2nd Edition. Boston: Addison-Wesley, 2004.

5   Ken Schwaber and Mike Beedle. *Agile Software Development with Scrum*. Upper Saddle River, NJ: Prentice Hall, 2002.

6   Jeff Sutherland and Ken Schwaber. "The Scrum Guide: The Definitive Guide to Scrum." www.scrumguides.org.

7   Thompson, 2013.

8   Kevin Thompson. "The Agile PMO." cPrime, Inc., April 2012.

9   *A Guide to the Project Management Body of Knowledge (PMBOK® Guide)*. 4th Edition. Atlanta: Project Management Institute, Inc., 2008. Referred to as PMBOK4 throughout.

10   *The Standard for Program Management*. 2nd Edition. Atlanta: Project Management Institute, Inc., 2008. Referred to as SProgMan2 throughout.

11   *The Standard for Portfolio Management*. 2nd Edition. Atlanta: Project Management Institute, Inc., 2008. Referred to as SPortMan2 throughout.

12   PMBOK4, 2008.

13   SProgMan2, 2008.

14 SPortMan2, 2008.

15 W. Edwards Deming. *Out of the Crisis.* Cambridge, MA: MIT Center for Advanced Engineering Study, 1986.

16 Frans Osinga. *Science, Strategy and War: The Strategic Theory of John Boyd.* London, UK: Routledge, 2006.

17 Inspired by Hubert Smits, "5 Levels of Agile Planning: From Enterprise Product Vision to Team Stand-Up." Rally Software Development Corporation Whitepaper, 2006.

18 Winston W. Royce. "Managing the Development of Large Software Systems." Proc. *IEEE WESCON*. Institute of Electrical and Electronics Engineers, August 1970. This paper originated the Waterfall process in concept, if not in name.

19 Ibid.

20 David Anderson. *Agile Management for Software Engineering: Applying the Theory of Constraints for Business Results.* Upper Saddle River, NJ: Prentice Hall, 2003.

21 Gerald Weinberg. *Quality Software Management, Volume 1: Systems Thinking.* New York: Dorset House, 1992.

22 PLANNING POKER® is a registered trademark of Mountain Goat Software, LLC.

23 Anderson, 2003.

24 I first encountered this term in Craig Larman and Bas Vodde's *Practices for Scaling Lean & Agile Development* (Boston: Addison-Wesley, 2010). I prefer it over the analogous "Chief Product Owner," as the latter does not work as well in a multilevel hierarchy.

25 Conteneo is a US-based company (www.conteneo.co).

26 Paul Hansen and Franz Ombler. "A New Method for Scoring Additive Multi-attribute Value Models Using Pairwise Rankings of Alternatives." *Journal of Multi-Criteria Decision Analysis* 15 (3–4, May–August 2008): 87–107.

27 1000minds is a New Zealand–based company (www.1000minds.com).

28 Figures 6.20, 6.21, and 6.22 courtesy of Planview, Inc.

29 Geoffrey Moore. *Crossing the Chasm: Marketing and Selling Disruptive Products to Mainstream Consumers.* New York: HarperBusiness, 1998.

Index

Release cycles, 104–5; team types and organization, 112–16; tracking and metrics, 127–29

alignment: Portfolio Management, 132–33, 135

Analogous Estimation technique, 162

anchoring, 50, 59, 60

Andres, Cynthia: *Extreme Programming Explained*, 5

Area Product Owner: Business Case and, 140; Initiative scope and, 134; number of teams under, 112; Portfolio Planning meeting, 138; Portfolio Refinement meeting, 137; Portfolio Review meeting, 139; Product Owner Scrum-of-Scrums meeting, 123–24; Release Backlog Refinement meeting, 123; Release Planning meeting, 120, 121, 123; Release Retrospective meeting, 125; Release Review meeting, 125; Risk Management and, 163; roles and responsibilities, 108, 109, 134–35, 136

Artifacts: in Agile governance, 14

Artifacts (Scrum), 60–68; Defects, 65; Definition of Done, 67–68; Epics, 66–67; Product Backlog, 67; Product Backlog Items, 60–65; Sprint Backlog, 67; Technical Stories, 63–65; User Stories, 61–63

Artifacts, Requirements-Definition (Kanban): flow of a mix of tasks and deliverables, 97; flow of dissimilar deliverables, 95; flow of similar deliverables, 91–93; flow of tasks, 89

Backlog, 81

Backlog Item, 81, 87

Backlog Owner: Backlog Refinement meeting, 84; Daily Stand-Up meeting, 85; Retrospective meeting, 86; roles and responsibilities, 81, 82

Backlog Refinement meeting (Kanban), 84–85

Backlog Refinement meeting (Scrum), 31, 36, 37–38, 195

Beck, Kent: *Extreme Programming Explained*, 5

"Big Up-Front" (BUF) approach, 200

Break Out a Spike pattern, 209–10, 211–12

budgeting, 185–86. *See also* capitalization

Burndown chart, 69–71, 72

Burn-Up chart, 127–29, *128, 183–84*

Business Case, 140–44; introduction, 140–41; audience, 140–41; definition, 133, 140; format, 141, *142–43,* 143–44; length, 140; Portfolio Planning meeting and, 138; Portfolio Refinement meeting and, 137; responsibility for writing, 134, 140

Business-Rules Variation pattern, 208

"Buy a Feature" method, 170

capitalization, 185, 187–89

categories, for Initiatives, 144

Ceremonies: in Agile governance, 14; definition, 35

Ceremonies (Agile Portfolio Management), 136–39; introduction, *136–137;* Portfolio Planning, 135, 138–39; Portfolio Refinement, 134, 137, 173–74; Portfolio Retrospective, 135, 139; Portfolio Review, 135, 139, 183

Ceremonies (Agile Program Management), 116–25; introduction, 116–17, *117–18,* 118–19; Product Owner Scrum-of-Scrums, 108, 123–24, 192; Release Backlog Refinement, 123, 192; Release Planning, 108, 118–19, 119–23; Release Retrospective, 108, 119, 125, 192; Release Review, 108, 119, 125, 192; Scrum-of-Scrums, 108, 119, 124

Ceremonies (Kanban), 83–87; introduction, 83–84; Backlog Refinement, 84–85; Daily Stand-Up, 82, 84, 85; Retrospective, 82, 84, 86–87; Sidebar meeting, 85

Ceremonies (Scrum), 35–49; introduction, 35–37; adaptions for geographically split groups, 195–97; attendance, 47–49; Backlog Refinement, 31, 36, 37–38, 195; Daily Stand-Up, 32, 36, 37, 43–44, 196; Retrospective, 37, 45–47, 48–49, 196–97; Sidebar meeting, 44; Sprint Planning, 32, 36, 38–43; Sprint Review, 36–37, 44–45, 48, 196

Chore, 65

57957665R00163

Made in the USA
Middletown, DE
03 August 2019